TRANSFORMER,
BERT, AND GPT

LICENSE, DISCLAIMER OF LIABILITY, AND LIMITED WARRANTY

TRANSFORMER, BERT, AND GPT
Including ChatGPT and Prompt Engineering

Oswald Campesato

MERCURY LEARNING AND INFORMATION
Boston, Massachusetts

Publisher: David Pallai
MERCURY LEARNING AND INFORMATION
121 High Street, 3rd Floor
Boston, MA 02110
info@merclearning.com
www.merclearning.com
800-232-0223

O. Campesato. *Transformer, BERT, and GPT: Including ChatGPT and Prompt Engineering.*
ISBN 978-1-68392-898-0

Library of Congress Control Number: 2023945517

232425321   This book is printed on acid-free paper in the United States of America.

I'd like to dedicate this book to my parents
— may this bring joy and happiness into their lives.

CONTENTS

*P*REFACE

WHAT IS THE VALUE PROPOSITION FOR THIS BOOK?

This book begins with foundational concepts such as the attention mechanism, covers tokenization techniques, explores the nuances of Transformer and BERT architectures, and culminates in advanced topics related to the latest in the GPT series, including ChatGPT.

Key chapters provide insights into the evolution and significance of attention in deep learning, the intricacies of the Transformer architecture, a two-part exploration of the BERT family, and hands-on guidance on working with GPT-3. The concluding chapters present an overview of ChatGPT, GPT-4, and the world of visualization using DALL-E and generative AI.

In addition to the primary topics, the document also describes influential AI organizations such as DeepMind, OpenAI, Cohere, Hugging Face, and more. Through this guide, readers will gain a comprehensive understanding of the current landscape of NLP models, their underlying architectures, and practical applications.

THE TARGET AUDIENCE

This book is intended primarily for people who have a basic knowledge of machine learning or software developers who are interested in working with LLMs. Specifically, this book is for readers who are accustomed to searching online for more detailed information about technical topics. If you are a beginner, there are other books that may be more suitable for you, and you can find them by performing an online search.

This book is also intended to reach an international audience of readers with highly diverse backgrounds in various age groups. In addition, this book uses standard English rather than colloquial expressions that might be confusing to those readers. This book provide a comfortable and meaningful learning experience for the intended readers.

DO I NEED TO LEARN THE THEORY PORTIONS OF THIS BOOK?

Once again, the answer depends on the extent to which you plan to become involved in working with LLMs and generative AI. In addition to creating a model, you will use various algorithms to see which ones provide the level of accuracy (or some other metric) that you need for your project. In general, it's probably worthwhile to learn the more theoretical aspects of LLMs that are discussed in this book.

GETTING THE MOST FROM THIS BOOK

Some people learn well from prose, others learn well from sample code (and lots of it), which means that there's no single style that can be used for everyone.

Moreover, some programmers want to run the code first, see what it does, and then return to the code to delve into the details (and others use the opposite approach).

Consequently, there are various types of code samples in this book: some are short, some are long, and other code samples "build" from earlier code samples.

WHAT DO I NEED TO KNOW FOR THIS BOOK?

Although this book is introductory in nature, some knowledge of `Python` 3.x with certainly be helpful for the code samples. Knowledge of other programming languages (such as `Java`) can also be helpful because of the exposure to programming concepts and constructs. The less technical knowledge that you have, the more diligence will be required in order to understand the various topics that are covered.

If you want to be sure that you can grasp the material in this book, glance through some of the code samples to get an idea of how much is familiar to you and how much is new for you.

DOES THIS BOOK CONTAIN PRODUCTION-LEVEL CODE SAMPLES?

This book contains basic code samples that are written in `Python`, and their primary purpose is to show you how to access the functionality of LLMs such as BERT and GPT-3. Moreover, clarity has higher priority than writing more compact code that is more difficult to understand (and possibly more prone to bugs). If you decide to use any of the code in this book, you ought to subject that code to the same rigorous analysis as the other parts of your code base.

WHAT ARE THE NON-TECHNICAL PREREQUISITES FOR THIS BOOK?

Although the answer to this question is more difficult to quantify, it's important to have a desire to learn about `NLP`, along with the motivation and discipline to read and understand the code samples. As a reminder, even simple APIs can be a challenge to understand them the first time you encounter them, so be prepared to read the code samples several times.

HOW DO I SET UP A COMMAND SHELL?

If you are a Mac user, there are three ways to do so. The first method is to use `Finder` to navigate to `Applications > Utilities` and then double click on the `Utilities` application. Next, if you already have a command shell available, you can launch a new command shell by typing the following command:

```
open /Applications/Utilities/Terminal.app
```

A second method for Mac users is to open a new command shell on a MacBook from a command shell that is already visible simply by clicking `command+n` in that command shell, and your Mac will launch another command shell.

If you are a PC user, you can install Cygwin (open source https://cygwin.com/) that simulates bash commands, or use another toolkit such as MKS (a commercial product). Please read the online documentation that describes the download and installation process. Note that custom aliases are not automatically set if they are defined in a file other than the main start-up file (such as .bash_login).

COMPANION FILES

All the code samples and figures in this book may be obtained by writing to the publisher at info@merclearning.com.

WHAT ARE THE "NEXT STEPS" AFTER FINISHING THIS BOOK?

The answer to this question varies widely, mainly because the answer depends heavily on your objectives. If you are interested primarily in NLP, then you can learn about other LLMs (large language models).

If you are primarily interested in machine learning, there are some subfields of machine learning, such as deep learning and reinforcement learning (and deep reinforcement learning) that might appeal to you. Fortunately, there are many resources available, and you can perform an Internet search for those resources. One other point: the aspects of machine learning you need depend on who you are: the needs of a machine learning engineer, data scientist, manager, student or software developer are all different.

## CHAPTER 1

INTRODUCTION

This chapter provides a fast-paced introduction to generative artificial intelligence (AI), focusing on the attention mechanism, which is a critical component of the transformer architecture. You will also learn about some influential companies in the AI space.

The first part of this chapter introduces you to generative AI, including its most important features and techniques. You will also learn about the difference between conversational AI and generative AI.

The second part of this chapter starts with a brief introduction to several companies making significant contributions in AI and natural language processing (NLP). You will become very familiar with these companies if you plan to pursue a career in NLP.

The third part of this chapter introduces the concept of LLMs (large language models), which is relevant for all the chapters in this book.

The fourth part of this chapter introduces the concept of *attention*, which is a powerful mechanism for generating word embeddings that contain context specific information for words in sentences. The concept of the inner product of vectors underlies the main principle of attention, as well as word2vec and support vector machines (i.e., the so-called "kernel trick").

WHAT IS GENERATIVE AI?

Generative AI refers to a subset of artificial intelligence models and techniques designed to generate new data samples that are similar in nature to a given set of input data. The goal is to produce content or data that was not part of the original training set but is coherent, contextually relevant, and in the same style or structure.

Generative AI is unique in its ability to create and innovate, as opposed to merely analyzing or classifying. The advancements in this field have led to breakthroughs in creative domains and practical applications, making it a cutting-edge area of AI research and development.

Key Features of Generative AI

The following list contains the most important features of generative AI, followed by a brief description for each item:

- Data Generation
- Synthesis
- Learning Distributions

Data Generation refers to the ability to create new data points that are not part of the training data but resemble it. This can include text, images, music, videos, or any other form of data.

Synthesis means that generative models can blend various inputs to generate outputs that incorporate features from each input, like merging the styles of two images.

Learning Distributions means that generative AI models aim to learn the probability distribution of the training data so they can produce new samples from that distribution.

Popular Techniques in Generative AI

Generative Adversarial Networks (GANs) consist of two networks, a generator and a discriminator, that are trained simultaneously. The *generator* tries to produce fake data, while the *discriminator* tries to distinguish between the real data and fake data. Over time, the generator gets better at producing realistic data.

Variational Autoencoders (VAEs) are probabilistic models that learn to encode and decode data so that the encoded representations can be used to generate new data samples.

Recurrent Neural Networks (RNNs) are used primarily for sequence generation, such as text or music.

What Makes Generative AI Different

Creation vs. Classification: While most traditional AI models aim to classify input data into predefined categories, generative models aim to create new data.

Unsupervised Learning: Many generative models, especially GANs and VAEs, operate in an unsupervised manner, meaning they do not require labeled data for training.

Diverse Outputs: Generative models can produce a wide variety of outputs based on learned distributions, making them ideal for tasks like art generation and style transfer.

Challenges: Generative AI poses unique challenges, such as mode collapse in GANs or ensuring the coherence of generated content.

There are numerous areas that involve generative AI applications, some of which are given in the following list:

- Art and music creation
- Data augmentation
- Style transfer
- Text generation
- Image synthesis
- Drug discovery

Art and music creation includes generating paintings, music, or other forms of art. *Data augmentation* involves creating additional data for training models, especially when the original dataset is limited. *Style transfer* refers to applying the style of one image to the content of another. *Text generation* involves creating coherent and contextually-relevant text. *Image synthesis* involves generating realistic images, faces, or even creating scenes for video games. *Drug discovery* pertains to generating molecular structures for new potential drugs.

CONVERSATIONAL AI VERSUS GENERATIVE AI

Both conversational AI and generative AI are prominent subfields within the broader domain of artificial intelligence. However, these subfields have a different focus regarding their primary objective, the technologies that they use, and applications. Please refer to the following site for more information:

https://medium.com/@social_65128/differences-between-conversational-ai-and-generative-ai-e3adca2a8e9a

The primary differences between the two subfields are in the following sequence of points:

- Primary Objective
- Applications

- Technologies Used
- Training and Interaction
- Evaluation
- Data Requirements

Primary Objective

The main goal of conversational AI is to facilitate human-like interactions between machines and humans. This includes chatbots, virtual assistants, and other systems that engage in dialogue with users.

The primary objective of generative AI is to create new content or data that was not in the training set but is similar in structure and style. This can range from generating images, music, and text to more complex tasks, like video synthesis.

Applications

Common applications for conversational AI include customer support chatbots, voice-operated virtual assistants (like Siri or Alexa), and interactive voice response (IVR) systems.

There are numerous generative AI applications, such as those for creating art or music, generating realistic video game environments, synthesizing voices, and producing realistic images or deep fakes.

Technologies Used

Conversational AI often relies on natural language processing (NLP) techniques to understand and generate human language. This includes intent recognition, entity extraction, and dialogue management.

Generative AI commonly utilizes Generative Adversarial Networks (GANs), Variational Autoencoders (VAEs), and other generative models to produce new content, such as ChatGPT and GPT-4.

Training and Interaction

While training can be supervised, semi-supervised, or unsupervised, the primary interaction mode for conversational AI is through back-and-forth dialogue or conversation.

The training process for generative AI, especially with models like GANs, involves iterative processes where the model learns to generate data by trying to fool a discriminator into believing the generated data is real.

Evaluation

Conversational AI evaluation metrics often revolve around understanding and response accuracy, user satisfaction, and the fluency of generated responses.

Generative AI evaluation metrics for models like GANs can be challenging and might involve using a combination of quantitative metrics and human judgment to assess the quality of the generated content.

Data Requirements

Data requirements for conversational AI typically involve dialogue data, with conversations between humans or between humans and bots. Large datasets of the kind of content the AI is supposed to generate (such as images, text, and music) are necessary.

Although both conversational AI and generative AI deal with generating outputs, their primary objectives, applications, and methodologies can differ significantly. Conversational AI is designed for interactive communication with users, while generative AI focuses on producing new, original content.

IS DALL-E PART OF GENERATIVE AI?

DALL-E and similar tools that generate graphics from text are indeed examples of generative AI. In fact, DALL-E is one of the most prominent examples of generative AI in the realm of image synthesis.

Here's a list of generative characteristics of DALL-E, followed by brief descriptions of each item:

- Image generation
- Learning distributions
- Innovative combinations
- Broad applications
- Transformer architecture

Image generation is a key feature of DALL-E, which was designed to generate images based on textual descriptions. Given a prompt like "a two-headed flamingo," DALL-E can produce a novel image that matches the description, even if such an image was not included in its training data.

Learning distributions: Like other generative models, DALL-E learns the probability distribution of its training data. When it generates an image, it samples from this learned distribution to produce visuals that are plausible based on its training.

Innovative combinations: DALL-E can generate images that represent novel or abstract concepts, showcasing its ability to combine and recombine learned elements in innovative ways.

In addition to image synthesis, DALL-E has provided broad application support in areas like art generation, style blending, and creating images with specific attributes or themes, highlighting its versatility as a generative tool. DALL-E leverages a variant of the transformer architecture, similar to models like GPT-3, but adapted for image generation tasks.

Other tools that generate graphics, art, or any form of visual content based on input data (whether it is text, another image, or any other form of data) and can produce outputs not explicitly present in their training data are also considered generative AI. They showcase the capability of AI models to not just analyze and classify, but to create and innovate.

ARE CHATGPT-3 AND GPT-4 PART OF GENERATIVE AI?

Both ChatGPT-3 and GPT-4 are LLMs and are examples of generative AI. They belong to a class of models called "transformers," which are particularly adept at handling sequences of data, such as text-related tasks.

The following list provides reasons why these LLMs are considered generative, followed by a brief description of each item:

- Text generation
- Learning distributions
- Broad applications
- Unsupervised learning

Text generation: These models can produce coherent, contextually relevant, and often highly sophisticated sequences of text based on given prompts. They generate responses that were not explicitly present in their training data, but are constructed based on the patterns and structures they learned during training.

Learning distributions: GPT-3, GPT-4, and similar models learn the probability distribution of their training data. When generating text, they are essentially sampling from this learned distribution to produce sequences that are likely based on their training.

Broad applications: Beyond just text-based chat or conversation, these models can be used for a variety of generative tasks, like story writing, code generation, poetry, and creating content in specific styles or mimicking certain authors, showcasing their generative capabilities.

Unsupervised learning: While they can be fine-tuned with specific datasets, models like GPT-3 are primarily trained in an unsupervised manner on vast amounts of text, learning to generate content without requiring explicit labeled data for every possible response.

In essence ChatGPT-3, GPT-4, and similar models by OpenAI are quintessential examples of generative AI in the realm of natural language processing and generation.

The next several sections briefly introduce some of the companies that have a strong presence in the AI world.

DEEPMIND

DeepMind has made significant contributions to AI, including the creation of various AI systems. DeepMind was established in 2010 and became a subsidiary of Google 2014. Its home page is *https://deepmind.com/*.

DeepMind created the 280 GB language model Gopher that significantly outperforms its competitors, including GPT-3, J1-Jumbo, and MT-NLG. DeepMind also developed AlphaFold, which solved a protein folding task in 30 minutes that had eluded researchers for ten years. DeepMind made AlphaFold available for free for everyone in July 2021. DeepMind has made significant contributions in the development of AI game systems, some of which are discussed in the next section.

DeepMind and Games

DeepMind is the force behind the AI systems AlphaStar, which plays StarCraft, and AlphaGo, which defeated the best human players in Go (which is considerably more difficult than chess). These games provide "perfect information," whereas games with "imperfect information" (such as poker) have posed a challenge for machine learning (ML) models.

AlphaGo Zero (the successor of AlphaGo) mastered the game through self-play in less time and with less computing power. AlphaGo Zero exhibited extraordinary performance by defeating AlphaGo 100–0. Another powerful system is AlphaZero, which also used a self-play technique to play Go, chess, and shogi; the system achieved SOTA ("State Of The Art") performance results.

By way of comparison, ML models that use tree search are well-suited for games with perfect information. By contrast, games with imperfect information (such as poker) involve hidden information that can be leveraged to devise counter strategies to counteract the strategies of opponents. In particular, AlphaStar is capable of playing against the best players of StarCraft II and became the first AI to achieve SOTA results in a game that requires "strategic capability in an imperfect information world."

Player of Games (PoG)

The DeepMind team at Google devised the general-purpose PoG (Player of Games) algorithm that is based on the following techniques:

- CFR (counterfactual regret minimization)
- CVPN (counterfactual value-and-policy network)
- GT-CFT (growing tree CFR)
- CVPN

The counterfactual value-and-policy network (CVPN) is a neural network that calculates the counterfactuals for each state belief in the game. This is critical for evaluating the different variants of the game at any given time.

Growing tree CFR (GT-CFR) is a variation of CFR that is optimized for game-trees trees that grow over time. GT-CFR is based on two fundamental phases, which is discussed in more detail online:

https://medium.com/syncedreview/deepminds-pog-excels-in-perfect-and-imperfect-information-games-advancing-research-on-general-9dbad5c04221

OPENAI

OpenAI is an AI research company that has made significant contributions to AI, including DALL-E and ChatGPT. Its home page is online: *https://openai.com/api/*.

OpenAI was founded in San Francisco by Elon Musk and Sam Altman (as well as others), and one of its stated goals is to develop AI that benefits humanity. Given Microsoft's massive investments in and deep alliance with the organization, OpenAI might be viewed as part of Microsoft. OpenAI is the creator of the GPT-x series of LLMs, as well as ChatGPT, which was made available on November 30, 2022.

OpenAI made GPT-3 (discussed in Chapter 7) commercially available via API for use across applications, charging on a per-word basis. GPT-3 was announced in July 2020 and was made available through a beta program. Then, in November 2021, OpenAI made GPT-3 open to everyone. More details are accessible online:

https://openai.com/blog/api-no-waitlist/

In addition, OpenAI developed DALL-E, which generates images from text. OpenAI initially did not permit users to upload images that contained realistic faces. Later, OpenAI changed its policy to allow users to upload faces into its online system. (Check the OpenAI website for more details.) Incidentally, diffusion models (discussed in Chapter 10) have superseded the benchmarks of DALL-E.

OpenAI has released a public beta of Embeddings, which is a data format that is suitable for various types of tasks with machine learning, as described online:

https://beta.openai.com/docs/guides/embeddings

OpenAI is the creator of Codex, which provides a set of models that were trained on NLP. The initial release of Codex was in private beta; more information is accessible online: *https://beta.openai.com/docs/engines/instruct-series-beta*.

OpenAI provides four models that are collectively called their "Instruct Models," which support the ability of GPT-3 to generate natural language. These models will be deprecated in early January 2024, and replaced with updated versions of GPT-3, ChatGPT, and GPT-4, as discussed in Chapter 7.

If you want to learn more about the features and services that OpenAI offers, navigate to the following link: *https://platform.openai.com/overview*.

COHERE

Cohere is a start-up and a competitor of OpenAI; its home page is *https://cohere.ai/*.

Cohere develops cutting-edge NLP technology that is commercially available for multiple industries. Cohere is focused on models that perform textual analysis instead of models for text generation (such as GPT-based models). The founding team of Cohere is impressive: CEO Aidan Gomez is one of the co-inventors of the transformer architecture, and CTO Nick Frosst is a protege of Geoff Hinton.

HUGGING FACE

Hugging Face is a popular community-based repository for open-source NLP technology; its home page is *https://github.com/huggingface*.

Unlike OpenAI or Cohere, Hugging Face does not build its own NLP models. Instead, Hugging Face is a platform that manages a plethora of open-source NLP models that customers can fine-tune and then deploy those fine-tuned models. Indeed, Hugging Face has become the eminent location for people to collaborate on NLP models, and it is sometimes described as "GitHub for machine learning and NLP."

Hugging Face Libraries

Hugging Face provides three important libraries: datasets, tokenizers, and transformers (discussed in Chapter 3). The Accelerate library supports PyTorch models. The datasets library provides an assortment of libraries for NLP. The tokenizers library enables you to convert text data to numeric values. Perhaps the most impressive library is the transformers library, which provides an enormous set of pre-trained BERT-based models (discussed in Chapter 5) to perform a wide variety of NLP tasks. The Github repository is at *https://github.com/huggingface/transformers*.

Hugging Face Model Hub

Hugging Face provides a model hub that provides a plethora of models that are accessible online. Moreover, the website supports online testing of its models, which includes the following tasks:

- Masked word completion with BERT
- Named Entity Recognition with Electra
- Natural Language Inference with RoBERTa
- Question answering with DistilBERT
- Summarization with BART
- Text generation with GPT-2
- Translation with T5

Navigate to the following link to see the text generation capabilities of "write with transformer:" *https://transformer.huggingface.co*.

In a subsequent chapter, you will see Python code samples that show how to list all the available Hugging Face datasets and how to load a specific dataset.

AI21

`AI21` is a company that provides proprietary large language models via API to support the applications of its customers. The current SOTA model of `AI21` is called `Jurassic-1` (roughly the same size as `GPT-3`), and `AI21` also creates its own applications on top of `Jurassic-1` and other models. The current application suite of `AI21` involves tools that can augment reading and writing.

`Primer` is an older competitor in this space, founded two years before the invention of the transformer. The company primarily serves clients in government and defense.

INFLECTIONAI

A more recent company in the `AI` field is `InflectionAI`, whose impressive founding team includes

- Reid Hoffman (LinkedIn)
- DeepMind cofounder Mustafa Suleyman
- DeepMind researcher Karen Simonyan

`InflectionAI` is committed to a challenging task: enabling humans to interact with computers in much the same way that humans communicate with each other.

ANTHROPIC

Anthropic was created in 2021 by former employees of OpenAI, and its home page is *https://www.anthropic.com/*.

Anthropic has significant financial support from an assortment of companies, including Google and Salesforce. As this book goes to print, Anthropic released Claude 2 as a competitor to ChatGPT. Expect Anthropic to make its API available by Q4 of 2023.

Claude 2 has the ability to summarize as much as 75,000 words of text-based content, whereas ChatGPT currently has a limit of 3,000 words. Moreover, Claude 2 achieved a score of 76.5% on portions of the bar exam and 71% in a `Python` coding test. Claude 2 also has a higher rate than `ChatGPT` in terms of providing "clean" responses to queries from users.

This concludes the portion of the chapter regarding the AI companies making important contributions in AI. The next section provides a high-level introduction to LLMs.

WHAT ARE LLMS?

Large language models, LLMs, are based on the transformer architecture. There are many LLMs of varying sizes, many of which are larger than BERT-based models (discussed in Chapters 5 and 6). As such, this section provides a very brief overview of the LLM landscape.

LLMs are known for their size, which is typically at least 10 billion parameters (BERT has "only" 1.5 billion parameters). Moreover, they involve very large datasets for the training step, which can require weeks of training time at a cost of millions of dollars. Unfortunately, there is an associated environment cost. According to the following article, the carbon footprint of training GPT-3 is comparable to a car's round-trip visit to the moon:

https://www.theregister.com/2020/11/04/gpt3_carbon_footprint_estimate/

Outside of BERT and the BERT family, perhaps the most well-known LLM that generated tremendous interest is GPT-3. GPT-3 consists of 175 billion parameters, which is almost 120 times larger than BERT. However, there are models that are much larger: Switch used 540 billion parameters and DAO used more than 1.2 trillion parameters. More recently (November, 2022) ChatGPT created a sensational impact on the general public (100 million registered users in two months), which is discussed in chapter 9.

Model Size Versus Training Set Size

Although it might be tempting to think that sheer size is the most important factor, the size of the training data set is more significant. This statement contravenes the results from Kaplan and his team, who researched the training set size versus the model size. (This is an important point, and it is discussed in more detail in Chapter 9.) Let's take a brief look at some LLMs that have been developed.

The `Chinchilla` LLM from DeepMind consists of 70 billion parameters, and it is able to outperform GPT-3, Jurassic-1 (178 billion), and Megatron-Turing (530 billion) because its training dataset was five times larger than the training datasets for the other LLMs.

Despite the impressive results of LLMs and the highly anticipated functionality of GPT-4 (released on March 14, 2023), LLMs are not capable of understanding language in the manner of human beings. The ability of an entity to make intelligent choices that are comparable to those made by humans does not prove that that entity truly understands those choices in the same way as a human.

Do LLMs Understand Language?

As a whimsical and partially related analogy, consider the following story that involves two chess grand masters, a confidence man, and a 12-year-old boy who are traveling on a cross-Atlantic ship during the early 1900s.

When the ship was several hours from its destination, the confidence man made an audacious bet that in the span of two hours, he could train the young boy to play chess so that the matches would result in either a draw or win for the boy. However, the grand masters and the boy were required to play in a closet-like cloaked area, and the three participants were not permitted to communicate in any manner with each other.

The grand masters accepted the challenge, expecting that they would leverage their tremendous knowledge over the young competitor. However, as the games progressed, the grand masters were shocked by the speed and sophistication of the chess moves of the boy. Their confidence was quickly replaced by concern and then by desperation. Eventually, one grand master offered a draw, and the other grand master conceded the match.

The deception was exceedingly simple: whenever one grand master made a chess move, the boy would make the same chess move against the *other* grand master, which effectively meant that the grand masters were competing against each other. Fortunately for the confidence man, the ship reached its destination, and he managed to collect the reward and the boy and then disembark before the chess grand masters realized that they had been swindled.

The point of the preceding story is that the boy made extremely intelligent chess moves, but did not necessarily understand the logic for making those chess moves. Hence, if a human being does not understand the logic behind an action, it suggests that it is even less likely for an LLM to have a human-level understanding of the reasons for its recommendations.

Caveats Regarding LLMs

Although LLMs are capable of impressive results, keep in mind the following points:

- smaller models can outperform larger models (in some tasks)
- models generate false results ("hallucinating")
- Some models process long documents and others are more conversational.
- the increasing relevance of vector databases
- Most models are not trained on up-to-date datasets (only up to a certain point in time).

For example, ChatGPT was trained on data prior to September 2021. Two features that are becoming increasing important to address are

1. the ability to maintain the history of previous conversations

2. the ability to perform on-the-fly Internet searches for information

Moreover, it is worth comparing the features of open source models to closed source models. Indeed, Yann LeCunn supposedly remarked that "open-source will eventually win the AI race."

Loss Functions

Deep learning models include models that are based on the transformer architecture. Such models rely on a loss function to train them. Specifically, a *loss function* is a differentiable function that determines the error arising from the predictions of a given model.

During each backward pass (called "backward error propagation" or "back prop") in a model, the loss function calculates a gradient (i.e., a vector of partial derivatives) of the model's parameters to update the weights of the parameters for the purpose of improving the accuracy of the model.

During the training process, the sequence of numbers regarding the accuracy of the model is not always a monotonically increasing set of numbers: some iterations perform worse than their immediate predecessors and sometimes there is no improvement whatsoever.

WHAT IS AI DRIFT?

The term *AI drift* refers to the scenario in which LLMs respond to inputs in an unexpected manner. AI drift may be different from hallucinating:

the former involves regular or consistently unexpected behavior, whereas *hallucinating* can occur randomly but not necessarily in a consistent pattern. In fact, you can even "induce" hallucinating-like behavior in LLMs when you invoke the `Completion.create()` method (see the Python examples in Chapter 8) in which the temperature parameter is set to a value that is larger than 1.0.

One potential cause of AI drift might be the unintended result of improving one area of LLMs that inadvertently results in worse performance in other areas of an LLM.

Another potential cause of drift involves *model drift*, which can occur when the production data is substantively different from training data. In this scenario, monitor production data and training data as well as predictions.

The consequences of AI drift can be significant. For instance, your decision-making process is vulnerable to AI drift, which can lead to decisions formed from incorrect assumptions. This, in turn, can result in lower quality predictions and recommendations, as well as adversely affecting customer satisfaction.

MACHINE LEARNING AND DRIFT (OPTIONAL)

In machine learning terms, *drift* refers to any type of change in distribution over a period of time. *Model drift* refers to a change (drift) in the accuracy of a model's prediction, whereas *data drift* refers to a change in the type of data that is collected. (Note that data drift is also called input drift, feature drift, or covariate drift.)

There are several factors that influence the value of data, such as accuracy, relevance, and age. For example, physical stores that sell mobile phones are much more likely to sell recent phone models than older models. In some cases, data drift occurs over a period of time, and in other cases, it is because some data is no longer relevant due to feature-related changes in an application. There might be multiple factors that can influence data drift in a specific dataset.

Two techniques for handling data drift are *domain classifier* and the *black-box shift detector*, both of which are discussed online:

https://blog.dataiku.com/towards-reliable-mlops-with-drift-detectors

In addition to the preceding types of drift, other types of changes can occur in a dataset:

• Concept shift
• Covariate shift

- Domain shift
- Prior probability shift
- Spurious correlation shift
- Subpopulation shift
- Time shift

See *https://arxiv.org/abs/1912.08142* for additional information on changes in datasets.

Perform an online search to find more information about the topics in the preceding list of items. Finally, the following list contains websites for open-source `Python`-based tools that provide drift detection:

- alibi-detect (*https://github.com/SeldonIO/alibi-detect*)
- evidently (*https://github.com/evidentlyai/evidently*)
- Torchdrift (*http://torchdrift.org/*)

With the preceding topics in mind, let's shift our focus to the concept of attention, which is the topic of the next section. For additional insights into this topic, read the following article:

https://sebastianraschka.com/blog/2023/self-attention-from-scratch. html

WHAT IS ATTENTION?

Attention is a mechanism in the transformer architecture by which contextual word embeddings are determined for words in a corpus. Unlike `word2vec` or `gloVe`, the attention mechanism takes into account *all* the words in a sentence during the process of creating a word embedding for a given word in a given sentence. For example, consider the following list of sentences:

I went to the bank.

I sat on the river bank.

The road will bank to the right.

As you can see, the word "bank" is overloaded in the sense that it has a different meaning in each of the three sentences (and twice as a noun and once as a verb). The attention mechanism in the transformer architecture generates a different context vector (i.e., a one-dimensional vector with floating point numbers). Hence, the same word in different (and distinct) sentences will have a different word embedding in each of those sentences. Interestingly, the attention mechanism existed before the transformer architecture: the use of attention in the latter is where the attention mechanism achieved its prominence.

By contrast, the `word2vec` algorithm (developed in 2013 by Google) creates a single word embedding (vector) for the word "bank" (as well as any other word in a given sentencr). This is not intended as a criticism of `word2vec`, which was an important breakthrough for NLP at the time of its creation.

The Origin of Attention

Before the attention mechanism was devised, popular architectures were based on other deep learning architectures such as RNNs, LSTMs, or bi-LSTMs. In fact, the attention mechanism was initially used in conjunction with RNNs or LSTMs. However, the Google team performed some experiments involving machine translation tasks on models that relied solely on the attention mechanism and the transformer architecture, and discovered that those models achieved higher performance that models that included CNNs, RNNs, or LSTMs. This result led to the expression "attention is all you need," which happens to be the title of the seminal paper regarding the transformer architecture:

https://papers.nips.cc/paper/2017/file/3f5ee243547dee91fbd053c1c4 a845aa-Paper.pdf

Interestingly, the removal of RNNs provided two additional benefits. First, RNNs were relatively slow due to sequential computation that cannot be parallelized. Second, RNNs suffered from the vanishing gradient problem. Consequently, removing RNNs eliminated both of these disadvantages.

In highly simplified terms, a transformer consists of an encoder and a decoder, each of which involves a stack of attention layers that perform attention-related operations, which you will learn about in Chapter 4.

Self-Attention

Self-attention can be parallelized so that calculations are performed independently. Hence, implementations of self-attention involve $O(N**2)$ complexity for time as well as memory. Google researchers devised an algorithm that significantly reduces memory complexity to $O(\log N)$.

Although standard implementations of self-attention have time and memory complexity, recent work by Google researchers shows that the memory complexity can be reduced to via a simple reordering of the operations.

If you are familiar with RNNs and LSTMs, you know that both architectures process tokens sequentially, and they can keep track of the order in which tokens appear in an input sequence. By contrast, the transformer architecture can process words in a sentence in a parallelized manner, and the sequence in which words appear in an input sequence is not maintained. The transformer architecture uses a mechanism called *positional encodings* (discussed in Chapter 3) to keep track of the sequence of words in an input sequence.

GAtt (Ghost Attention)

GAtt is an algorithm used for fine tuning the LLM LlaMa 2 Chat from Meta (discussed in Chapter 9). GAtt was developed to address the problem in which ChatGPT has a tendency to "forget" instructions during the course of long conversations. More information regarding GAtt is accessible online:

https://betterprogramming.pub/the-dawn-of-a-new-era-llama2-b0b1a9175029

Types of Attention and Algorithms

In addition to hierarchical attention, there are additional types of attention mechanisms, three of which are

1. self-attention
2. global/soft
3. local/hard

Self-attention tries to determine how words in a sentence are interconnected with each other. *Multi-headed attention* uses a block of multiple self-attention instead of just one self-attention. However, each head processes a different section of the embedding vector. In addition to the preceding attention mechanisms, there are also several attention algorithms available:

- Additive
- Content-based
- Dot Product
- General
- Location-base
- Scaled Dot Product <= a transformer uses this algorithm

The formulas for attention mechanisms fall into two categories: formulas that involve a dot product of vectors (and sometimes with a scaling factor) and formulas that apply a `softmax()` function or a `tanh()` function to the products of matrices and vectors.

The transformer architecture uses a scaled dot-product mechanism to calculate the attention. There are several attention types available, and the following article contains a list of more than 20 attention types:

https://paperswithcode.com/methods/category/attention-mechanisms-1

A benefit of attention is the parallelization of the calculations involving inner products between pairs of word vectors, whereas RNNs and LSTMs involve sequential calculations instead of parallelization.

Note: The transformer architecture uses a scaled dot-product mechanism to calculate the attention.

Attention in GPT-2 Versus BERT

LLMs can differ in terms of their self-attention mechanism. For instance, self-attention in a GPT-2 decoder component (discussed in Chapter 7) differs from self-attention in a BERT encoder component (discussed in Chapter 5). For more details regarding these different attention mechanisms, read Jay Allamar's Illustrated GPT-2 post that is accessible online:

https://www.linkedin.com/pulse/illustrated-gpt-2-visualizing-transformer-language-jay/

CALCULATING ATTENTION: A HIGH-LEVEL VIEW

The calculation of attention-based values involves multiple steps. To facilitate an understanding of this process, let's review the forward propagation step in neural networks.

Forward Propagation in Neural Networks

The forward propagation step in neural networks can help us understand the role of the matrices Q, K, and V in the attention mechanism for the transformer architecture. Recall that a neural network consists of an input layer, one or more hidden layers, and an output layer. Given any pair of adjacent layers in a neural network, the weights of the parameters (i.e., edges) between the adjacent layers are represented by a matrix W.

Of course, the content of matrix W is different for different pairs of adjacent layers in the neural network.

The forward pass starts from the input layer and proceeds as follows until we reach the output layer:

1. the input layer is a vector v1

2. v2 = matrix W multiplied by vector v1

3. v3 = activation function applied to v2

4. repeat steps 2, 3, and 4

The matrix W can be initialized with small random values (or you can use the He algorithm) and those values are updated during backward error propagation (which happens after the forward pass has completed). Hence, the values in the matrix W are tuned during the training process involving a neural network.

The Matrices Q, K, and V of the Transformer

One way to think of these three matrices is their role in performing an Internet search through a search engine. The typical use case involves the following:

- Specifying a search string (query)
- Selecting one of the options returned by the search engine (key)
- Viewing the contents of the selected option (value)

Although you might not think of the middle step when you perform a search, it is important to think of a search as the three steps in the preceding list. Let's think of the query, key, and value as vectors in the Euclidean plane (just to keep things simple).

When you view the results returned for a query string, you will see a list of multiple links (and many additional pages containing multiple links). Think of each link as a key that has a corresponding vector in the Euclidean plane. Conceptually, the link that you select corresponds to the vector that is closest to the query vector. Moreover, the act of selecting (i.e., clicking on) that link causes the search engine to retrieve the *value* of that link (key), which is the content of the associated link.

To summarize, an input string (query) is matched with the closest vector (key) of a set of vectors (keys) to retrieve the content (value) associated with the selected vector (key).

The Steps for Calculating Attention

Although the process for calculating attention values is different from the calculations of the matrix W in the example involving neural networks that was discussed in an earlier section, the counterpart to the matrix W involves three matrices Q, K, and V, each of which is randomly initialized. The sequence of steps for calculating the attention matrix are listed here:

- Tokenize an input sentence.
- Generate an embedding vector for each token.
- Create matrix X from the embedding vectors.
- Initialize three matrices: Q, K, and V.
- Calculate Q*Kt with pairwise values.
- Divide by the scalar dk2 = sqrt (dimensionality of the key vector).
- Apply a softmax() function to Q*Kt/dk2.
- Calculate the attention matrix Z.

An alternate (and shorter) way to describe the sequence of steps for calculating the attention matrix that includes the dimensionality of the matrices is shown here:

```
    X        Wq/Wk/Wv    ⌐ Q/K/V
4x512  *   512x64     = 4x64


1) Q*Kt                        [4x64 * 64x4 = 4x4]
2) Q*Kt/sqrt(dk)               [4x4]
3) softmax[Q*Kt/sqrt(dk)]      [4x4]
4) softmax[Q*Kt/sqrt(dk)]*V    [4x4 * 4x64 = 4x64]
```

The next section contains an example of performing each step in the preceding list.

AN EXAMPLE OF SELF ATTENTION

Consider the input sentence "I love Chicago pizza," which contains four tokens, and calculate the word embeddings (i.e., floating-point vectors) for each token.

The initial values for each word embedding can be random numbers, and the correct values for the floating-point numbers in each word vector are determined during the training step. Recall that the weights of the parameters in two adjacent layers in a neural network can be initialized with random numbers, and those values are updated during backward error propagation during the training phase.

Let's assume that the width of each vector is 512 and arbitrarily assign the embeddings y1, y2, y3, and y4 to the words "I," "love," "Chicago," and "pizza," respectively, as follows:

```
y1 = [5.32 7.56 . . . 0.234]
y2 = [8.65 0.58 . . . 2.085]
y3 = [0.95 3.47 . . . 6.813]
y4 = [3.91 5.72 . . . 7.055]
```

Now we can create a matrix X whose rows consist of the vectors y1, y2, y3, and y4, as shown here:

```
    |5.32 7.56 . . . 0.234|
X = |8.65 0.58 . . . 4.085|
    |0.95 3.47 . . . 6.813|
    |3.91 5.72 . . . 7.055|
```

Matrix X is a 4x512 matrix of floating point numbers, and if the input sentence has P words, then matrix X is a Px512 matrix.

We generate three matrices with randomly initialized values that we name Wq, Wk, and Wv, after which we can initialize the three matrices Q, K, and V that are used in self-attention, as shown here:

- a query matrix Q = X*Wq
- a key matrix   K = X*Wk
- a value matrix V = X*Wv

The matrices Q, K, and V are somewhat analogous to the matrix W in the previous section: they are initialized with random values and updated during the training step. The next details to observe are as follows:

- The 1st row in Q/K/V: the query/key/value vectors of the word I
- The 2nd row in Q/K/V: the query/key/value vectors of the word love
- The 3rd row in Q/K/V: the query/key/value vectors of the word Chicago
- The 4th row in Q/K/V: the query/key/value vectors of the word pizza 6.

Calculate the Matrix Q*Kt

Now we are ready to calculate a matrix that equals the product of the matrix Q and the matrix Kt (the transpose of matrix K). The product of these two matrices results in a matrix whose cell values contain all possible dot (inner) products between every pair of words in the original sentence. Recall that the inner product of two vectors provides a measure of the similarity between the two vectors.

For example, the *first* row of Q*Kt is the inner product of the query vector "I" with the key vectors I, love, Chicago, and pizza.

The *second* row of Q*Kt is the inner product of the query vector "love" with the key vectors I, love, Chicago, and pizza.

The *third* row of Q*Kt is the inner product of the query vector "Chicago" with the key vectors I, love, Chicago, and pizza.

The *fourth* row of Q*Kt is the inner product of the query vector "pizza" with the key vectors I, love, Chicago, and pizza.

Just to emphasize the earlier statement regarding the contents of Q*Kt: the product matrix contains the inner product of the word embedding for every token (word) in the original sentence "I love Chicago pizza" with every other word embedding in this sentence.

The preceding calculation has complexity O(N**2), where N is the number of tokens in the input sentence. However, these computations are independent of each other, which means that they can be performed in parallel, which is not possible with RNNs and LSTMs. Moreover, there are variations of the transformer architecture, such as the Reformer architecture, that have achieved lower than quadratic complexity.

Divide by the Square Root of the Vector Dimensionality

The vector dimensionality dk equals 64, so its square root is 8. We need to divide Q*Kt by this value to "scale down" its values. Note that the dk term was empirically determined, and it works well as a scaling factor.

Apply a Softmax Function to Q*Kt/dk

Applying a softmax() function to the rows of the matrix Q*Kt/dk accomplishes two things: 1) all values lie between 0 and 1, and 2) each row is a discrete probability distribution.

The values in the matrix Q*Kt/dk provide a relative measure of how any pair of words are related. For example, suppose that the first row contains the following values:

```
[0.88 0.06 0.03 0.03]
```

Keeping in mind that the rows and the columns are labeled with the tokens in the sentence "I love Chicago pizza," we now know that the values in the first row provide the following information:

```
0.88 is the correlation between I and I
0.06 is the correlation between I and love
```

```
0.03 is the correlation between I and Chicago
0.03 is the correlation between I and pizza
```

Similar results can be obtained from rows 2, 3, and 4 of the matrix
Q*Kt/dk.

Calculate the Attention Matrix Z

We can now define the attention matrix Z, which is the product of two
matrices:

```
Z = softmax [(Q*Kt/dk)] * V
```

The labels for the rows and columns in the matrix Q*Kt/dk and the
matrix V are all the same: they consist of the tokens in the sentence "I
love Chicago pizza." The self-attention values for each word equals the
weighted sum of product of each row in the Q*Kt/dk matrix with the
values in the V matrix.

The self-attention mechanism is also known as the *scaled dot product attention* because it equals the scaled values of the inner product of
Q and Kt.

For example, let y1, y2, y3, and y4 be the word embeddings for
the tokens "I," "love," "Chicago," and "pizza," respectively, which have
been arbitrarily assigned the following values:

```
y1: [0.823, 4.432, 2.789, . . ., 7.123]
y2: [2.382, 3.432, 8.786, . . ., 6.459]
y3: [3.569, 2.432, 5.783, . . ., 4.684]
y4: [5.277, 0.426, 0.123, . . ., 9.001]
```

Although the vectors for y1, y2, y3, and y4 consist of 512 components, and the actual values will be different from the values specified
above, they are still useful for the purpose of illustration. Next, let's create a matrix with these same four vectors, as shown here:

```
      |0.823, 4.432, 2.789, . . ., 7.123|
X  =  |2.382, 3.432, 8.786, . . ., 6.459|
      |3.569, 2.432, 5.783, . . ., 4.684|
      |5.277, 0.426, 0.123, . . ., 9.001|
```

We will also create three weight matrices Wq, Wk, and Wv, which are
initialized with random values that are updated during the training process, somewhat analogous to the training step for an MLP (multi-layer
perceptron). We create the three matrices' query matrix Q, key matrix K,
and value matrix V by multiplying X with their preceding counterparts,
as shown here:

```
Q = X*Wq
K = X*Wk
V = X*Wv
```

The Q, K, and V matrices have the dimensionality 4x64 because they are the product of a 4x512 matrix X with a 512x64 matrix: hence, the product is a 4x64 matrix. In addition, each row in Q, K, and V is associated with the corresponding word of our input sentence "I love Chicago pizza." However, the contents of Q, K, and V are different from the contents of X.

The product Q*Kt is a 4x4 self-attention matrix that contains the similarity of every input token y1, y2, y3, and y4 with *all the tokens* in the input sentence, as shown here:

```
        y1      y2      y3      y4
y1  |0.823,  4.432,  2.789,  123|
y2  |2.382,  3.432,  8.786,  456|
y3  |3.569,  2.432,  5.783,  789|
y4  |5.277,  0.426,  0.123,  432|
```

Thus, the diagonal entries in the preceding matrix represent the similarity of each input token with itself.

The next step involves *scaling* the entries in the preceding matrix, and based on the original attention paper, the matrix values are decreased by dividing by the square root of dk, which is the dimensionality of the key vector. In our case, dk equals 64, so the square root equals 8. The new matrix is shown here:

```
        y1      y2      y3      y4
y1  |0.104,  0.554,  0.348,  15.375|
y2  |0.297,  0.422,  1.098,  57.000|
y3  |0.446,  0.304,  0.724,  98.625|
y4  |0.659,  0.053,  0.015,  54.000|
```

MULTI-HEAD ATTENTION (MHA)

The preceding section discusses the steps for calculating self-attention for every word in an input sentence. Multi-head attention involves calculating *multiple* attention matrices instead of a single attention matrix. A single head processes one "stack" of the flow that starts with an embedding vector and progresses through each encoder component (which typically involves 6 or 12 such components). Please read the following article for additional information:

https://towardsdatascience.com/intuition-behind-transformers-architecture-nlp-c2ac36174047

The process for creating multiple attention matrices involves replicating the steps for creating the initial attention matrix, which means creating a new set of matrices Q, K, and V, which are multiplied by a new set of matrices Wq, Wk, and Wv, respectively.

The original attention research paper specifies 8 attention heads, which means that we would calculate the attention matrices Z1, Z2, ..., Z8. The next step is to concatenate Z1, Z2, ..., Z8 to create a final matrix Zf, and then multiply Zf by the concatenation of the set of matrices W1, W2, ..., W8, which results in a single matrix that we call MHA (multi-head attention).

In summary, scaled dot-product attention computes an inner product for each query Q with all the keys K, the result of which is divided by the dk (the square root of the dimension d) that is then passed through the softmax() activation function. The result of the preceding sentence is a matrix that is multiplied with the value matrix V, resulting in a matrix that is a scaled version of the matrix V.

Check the diagram for the transformation architecture and notice that there are three inputs to the multi-head attention: these inputs are the Q, K, and V vectors.

In addition, the formula for single-head attention does not involve weights for the softmax() attention, and in the case of multi-head attention, the weights appear before the actual scaled dot-product attention is performed. In fact, the weights appear in the linear layers that are placed lower in the diagram and prior to the calculation of the scaled dot-product attention.

Note that inner products can become large and can result in a "vanishing gradient" type of effect (hence, the introduction of a scaling factor dk to produce scaled values that avoid this effect).

The preceding sections showed you how to compute the attention values from the matrices Q, K, and V. We can also calculate multiple attention matrices, each of which is based on a different set of values for the matrices Q, K, and V. While this might seem unnecessary, consider the analogous situation in CNNs (convolutional neural networks), which is discussed in more detail in the next section.

While this might seem unnecessary, consider the analogous operation in CNNs (convolutional neural networks) that involves performing convolutions of multiple independent small randomly generated filters (typically 3x3) with an array of pixel values for a PNG.

CNN Filters and Multi-Head Attention

Recall that the convolution process involves specifying a number of filters, which are square matrices that are initialized with random values. Next, we apply a convolution, the ReLU activation function, and max pooling that can be performed multiple times. This sequence of operations is performed for every filter, and after those operations are completed, we concatenate the results obtained from each filter. The concatenated result can be passed to one or more fully connected layers, and the last step involves applying a softmax() function to obtain the output later.

Now, let's again consider multi-head attention. Suppose we want to calculate 8 multi-head attention values. Analogous to the filters in a CNN, we need to calculate 8 attention matrices {Z1, Z2, . . . , Z8}, where each of these values is calculated in the same fashion as you saw previously. In the case of CNNs, this would involve 8 different filters, and in the case of attention values, this involves 8 sets of triples {Q, K, V}, all of which are independently initialized with random values.

The final step involves concatenating the matrices in {Z1, Z2, . . . , Z8} and then multiplying by the matrix W to obtain a final attention matrix, as shown here:

```
MHA = concatenation(Z1, Z2, . . ., Z8) * W
```

SUMMARY

This chapter started with a brief description of several companies, such as DeepMind, OpenAI, and Hugging Face, that are leaders in AI. Next, you learned about LLMs (large language models) and model size versus training set size.

You learned about the attention mechanism, which is a vitally important component of the Transformer architecture (discussed in Chapters 3 and 4), and how this mechanism is useful for obtaining contextual information from text. You also learned about self-attention and the some of the details for calculating attention.

Finally, you learned about the use of the softmax() function in conjunction with the attention mechanism in the transformer architecture.

2

TOKENIZATION

This chapter introduces you to various types of tokenization for splitting words into one or more tokens because there is a one-to-many relationship between words and tokenization.

The first section discusses pre-tokenization, the concept of a word, and the difference between pre-tokenization and tokenization. This section also contains a Python code sample involving pre-tokenization.

The second section discusses word-based, character-based, and subword tokenization, along with the trade-offs of these tokenization techniques. You will also learn about a tokenizer for BERT and a tokenizer for GPT-2, even though they are introduced later in this book, so that you can see that their tokenizers operate differently. You will also see Python-based code samples that show the actual tokenization that is generated by these language models.

Note that the Python-based code samples in this chapter currently require Python 3.7, which you can download from the Internet if you have not already done so. As this book goes to print, you might be able to use Python 3.9 (or later) for the code samples in this book.

WHAT IS PRE-TOKENIZATION?

Pre-tokenization is the first of several tasks to perform when you need to process a text-based corpus, which typically includes some subset of the following:

- Pre-tokenization
- Tokenization tasks
- Word-based tokenization
- Character-based tokenization
- Subword tokenization

Before we delve into pre-tokenization, the next section discusses something fundamental: the definition of a word.

What is a Word?

A *word* is essentially a sequence of symbols that represent something that can be either tangible or an abstraction (it is what you have always known regarding a word). A word that contains only alphabetic characters is consistently treated as a word among different tokenizers. However, tokenizers can treat contractions in English differently, especially those that tokenize on white space.

As an example, the word "I've" is a contraction of "I and "have," and is considered one word by tokenizers that split on white space, whereas tokenizers that use white space and punctuation treat "I've" as two words.

The following four methods are available for performing mapping operations between tokens, characters, and words:

- `word_to_chars()`
- `token_to_chars()`
- `char_to_word()`
- `char_to_token()`

Pre-tokenization Versus Tokenization

Hugging Face documentation makes a distinction between *pre-tokenization* and *tokenization*, whereas many online articles only use the term "tokenization." Pre-tokenization can be implemented in various ways, either individually or in combination, and three techniques are given here:

- space tokenization (such as RoBERTa and GPT-2)
- space and punctuation tokenization
- rule-based tokenization (such as FlauBERT and XLM)

The use of a space as a word separator (or a space and punctuation) in pre-tokenization coincides with "regular" tokenization that can be performed on English and most European languages. However, some European languages (such as French and German) use diacritical marks, and removing them can change the meaning of a word, as discussed in a later section.

Later in this book you will encounter the terms "uncased" and "cased" in reference to LLMs. An *uncased* LLM is an LLM in which all words are lowercase and all diacritical marks have been removed. Diacritical marks appear in several Indo-European languages, such as French, Spanish, German, and Scandinavian languages, but not in English. However, a *cased* LLM retains uppercase letters and diacritical marks (if any). Note that some languages, such as Mandarin and Japanese, do not have the concept of uppercase or lowercase letters. The choice between an uncased LLM and a cased LLM depends directly on your use case.

English is perhaps the easiest language for pre-tokenization because of the following features:

- No diacritical marks
- All words are separated by a space character
- No declension of articles or adjectives (versus German/Slavic languages)
- One form for every word in every grammatical case (e.g., Nominative and Accusative)

Moreover, an apostrophe in an English word can refer to possession or a contraction involving a verb (which can be irregular), as shown in the following sentences:

- Yes it's certainly true.
- I think that that's its true nature.
- Yes, it's true that its price is high.
- John's car is a convertible, it's new, and its top is red.
- Dave's buying a new car.
- Sara won't eat shrimp.
- Sara isn't finished yet.

Notice that the word "its" refers to *possession*, even though it does not contain an apostrophe, and it is the only exception to the rule regarding possession.

English can also treat nouns as verbs in conversations. When the context is clear, then people understand their meaning even when they hear such a construction for the first time, as illustrated in the following sentence:

"I need *to book* for an hour and then I can meet up you."

The word *book* in the previous sentence is a noun that is used as a substitute for the verb *study*. In standard English, verbs in the infinitive form are triggered by the preposition *to* that precedes a verb. However, the preceding sentence is non-standard English because it contains *to book*, and yet people can easily infer the intended meaning.

Now let's take a look at a Python-based code sample that illustrates pre-tokenization, which is discussed in the next section.

A Pre-tokenization Code Sample

Listing 2.1 displays the content of `pretokenizer1.py` that shows you how tokenizers perform tokenization for different models.

Listing 2.1: hf_transformer_mask.py

```
from transformers import AutoTokenizer

# notice the multiple white spaces:
sentence  = "I love Chicago deep dish      pizza
don't you?"

# instantiate a BERT-based tokenizer:
tokenizer = AutoTokenizer.from_pretrained
("bert-base-uncased")

# invoke the pre-tokenizer:
result1 = tokenizer.backend_tokenizer.pre_
tokenizer.pre_tokenize_str(sentence)
print("=> tokenizer: BERT")
print("sentence:  ",sentence)
print("tokenized: ",result1)
print()

# instantiate a GPT2-based tokenizer:
tokenizer = AutoTokenizer.from_pretrained("gpt2")
result2 = tokenizer.backend_tokenizer.pre_
tokenizer.pre_tokenize_str(sentence)

print("=> tokenizer: GPT2")
print("sentence:  ",sentence)
print("tokenized: ",result2)
print()
```

```
# instantiate a T5-based tokenizer:
tokenizer = AutoTokenizer.from_pretrained("t5-
small")
result3 = tokenizer.backend_tokenizer.pre_
tokenizer.pre_tokenize_str(sentence)


# instantiate a XLNetTokenizer-based tokenizer:
from transformers import XLNetTokenizer


tokenizer = XLNetTokenizer.from_pretrained
("xlnet-base-cased")
result4 = tokenizer.tokenize(sentence)


print("=> tokenizer: XLNetTokenizer")
print("sentence:   ",sentence)
print("tokenized: ",result4)
```

Listing 2.1 starts with an import statement as well as initializing the variable sentence with a text string. The rest of Listing 2.1 consists of four blocks of tokenization code for the models BERT, GPT-2, T5, and XLNetTokenizer. Each code block initializes the variable tokenizer as an instance of the model-specific tokenizer, tokenizes the text in the sentence variable, and then displays the results.

For example, the following code block illustrates the details of the preceding sentence for the BERT model:

```
# instantiate a BERT-based tokenizer:
tokenizer = AutoTokenizer.from_pretrained
("bert-base-uncased")


# invoke the pre-tokenizer:
result1 = tokenizer.backend_tokenizer.pre_
tokenizer.pre_tokenize_str(sentence)
print("=> tokenizer: BERT")
print("sentence:   ",sentence)
print("tokenized: ",result1)
print()
```

Now launch the code in Listing 2.1, and you will see the following output:

```
=> tokenizer: BERT
sentence:    I love Chicago deep dish        pizza,
don't you?
tokenized:  [('I', (0, 1)), ('love', (2, 6)),
('Chicago', (7, 14)), ('deep', (15, 19)), ('dish',
(20, 24)), ('pizza', (31, 36)), (',', (36, 37)),
('don', (38, 41)), ("'", (41, 42)), ('t', (42,
43)), ('you', (44, 47)), ('?', (47, 48))]


=> tokenizer: GPT2
sentence:    I love Chicago deep dish        pizza,
don't you?
tokenized:  [('I', (0, 1)), ('Ġlove', (1, 6)),
('ĠChicago', (6, 14)), ('Ġdeep', (14, 19)),
('Ġdish', (19, 24)), ('ĠĠĠĠĠĠ', (24, 30)),
('Ġpizza', (30, 36)), (',', (36, 37)), ('Ġdon',
(37, 41)), ("'t", (41, 43)), ('Ġyou', (43, 47)),
('?', (47, 48))]


=> tokenizer: T5-SMALL
sentence:    I love Chicago deep dish        pizza,
don't you?
tokenized:  [('_I', (0, 1)), ('_love', (2, 6)),
('_Chicago', (7, 14)), ('_deep', (15, 19)),
('_dish', (20, 24)), ('_pizza,', (31, 37)),
("_don't", (38, 43)), ('_you?', (44, 48))]


=> tokenizer: XLNetTokenizer
sentence:    I love Chicago deep dish        pizza,
don't you?
tokenized:  ['_I', '_love', '_Chicago', '_deep',
'_dish', '_pizza', ',', '_don', "'", 't', '_you',
'?']
```

WHAT IS TOKENIZATION?

In simplified terms, *tokenization* involves splitting the text of a corpus into words that can be mapped to numbers (e.g., word2vec) to process these numeric counterparts of those words by neural networks. There are several types of tokenization techniques that are discussed briefly in a later section, along with some of the trade-offs involved in these techniques.

Nuances of Tokenizers

Tokenizers perform different types of tokenization, and their characteristics depend on the NLP model that is used to instantiate the tokenizer. As such, this section briefly discusses the differences among tokenizers that are instantiated from BERT, GPT2, and T5 models.

A BERT-based tokenizer maintains the index of word offsets. Moreover, the pre-tokenization splits on whitespace and punctuation. However, a GPT2-based tokenizer splits on whitespace and punctuation and replaces spaces with a Ġ symbol, from which it is possible to recover the original spaces in a text string. This tokenizer differs from a BERT tokenizer because it recognizes the double space.

Another type of tokenizer is the T5-based tokenizer that is based on the SentencePiece algorithm and is also similar to a GPT2-2 tokenizer. However, this tokenizer maintains spaces and replaces them with an underscore (_) token. Moreover, a T5 tokenizer only splits on whitespace instead of punctuation, and also adds an initial whitespace. In Chapter 4, you will see Python-based examples of language models that involve instantiating a model-specific tokenizer.

A Generic Token-to-Index Mapping Algorithm

This section provides a simple algorithm for associating an integer for each word in a corpus, shown in Listing 2.2.

Listing 2.2: create_token2idx.py

```
token2idx = {}
curr_idx  = 0

docs = list()
docs.append("this is a simple document")
docs.append("this is a second document")
docs.append("the third short document")

# initialize word/integer pairs:
for doc in docs:
```

```
    for token in doc.split(" "):
      if token not in token2idx:
        token2idx[token] = curr_idx
        curr_idx += 1


  # display token/integer pairs:
  for token in token2idx.keys():
    print(f"token: {token:10} value:
  {token2idx[token]:4}")
  print()


  # create an integer-based counterpart
  int_docs = []
  for doc in docs:
    for doc in docs:
      tokens = [token2idx[word] for word in doc.split
  (" ")]
      int_docs.append(tokens)

  print("int_docs:",int_docs)
  print()


  # create integer-to-token mapping:
  idx2token = {v: k for k,v in token2idx.items()}
  for k,v in idx2token.items():
    print(f"key: {k:4} value: {v:10}")
```

Listing 2.2 starts by defining a Python dictionary `token2idx` and the scalar variable `curr_idx` that is initially 0. The next block of code initializes the variable `docs` with three documents, each of which is a short sentence.

The next portion of Listing 2.2 iterates through the documents in `docs`, and uses the `split()` function to tokenize each document. Next, conditional logic adds a new token/integer pair in the dictionary `token2idx` if the current token is not already in this dictionary.

The next code block displays the token/integer pairs in `token2idx`, followed by a code block that populates the variable `int_docs` with the integer values associated with each token in the dictionary `token2idx`, and then displays all the integer values. The final portion of Listing 2.2

creates an integer-to-token mapping called `idx2token`. The latter code block is relevant when we need to convert from predictions (involving token ID values) in neural networks to the associated tokens. Launch the code in Listing 2.2, and you will see the following output:

```
token: this       value:    0
token: is         value:    1
token: a          value:    2
token: simple     value:    3
token: document   value:    4
token: second     value:    5
token: the        value:    6
token: third      value:    7
token: short      value:    8


int_docs: [[0, 1, 2, 3, 4], [0, 1, 2, 5, 4], [6, 7,
8, 4], [0, 1, 2, 3, 4], [0, 1, 2, 5, 4], [6, 7, 8,
4], [0, 1, 2, 3, 4], [0, 1, 2, 5, 4], [6, 7, 8, 4]]


key:     0 value: this
key:     1 value: is
key:     2 value: a
key:     3 value: simple
key:     4 value: document
key:     5 value: second
key:     6 value: the
key:     7 value: third
key:     8 value: short
```

Again, the preceding code sample provides a generic process for associated words with integer values. Before discussing tokenization techniques that are used in language models, let's delve into some of the associated challenges, as described in the next section.

Tokenization Tasks and Their Challenges

Tokenization involves finding the tokens in sentences and documents, where tokens can be words, characters, or partial words. Tokenization must also take into account potential issues that can arise while performing the following subtasks:

- Convert text to lowercase (or not)
- Process punctuation that separates sentences
- Handle diacritical marks (such as French and German)
- Handle contractions ("won't" versus "will not")
- Processing unusual (infrequent) words

If you have not previously performed tokenization, it might seem like a simple task, but there are several non-trivial aspects of tokenization. Here is a list of points (in no particular order) to address while performing tokenization of a corpus:

- Common nouns versus proper nouns
- An optional word delimiter
- Diacritical marks and word meanings
- Different subword tokenization techniques
- Singular versus plural nouns
- Variants in word spellings
- Typographical errors
- False cognates in translation tasks

First, converting words to lowercase loses the distinction between common nouns and proper nouns (such as "Stone" versus "stone"). Second, the use of a white space to tokenize sentences into word tokens does not work correctly in languages such as Japanese, in which spaces are optional. Consequently, a sentence can be written as a single contiguous string of non-space characters: Thiscanbeapainandtediousinanylanguage. This example shows you that missing white spaces increases complexity (and perhaps you had to concentrate to parse the preceding string sans spaces).

Third, dropping diacritical (accent) marks can make a word ambiguous: *peche* has three possible meanings (i.e., peach, fish, or sin) depending on which diacritical mark appears in the word. As an extreme example, the following (uncommon) French phrase "le peche du peche" has multiple interpretations, which would be clear only from context.

Fourth, it is important to consider punctuation during tokenization, thereby ensuring that models are not required to learn different representations of a word combined with multiple punctuation symbols.

Fifth, different libraries and toolkits perform different types of subword tokenization. For example, it is possible to tokenize the word "Don't" as either ["Don", "'", "t"] or as ["Do", "n't"] (in this case, the spaCy library uses the latter approach).

Sixth, removing a final "s" from an English word can result in a word with a different meaning. For example, "birds" and "bird" are the plural and singular form of a noun, whereas "new" and "news" have different meanings. In general, adding the letter "s" to a noun creates the plural of that noun, whereas adding an "s" to an adjective can result in a noun that has a different meaning from the adjective.

While some of the preceding examples might seem insignificant (or even trivial), such details can affect the accuracy as well as the fluency of a text string that has been translated into a language that is different from the language of the input text.

Tokenization must also address other issues, such as handling alternate ways to spell a word (e.g., "favor" versus "favour," "tire" versus "tyre," and "color" versus "color"), different meanings of the same word (such as "to table" a discussion), and typographical errors (such as "dependent" versus the incorrect "dependant").

Other potential issues include variants in spelling and capitalization, irregular verbs, and the out-of-vocabulary tokenization problems. There is yet another issue pertaining to differences in pronunciation. Consider the different ways to pronounce the following words:

- Aluminum: "uh-LOO-minum" or "al-loo-MIN-ium"
- Privacy: "PRIV-acy" versus "PRY-vacy"
- Schedule: "SKEDjule" versus "SHEDjule"

An Alternative to Tokenization: ByT5 Model

Google introduced the ByT5 model that works directly with UTF-8 bytes instead of using subword tokenization. The advantage of this approach is that it dispenses with any form of text preprocessing. Moreover, this approach can be extended to handle byte sequences without adding excessive computational cost. However, byte sequences are considerably longer than word-level sequences.

The ByT5 model is derived from another Google model called mT5, which is an acronym for "Massively Multilingual Text-to-Text Transfer Transformer." Although mT5 is a token-based model, it can be made token-free by making a modest set of modifications to mT5. Details of the ByT5 model are available in the arxiv paper "Towards a Token-Free Future With Pre-Trained Byte-to-Byte Models," which is accessible at *https://arxiv.org/abs/2105.13626*.

WORD, CHARACTER, AND SUBWORD TOKENIZERS

In essence, tokenizers transform sentences and documents into a format that is suitable for processing by language models. Keep in mind that LLMs only process numeric values, which means that tokenizers must convert text strings into numeric data. In general, the goal of a tokenizer is two-fold: find the most meaningful representation and also (if possible) find the smallest representation.

There are several types of tokenizers that you will encounter in NLP:

- preword tokenizers (discussed previously)
- word tokenizers
- character tokenizers
- subword tokenizers

Each of the preceding tokenizer types is discussed in the following subsections, along with some of their trade-offs.

Word-Based Tokenizers

In general, word-based tokenizers are straightforward because they involve a limited number of rules, and they can achieve reasonably good results. One way to programmatically tokenize a text string based on whitespaces involves the split() function in Python, as shown here:

```
tokenized_text = "I love Chicago pizza".split()
print(tokenized_text)
['I', 'love', 'Chicago', 'pizza']
```

Some word tokenizers specify extra rules for punctuation, which can result in a large vocabulary (i.e., the number of tokens in a given corpus). In addition, words are assigned an ID that ranges from 0 to (N-1), where N is the number of tokens in the vocabulary. The model identifies a given word via its assigned id value.

Unfortunately, closely related words are treated as different words, which means they will be assigned different id values. For example, the following set of words are related in meaning:

- sing
- sang
- sung
- singing

Moreover, the model will treat the singular form of a noun differently from the plural form of that noun. This process is further complicated in languages (such as German and Slavic languages) that have a masculine, feminine, neuter, and plural form of nouns, all of which are treated as different nouns.

For example, English has only one form for the article "the," whereas the following shows you the declension of the definite article "der" in

German, with columns for the masculine, feminine, neuter, and plural, and rows for the nominative, genitive, dative, and accusative cases:

	Masculine	Feminine	Neuter	Plural
Nominative	der	die	das	die
Genitive	des	der	des	der
Dative	dem	der	dem	den
Accusative	den	die	das	die

As you will see in Chapter 5, BERT contains approximately 25,000 tokens that are words from the English language, which consists of more than half a million words. BERT uses a mechanism to split tokens into subtokens, which enables BERT to use those "word pieces" for other tokens. Moreover, BERT uses the special token UNK to represent unknown words (and other language models use the UNK token, as well).

Limitations of Word Tokenizers

A model only recognizes word tokens that are part of its training step, which means that compound words will not be recognized if they do not appear in the training step. For example, if the words "book" and "keeper" are part of the training step, but the word "bookkeeper" was not in the training step, then "bookkeeper" will not be recognized and hence it will be represented via the UNK token.

Another challenge for tokenizers pertains to contractions. For example, the English words "its" and "it's" have an entirely different meaning: "its" refers to possession whereas "it's" means "it is." In the case of nouns, the apostrophe also refers to possession (e.g., John's car). Thus, the sentence "It's true that John's pen is worth its weight in gold" can have only one interpretation.

As you can probably guess, acronyms in conjunction with slang pose challenges for tokenizers. Consider the following set of terms that some people use in their text messages:

```
AFAIK
IIRC
IDK
SMH
AFAICS
LMK
DOPE
BOMB
```

Tokenization for Languages with Multiple Alphabets

As you saw earlier, a space character between words is optional in languages such as Chinese and Japanese. Furthermore, Japanese has three alphabets: Hiragana, Katakana (used only for foreign words), and Romaji (for romanizing Japanese words). Japanese also has Kanji, which is a pictograph-based system for representing words. Japanese sentences and street signs can contain a combination of Hiragana and Kanji, which are even more difficult for non-Japanese people to understand.

One idea involves representing words via an encoding system. For example, ASCII is an encoding scheme that encodes words in the English language; however, ASCII cannot represent European languages (such as French) that have diacritical marks.

Another encoding scheme is ISO-159, which does support diacritical marks; however, this encoding scheme is limited primarily to Western European languages. Another encoding scheme is UTF-8, which supports a far larger set of characters. Perhaps the most extensive encoding scheme is the Unicode encoding scheme that supports all the letters, punctuation marks, and alphabets of every human language, which includes Arabic, Mandarin, and Japanese. Perform an online search for more information about encoding schemes, and you will find numerous free articles.

TRADE-OFFS WITH CHARACTER-BASED TOKENIZERS

Character-based tokenizers split a corpus into characters instead of individual words, which has two primary benefits:

- The vocabulary is smaller than word-based tokenization.
- There are fewer out-of-vocabulary tokens (every word can be built from characters).

However, there are also two limitations to character-based tokenization. First, a set of characters provides a limited substantive meaning. Words are the fundamental building blocks of sentences, and therefore they carry meaning (and sometimes multiple meanings). While the preceding is true for languages that are based on an alphabet (such as Indo-European languages), some southeast Asian languages are based on pictographs, which can convey complex concepts that require a sentence of explanation.

Second, character-based tokenization will generate a significantly larger number of tokens, which can easily be five times as large as a set of word-based tokens, resulting in much more processing time for training a model compared to the processing time for word-based tokens.

If we contrast the properties of characters with properties of words, we see that characters have no substantive meaning for many languages (excluding Asian languages). As a very simple example, the letter "s" is ambiguous in meaning because of the absence of context, whereas the context of the word "apples" is essentially unambiguous. However, words have the opposite property: a word can be overloaded with multiple meanings that depend on their context in sentences.

Limitations of Character-Based Tokenizers

As you learned in the previous section, character-based tokens involve more computational time and resources for training a model. If the average number of letters in a word is 5, then a 10-word sentence involves 50 tokens instead of 10.

In addition, there is the question of generating the correct spelling of a word, which is more difficult when tokens are characters instead of words. Furthermore, word-based tokenization is better suited for various NLP-related tasks, such as NER and text classification, and less suited for character-based tokenization.

While the preceding points favor word-based tokenization, this involves creating a vocabulary of modest size, which in turn raises the possibility of OOV (out-of-vocabulary) words in a corpus. As you will see in the BERT-based code samples, OOV words are represented with an UNK ("unknown") token.

Fortunately, there is a third hybrid-like technique for leveraging the advantages of character-based and word-based tokenization while avoiding their issues. This technique is called subword tokenization, which is the topic of the next section.

SUBWORD TOKENIZATION

Subword tokenization is typically based on algorithms, statistical rules, and an important heuristic: tokenize uncommon or infrequently appearing words into subwords, and do not split frequently occurring words.

Such tokenization can be easily performed for English adverbs with the suffix "ly:" replace the adverb with two tokens, where the second token is the combination "ly." Thus, "slowly" is split into "slow" and "ly," and "quickly" is replaced with "quick" and "ly," and so forth.

Likewise, the adjective "lonely" can be split into "lone" and "ly." In some cases, this decomposition into two tokens produces an actual word for the first token, which is the case for the preceding examples.

Moreover, subword tokenization can also yield tokens that have meaning, such as tokenization the word "internationalization" into "international" and "ization."

In addition to the preceding type of tokenization for handling a sub-set of English words, there are other algorithms for tokenization, some of which are listed here:

- Byte-level BPE (in GPT-2)
- WordPiece (in BERT)
- SentencePiece or Unigram (in several multilingual models)

A Subword Tokenizer Code Sample

Listing 2.3 displays the content of hf_subword_tokenizer. py that illustrates how to perform tokenization with the Hugging Face transformer.

Listing 2.3: hf_subword_tokenizer.py

```
from transformers import AutoTokenizer

tokenizer = AutoTokenizer.from_pretrained
("bert-base-cased")
sequence = "I love Chicago always deeply dished
pizzas!"
tokens = tokenizer.tokenize(sequence)

print("sequence:",sequence)
print("tokens:   ",tokens)

ids = tokenizer.convert_tokens_to_ids(tokens)
print("token ids:",  ids)

# ids = [146, 1567, 2290, 1579, 5585, 10478, 1174,
13473, 1116, 106]
decoded_ids = tokenizer.decode(ids)
print("decoded:   ",decoded_ids)
```

Listing 2.3 starts with an import statement and then initializes the variable tokenizer as an instance of AutoTokenizer. Next, the variable `sequence` is initialized as a text string, and then the variable `tokens` is initialized as the set of tokens in the variable `sequence`. Launch the code in Listing 2.3 with the following command:

```
python3 hf_tokenizer.py
```

The preceding command will display the following output:

```
sequence: I love Chicago always deeply dished
pizzas!
tokens:   ['I', 'love', 'Chicago', 'always',
'deeply', 'dish', '##ed', 'pizza', '##s', '!']
token ids: [146, 1567, 2290, 1579, 5585, 10478,
1174, 13473, 1116, 106]
decoded:   I love Chicago always deeply dished
pizzas!
```

Note that the `decode()` method in Listing 2.3 does two things: first, indices are converted to tokens; second, tokens that were part of the same words are grouped together, thereby producing a readable sentence. This behavior is extremely useful for models that predict new text (either text generated from a prompt, or for sequence-to-sequence problems like translation or summarization).

Key Points Regarding BERT Tokenization

Although BERT is discussed in Chapter 5, this section is included here because of the token-related information that this chapter contains regarding BERT. Whether or not you decide to read this section, you can always return to this portion of the chapter after you read the material regarding byte-pair encoding (BPE) and WordPiece in Chapter 5.

BERT has a fixed vocabulary of tokens, along with associated embeddings, which means that BERT *provides its own tokenizer*. Furthermore, you *cannot* replace BERT embeddings with a different set of embeddings (either yours or from someone else). Other key points about BERT are as follows:

· includes BPE and WordPiece (similar to BPE)
· includes a layer of likelihood calculation
· BERT-based models use the same special tokens
· generally trained on raw text with WordPiece
· does not require stemming and lemmatization
· lowercase model converts sentences into lowercase
· uppercase model makes no changes in sentence capitalization
· uses the transformer model

Since BERT uses the encoder component of the transformer architecture, the fine-tuning step only examines words that have an effect on the output and ignores words that are common in all data. Note that each BERT model uses its own input type: for example, unlike BERT, DistilBERT does not use `token_type_ids`. You now have sufficient knowledge of tokenizers to learn about the Hugging Face APIs, which are discussed in the next section.

Models such as BERT or GPT-2, as well as their variants, tokenize text either through some version of the BPE algorithm or via the unigram model.

SUBWORD TOKENIZATION ALGORITHMS

Subword tokenization involves splitting OOV tokens into smaller fragments. Recall that the previous section briefly describes of the following types of tokenizers:

- word tokenizers
- character tokenizers
- subword tokenizers

Subword tokenization algorithms are based on a heuristic, which means that they are based on intuitive reasoning that "makes sense" and can produce the correct answer. Specifically, words that appear more frequently are assigned unique IDs. However, lower frequency words are split into subwords that retain the meaning of the lower frequency words. The following list contains four important subword tokenization algorithms:

- BPE
- SentencePiece (used in ALBERT)
- unigram language model
- WordPiece (used in BERT and DistilBERT)

The Hugging Face transformers library supports the required tokenizers for most BERT variants. In fact, the BERT model in this library handles 11 types of NLP problems, which can also be combined to form a pipeline.

All four algorithms involve subword tokenization of text, though they differ in that they implement different algorithms for processing subwords.

The BERT authors did train a variant of BERT using a technique called *whole-word masking* that uses the following rule: if *one* of the subwords from "embeddings" was selected, then *all* of the subword tokens would be replaced.

What is BPE?

BPE (byte-pair encoding) is a versatile tool that initially served data compression needs but has become pivotal in modern NLP. By enabling subword tokenization, BPE allows models to handle a vast vocabulary efficiently and adaptively, making it a mainstay in many cutting-edge language models. BPE is a bottom-up subword tokenization algorithm that learns a subword vocabulary of a certain size (the vocabulary size is a hyperparameter). The core idea behind BPE is to iteratively merge the most frequent pair of bytes (or characters) in a dataset until a specified number of merges is reached.

The first step is called *initialization*, which involves tokenizing the text into characters, and then assigning a unique token to each character. The second step involves merging results in an iterative fashion. During each iteration, find the most frequent pair of adjacent tokens and then merge the tokens to create a new token. Repeat this process for a predefined number of iterations or until no more merges are possible. The resulting tokens represent common character or subword combinations in the data.

Let's look at the word "lowers" and see how to apply BPE to this word. Based on the preceding paragraph, the first step involves tokenizing the word into characters, and therefore the initial tokens are l, o, w, e, r, and s.

Next, if "lo" is the most frequent pair in your dataset, it might be the first merge, resulting in this new set of tokens: lo, w, e, r, and s. An additional merge could result in the tokens low, e, and rs. The final subword units depend on the frequency of pairs in the dataset and the number of merge operations performed. There is a drawback to using frequency in BPE: the outcome of the iterative merging step can result in ambiguous final encodings that might not be useful.

As a second example, consider the string `aaabdaaabac`. Since the byte pair `aa` occurs most often, we will replace it with a character that does not appear in the string, such as the letter `z`. Perform the replacement, which results in the following text string:

```
ZabdZabac (where Z=aa)
```

Repeat the substitution step, this time with the pair `ab`, and replace this pair with the letter `Y`, which results in the string `ZYdZYac (where Y=ab Z=aa)`. At this point, we can continue the preceding procedure by selecting ZY (which appears twice) and replacing this string with the letter X, which results in XdXac (where X=ZY Y=ab Z=aa).

What is WordPiece?

WordPiece is a greedy-based subword tokenization algorithm that became available when BERT was released in 2018 that has characteristics of BPE (i.e., the pairing of characters) as well as the unigram algorithm (i.e., selecting pairs to be merged).

Specifically, WordPiece uses a likelihood value instead of count frequency to merge the best pair of characters and uses count frequency for the choice of characters to be paired.

The main difference pertains to the specific manner in which bigrams are selected for the merging step. Interestingly, RoBERTa (which is based on BERT) also involves the use of WordPiece. Here are some examples of subword tokenization in BERT:

1. toppings is split into topping and ##s.

2. trimmings is split into trim, ##ming, and ##s.

3. misspelled is split into mis, ##spel, and ##led.

However, BERT does *not* provide a mechanism to re-construct the original word from its word pieces. By contrast, ELMo provides word-level (not subword) contextual representations for words, which is different from BERT. Later in this chapter, you will learn code samples that create BERT tokens from English sentences.

What is SentencePiece?

SentencePiece is another subword tokenizer and a detokenizer for NLP that performs subword segmentation, with support for BPE and unigram language models.

SentencePiece offers a unified, data-driven approach to text tokenization and detokenization. Its ability to work with raw text, generate subword units, and be language-agnostic makes it a popular choice for neural network-based text processing tasks, especially in scenarios that involve multiple languages or require consistent handling of text data.

SentencePiece has two main features. First, SentencePiece treats a text string as a sequence of Unicode characters, and replaces spaces with a _ character. In addition, SentencePiece can handle languages in which a space between words is optional (such as Chinese and Japanese).

Second, SentencePiece supports *reversible tokenization*, which means that the original text can be constructed by concatenating words and replacing all occurrences of a "_" character with a white space. By contrast, BERT does *not* support reversible tokenization because a BERT tokenizer removes multiple white spaces.

Third, traditional tokenizers are often designed for specific languages, and their performance might degrade when applied to others. By contrast, SentencePiece provides a consistent tokenization approach regardless of the language, making it suitable for multilingual models or languages with less NLP support.

Fourth, SentencePiece encapsulates tokenization and detokenization, offering an end-to-end workflow for text processing, which simplifies the pipeline for developers.

Fifth, SentencePiece can effectively handle rare words and out-of-vocabulary terms, representing them as a combination of known subword tokens. This capability is essential for models to generalize well to unseen data.

For additional insights, the original arxiv paper that describes SentencePiece in detail is at *https://arxiv.org/abs/1808.06226v1*.

HUGGING FACE TOKENIZERS AND MODELS

Hugging Face provides numerous classes for tokenizers and models. In particular, Hugging Face classes that contain the prefix Auto (e.g., AutoModel and AutoTokenizer) perform various tasks, such as accessing the configuration and pre-trained weights of a model that is included as a string in the from_pretrained() method.

For example, the following code snippet initializes the variable tokenizer as an instance of the AutoTokenizer class, and from the bert-base-uncased model:

```
tokenizer = AutoTokenizer.from_pretrained
("bert-base-uncased")
```

The following code snippet initializes the variable model as an instance of the bert-base-uncased model:

```
mymodel = TFAutoModel.from_pretrained
("bert-base-uncased")
```

For your convenience, the following list contains the set of tokenizers that are referenced in the Python code samples in this book, displayed as a list of import statements:

- from transformers import AutoTokenizer
- from transformers import BartTokenizer

- `from transformers import BertTokenizer`
- `from transformers import BertTokenizerFast`
- `from transformers import FlaubertTokenizer`
- `from transformers import GPT2Tokenizer`
- `from transformers import RobertaTokenizer`

- `# dall_e_tok tokenizers:`
- `from dall_e_tok import DALLETokenizer`
- `from dall_e_tok import DallEEncoder`
- `from dalle_pytorch.simple_tokenizer import tokenizer, HugTokenizer`
- `# pytorch tokenizers:`
- `from pytorch_transformers import GPT2Tokenizer, GPT2LMHeadModel`
- `# BPE tokenizer:`
- `from tokenizers import ByteLevelBPETokenizer`

The following list contains the set of model-related classes that are referenced in the Python code samples in this book, displayed as `import` statements:

- `from transformers import AutoModel`
- `from transformers import AutoModelForSeq2SeqLM`
- `from transformers import AutoModelForSequenceClassification`
- `from transformers import BartForConditionalGeneration`
- `from transformers import BertForQuestionAnswering`
- `from transformers import BertForSequenceClassification`
- `from transformers import BertModel`
- `from transformers import FlaubertModel`
- `from transformers import GPT2LMHeadModel`
- `from transformers import TFAutoModel`
- `from transformers import TFAutoModelForSequenceClassification`

Finally, the following list contains the configuration-related classes that are referenced in the Python code samples in this book, displayed as `import` statements:

- `from transformers import BertConfig`
- `from transformers import RobertaConfig`

The following subsections discuss how to save and load tokenizers, as well as how to tokenize strings via a Hugging Face transformer.

Loading and Saving Tokenizers

The task of loading and saving tokenizers is as simple as the corresponding task for models, and it is based on the same two methods: `from_pretrained()` and `save_pretrained()`. These methods will load or save the algorithm used by the tokenizer (a bit like the architecture of the model) as well as its vocabulary (a bit like the weights of the model).

We need to load the BERT tokenizer, which is trained with the same checkpoint as BERT for the step when the model is loaded, except we use the `BertTokenizer` class:

```
from transformers import BertTokenizer
tokenizer = BertTokenizer.from_pretrained
("bert-base-cased")
```

Similar to `AutoModel`, the `AutoTokenizer` class grabs the proper tokenizer class in the library based on the checkpoint name, and can be used directly with any checkpoint:

```
from transformers import AutoTokenizer
tokenizer = AutoTokenizer.from_pretrained
("bert-base-cased")
```

We can now use the tokenizer as shown in the previous section:

```
tokenizer("Using a Transformer network is simple")
```

```
{'input_ids': [101, 7993, 170, 11303, 1200, 2443,
1110, 3014, 102],
 'token_type_ids': [0, 0, 0, 0, 0, 0, 0, 0, 0],
 'attention_mask': [1, 1, 1, 1, 1, 1, 1, 1, 1]}
```

Saving a tokenizer is identical to saving a model:

```
tokenizer.save_pretrained("directoryname")
```

AutoTokenizer, BERTTokenizer, and GPT2Tokenizer

Although BERT and GPT are discussed in Chapters 5 through 8, respectively, their tokenizer classes for BERT and GPT2 are introduced here:

```
AutoTokenizer
BERTTokenizer
GPT2Tokenizer
```

For example, consider the following code snippets for instantiating a BERT-based tokenizer:

```
tokenizer = transformers.BertTokenizer.from_
pretrained('bert-base-uncased', do_lower_case=True)
tokenizer = AutoTokenizer.from_pretrained
("bert-base-uncased")
tokenizer = GPT2Tokenizer.from_pretrained("gpt2")
```

In the three preceding code snippets, the desired architecture can be inferred from the name of the pre-trained model you are supplying to the `from_pretrained()` method. By convention, the snippet "uncased" means that the words in a model are all in lowercase form.

What are AutoClasses?

Classes that have the prefix `AutoClass` automatically retrieve the relevant model given the name/path to the pre-trained weights/config/vocabulary. Moreover, instantiating `AutoModel`, `AutoConfig`, or `AutoTokenizer` creates a class of the relevant architecture. For example, the following code snippet creates an instance of `BertModel`:

```
model = AutoModel.from_pretrained('bert-base-
cased')
```

Thus, if the string specified in the `from_pretrained()` method is a BERT checkpoint (such as `bert-base-uncased`), then the following code snippets have the same effect:

```
AutoTokenizer.from_pretrained("bert-base-uncased")
BertTokenizer.from_pretrained("bert-base-uncased")
```

The `Auto*` classes also enable you to specify any checkpoint, and the correct model will be loaded, an example of which is here:

```
# this returns the correct GPT2Tokenizer instance:
AutoTokenizer.from_pretrained("gpt2")

# this will fail (model mismatch):
BertTokenizer.from_pretrained("gpt2")
```

HUGGING FACE TOKENIZERS

This section describes the outcome of training with the following tokenizers using Hugging Face:

- Slow Versus Fast Tokenizers
- BPE (frequency-based model)
- WordPiece
- Unigram Tokenizers (probability-based model)

We will also compare the tokens generated via Hugging Face with the SOTA (state of the art) tokenization algorithms.

The primary distinction among these algorithms pertains to the choice of character pairs to merge as well as the merging policy that these algorithms use to generate the final tokens.

Slow and Fast Tokenizers

There is a difference between slow and fast tokenizers. Slow tokenizers are written in Python and are located in the Hugging Face Transformers library. By contrast, fast versions are located in Hugging Face Tokenizers and are written in the Rust programming language.

In addition, keep in mind the following point regarding slow and fast tokenizers: the difference in the speed of tokenization is most apparent when a significant amount of text is being processed in parallel. In fact, slow tokenizers can be faster than fast tokenizers while processing a small amount of text.

Fast tokenizers support two other important features: parallelization and *offset mapping*, which refers to recording the index position of tokens. The latter functionality supports mapping words to their generated tokens, as well as the ability to map text characters to the token in which they are embedded.

Token Classification Pipelines

Listing 2.4 displays the content of `tokens_classify1.py` that shows you how to perform token classification.

Listing 2.4: tokens_classify1.py

```
from transformers import pipeline

sentence = "I Love Chicago Deep Dish Pizza"
token_classifier = pipeline("token-classification")
```

```
tokens = token_classifier(sentence)
print("sentence:",sentence)
print()
print("tokens:   ",tokens)
```

Listing 2.4 starts with an `import` statement, and initializes the variable `sequence` as a text string. Then, the variable `token_classifier` is initialized as an instance of the `pipeline` class, which also specifies `token-classification` as the task type. Then the variable `tokens` is initialized with the result of invoking the `token_classifier()` method with the variable `sentence`.

The final portion of Listing 2.4 displays the contents of the variable `sentence` as well as the variable `tokens`. Launch the code in Listing 2.4, and you will see the following output:

```
sentence: I Love Chicago Deep Dish Pizza


tokens:   [{'entity': 'I-MISC', 'score':
0.59600025, 'index': 1, 'word': 'I', 'start': 0,
'end': 1}, {'entity': 'I-MISC', 'score': 0.500077,
'index': 2, 'word': 'Love', 'start': 2, 'end':
6}, {'entity': 'I-ORG', 'score': 0.8103038,
'index': 3, 'word': 'Chicago', 'start': 7, 'end':
14}, {'entity': 'I-ORG', 'score': 0.56864274,
'index': 4, 'word': 'Deep', 'start': 15, 'end':
19}, {'entity': 'I-ORG', 'score': 0.71021026,
'index': 5, 'word': 'Di', 'start': 20, 'end': 22},
{'entity': 'I-ORG', 'score': 0.771432, 'index': 6,
'word': '##sh', 'start': 22, 'end': 24}, {'entity':
'I-ORG', 'score': 0.8432511, 'index': 7, 'word':
'Pizza', 'start': 25, 'end': 30}]
```

The preceding output has been realigned with a smaller font so that you can easily examine the entity types and the various values associated with the tokens:

```
[
{'entity': 'I-MISC','score': 0.59600025,'index':
1,'word':'I',      'start': 0, 'end': 1},
{'entity': 'I-MISC','score': 0.500077,  'index':
2,'word':'Love', 'start': 2, 'end': 6},
{'entity': 'I-ORG', 'score': 0.8103038, 'index':
3,'word':'Chicago','start':7,'end': 14},
```

```
{'entity': 'I-ORG', 'score': 0.56864274,'index':
4,'word':'Deep','start': 15, 'end': 19},
{'entity': 'I-ORG', 'score': 0.71021026,'index':
5,'word':'Di',   'start': 20, 'end': 22},
{'entity': 'I-ORG', 'score': 0.771432,  'index':
6,'word':'##sh', 'start':22, 'end': 24},
{'entity': 'I-ORG', 'score': 0.8432511, 'index':
7,'word':'Pizza','start':25, 'end': 30}
]
```

Launch the code in Listing 2.4 with Python 3.7. If you launch the code with Python 3.9, you will see the following error message that displays all the available tasks:

```
KeyError: "Unknown task token-classification,
available tasks are ['feature-extraction',
'sentiment-analysis', 'ner', 'question-
answering', 'table-question-answering', 'fill-
mask', 'summarization', 'translation', 'text2text-
generation', 'text-generation', 'zero-shot-
classification', 'conversational', 'translation_XX_
to_YY']"
```

TOKENIZATION FOR THE DISTILBERT MODEL

When you write Python code for various BERT-based models, make sure that you combine tokenizers and models that belong to the same model. For example, if you reference a tokenizer from the BertTokenizer class, you also need to instantiate a BERT-based model instead of a DistilBERT model. While the latter is obvious, you will not see an error message if you mix them; instead, you will see warning messages about "unexpected tokenization."

Listing 2.5 displays the content of distilbert_tokenizer1.py that shows you what happens when you "mix" tokenizers and models.

Listing 2.5: distilbert_tokenizer1.py

```
# notice the mismatch in this code snippet:
from transformers import DistilBertTokenizer,
BertModel
```

```
tokenizer = DistilBertTokenizer.from_pretrained
('bert-base-uncased')
print("tokenizer size:    ",tokenizer.vocab_size)
print("model max length: ",tokenizer.model_max_
length)
print("model input names:",tokenizer.model_input_
names)
print()


text1 = "Pizza with four toppings and trimmings."
marked_text1 = "[CLS] " + text1 + " [SEP]"
tokenized_text1 = tokenizer.tokenize(marked_text1)

print("input sentence #1:")
print(text1)
print()

print("Tokens from input sentence #1:")
print(tokenized_text1)
print()

print("Some tokens in BERT:")
print(list(tokenizer.vocab.keys())[1000:1020])
print()
```

Listing 2.5 starts with an `import` statement, and then initializes the variable `tokenizer` as an instance of the tokenizer that is associated with the dataset `bert-base-uncased`, which consists of all lowercase letters and no diacritical marks. This variable enables us to display the maximum length of the model as well as the input names for the model.

The next portion of Listing 2.5 initializes the string variable `text1`, and then the variable `marked_text1` has an initial and terminal special token. The variable `tokenized_text1` is initialized with the result of tokenizing the text in the string `marked_text1`.

Next, the contents of the variables `text1` and `tokenized_text1` are displayed, followed by a list of existing tokens. Launch the code in Listing 2.5, and you will see the following output. Notice the incorrect value for the maximum length that is shown in bold, and also the sub-word tokenization for `toppings` and `trimmings`:

```
tokenizer size:      30522
model max length:    1000000000000000019884624838656
model input names: ['input_ids', 'attention_mask']

input sentence #1:
Pizza with four toppings and trimmings.

Tokens from input sentence #1:
['[CLS]', 'pizza', 'with', 'four', 'topping',
'##s', 'and', 'trim', '##ming', '##s', '.',
'[SEP]']

Some tokens in BERT:
['"', '#', '$', '%', '&', "'", '(', ')', '*', '+',
',', '-', '.', '/', '0', '1', '2', '3', '4', '5']
```

In addition, you will also see the following warning messages:

```
The tokenizer class you load from this checkpoint
is not the same type as the class this function
is called from. It may result in unexpected
tokenization.
The tokenizer class you load from this checkpoint
is 'BertTokenizer'.
The class this function is called from is
'DistilBertTokenizer'.
```

Notice that the warning message does not state that errors will necessarily occur; however, you need to check your code if you see any unusual or unexpected results.

Listing 2.6 displays the content of distilbert_tokenizer2.py that shows you how to correct the mismatched classes and models in Listing 2.5.

Listing 2.6: distilbert_tokenizer2.py

```
# notice the corrections in this code sample
from transformers import DistilBertTokenizer,
DistilBertModel
tokenizer = DistilBertTokenizer.from_pretrained
('distilbert-base-uncased')
print("tokenizer size:    ",tokenizer.vocab_size)
```

```
print("model max length: ",tokenizer.model_max_
length)
print("model input names:",tokenizer.model_input_
names)
print()


text1 = "Pizza with four toppings and trimmings."
marked_text1 = "[CLS] " + text1 + " [SEP]"
tokenized_text1 = tokenizer.tokenize(marked_text1)

print("input sentence #1:")
print(text1)
print()

print("Tokens from input sentence #1:")
print(tokenized_text1)
print()

print("Some tokens in BERT:")
print(list(tokenizer.vocab.keys())[1000:1020])
print()
```

Listing 2.6 is almost identical to Listing 2.5; the only differences involve the first two lines that are shown in bold. Launch the code in Listing 2.6, and you will see almost the same output as Listing 2.5, but this time with the correct maximum length value and also without the warning messages.

```
tokenizer size:     30522
model max length:   512
model input names: ['input_ids', 'attention_mask']

input sentence #1:
Pizza with four toppings and trimmings.

Tokens from input sentence #1:
['[CLS]', 'pizza', 'with', 'four', 'topping',
'##s', 'and', 'trim', '##ming', '##s', '.',
'[SEP]']
```

```
Some tokens in BERT:
['"', '#', '$', '%', '&', "'", '(', ')', '*', '+',
',', '-', '.', '/', '0', '1', '2', '3', '4', '5']
```

TOKEN SELECTION TECHNIQUES IN LLMS

LLMs and neural networks have several parameter types. For instance, *parameters* in neural networks are the edges that connect neurons in two different layers. The parameters are assigned numeric weights that are updated *during* the training step of an LLM or neural network. Please see the following article for more information:

https://medium.com/@mlubbad/the-ultimate-guide-to-gpt-4-parameters-everything-you-need-to-know-about-nlps-game-changer-109b8767855a

Second, LLMs and neural networks usually have hyperparameters whose values are set *prior* to the training step for an LLM or neural network.

Third, many LLMs, such as GPT-x models and other decoder-based LLMs, provide adjustable inference parameters that influence the output of the model, some of which are as follows:

- Max new tokens
- Token length
- Stop tokens
- Sample top K
- Sample top P
- Temperature

Since inference parameters will make more sense after you learn about fine tuning an LLM, the discussion of the preceding list of inference parameters is postponed until Chapter 5.

SUMMARY

This chapter started with an introduction to the concept of pre-tokenization, as well as the difference between pre-tokenization and tokenization, along with a Python code sample. Then you learned about some of the nuances of tokenizers and a generic token-to-index mapping algorithm.

In addition, you learned about word, character, and subword tokenizers. Then you learned about the limitations of word-based tokenizers and languages that have multiple alphabets (such as Japanese), as well as limitations of character-based tokenizers.

In addition, you learned about subword tokenization algorithms such as BPE, as well as the WordPiece and SentencePiece algorithms. You were introduced to Hugging Face tokenizers and the difference between slow and fast tokenizers. Then you learned about token selection techniques.

This chapter provided foundational information to prepare you for learning about the transformer architecture, which is discussed in the next chapter.

## CHAPTER 3

TRANSFORMER ARCHITECTURE INTRODUCTION

This chapter is the first of two chapters that discusses the transformer architecture, which is the foundation for a plethora of language models, such as BERT and its variants (discussed in Chapters 5 and 6), as well as the GPT-x family from OpenAI (discussed in Chapters 7 and 8).

This chapter describes the main components of the original transformer, along with Python-based transformer code samples for various NLP tasks, such as NER, QnA, and mask-filling tasks.

The first part of this chapter introduces the transformer architecture that was developed by Google and released in late 2017. This section also discusses some transformer-based models.

The second part of this chapter discusses the transformers library from Hugging Face, which is a company that provides a repository of more than 20,000 transformer-based models. This section also contains Python-based transformer code samples that perform various NLP tasks, such as NER, QnA, and mask-filling tasks.

The third part of this chapter provides more details regarding the encoder component, along with additional details regarding the attention mechanism, as well as the decoder component, which is the other main component of the transformer architecture.

Before you read this chapter, keep in mind that there are cases of "forward referencing" concepts that are discussed in later chapters, which provide context for a given concept. Of course, if you are unfamiliar with a concept discussed in a later chapter, then it will also be challenging to fully understand the topic under discussion. As a result, you will probably need to read some topics more than once, after which concepts become easier to grasp when you understand the current context and the context of referenced material in later chapters (fortunately, this reading process is finite).

The following article examines transformers before asking whether they are likely to overtake AI:

https://www.quantamagazine.org/will-transformers-take-over-artificial-intelligence-20220310

SEQUENCE-TO-SEQUENCE MODELS

The terms "seq2seq" and "encoder-decoder" are closely related and are often used interchangeably in the context of neural network architectures for sequence-to-sequence tasks. As a result, you will find online articles that use both of these terms, and sometimes they do not make a distinction between them.

In brief, a sequence-to-sequence model (also referred to as `Seq2Seq` or `seq2seq`) processes an input sequence and outputs a (possibly different type of) sequence. In the case of the transformer architecture, the process of training the encoder and decoder together creates a sequence-to-sequence model.

If you have studied a foreign language, then you undoubtedly know that there is rarely a word-for-word translation of a sentence to a different language. In addition, sometimes a sequence of multiple words in one language can have a single-word translation (and vice versa). Consequently, the length of a sentence in the source language can have a different length in the target language.

As a result, in 2014, Richard Sutskever (and others) developed a sequence-to-sequence or Seq2Seq architecture whose main components are an encoder and a decoder. This seq2seq architecture relies on two multilayer LSTMs: one LSTM maps the input sequence to a fixed sized vector (the context vector), and the second LSTM decodes the fixed-size vector to produce a sequence in the target language (one word at a time). This approach proved sufficiently successful that in 2016 Google translate switched to a seq2seq model.

The seq2seq model has been generalized in the sense that it can consist of multiple LSTMs that also allows for Gated Recurrent Unit (GRU) components. However, the fundamental structure consisting of an encoder component and a decoder component remains intact. It is worth mentioning again that the encoder component summarizes information and generates a fixed-length vector that the decoder component uses to generate the sentence in the target language.

Note that seq2seq models can be used for speech, video, text, machine translation, and question-answering. Moreover, seq2seq models are well-suited for text generation: they can handle one type of sequence as input and then generate a different type of sequence as output.

If only one component (i.e., encoder or decoder) is trained, the result is either an autoencoding model or an autoregressive model, respectively (more details about both of these are provided later). In addition, the length of the input sequence can be different from the length of the output sequence.

Types of seq2seq Models

There are several types of seq2seq architectures, some of which are listed here:

- Recurrent Neural Network (RNN)-based seq2seq
- Long Short-Term Memory (LSTM)-based seq2seq
- Attention-based seq2seq

Recall that an RNN relies on the tanh() activation function for processing an input sequence, as well as combining the input at step t with the output from step (t-1) to generate an output that is used as input for step (t+1).

An LSTM cell is a specialized type of RNN that has the following characteristics:

- the sigmoid() and tanh() activation functions
- a forget gate, an input gate, and an output gate
- a long-term cell state that is updated via the preceding gates

Notice that DNNs (deep neural networks) are *not* in the previous bullet list: that is because DNNs cannot be used to map sequences to sequences.

You might see seq2seq described as a specific type of RNN that is often implemented by an encoder-decoder architecture. As you will see later, the transformer architecture is an encoder-decoder architecture that was *originally* based on RNNs. However, the transformer architecture has dispensed with RNNs and relies on the attention mechanism (discussed later).

In other words, seq2seq architectures and encoder-decoder architectures both involve input sequence and output sequences. The difference is that early seq2seq architectures relied on RNNs, whereas newer encoder-decoder architectures favor attention instead of RNNs.

The original transformer is a seq2seq model that comprises an encoder component and a decoder component. The encoder component contains N layers, each of which encodes input data into a 1x512 vector. Although the decoder also contains N decoder layers, the decoder is not simply a mirror image of the encoder. In fact, each decoder block in the decoder component processes input data from the following sources:

- the output from the entire encoder component
- the output of the previous decoder block

Sequence-to-Sequence Prediction Problems

Sequence prediction often involves either 1) forecasting the next value in a real valued sequence or 2) outputting a class label for an input sequence. As such, there are several types of sequence predictions:

- one input time step to one output time step (one-to-one)
- multiple input time steps to one output time step (many-to-one)
- a sequence as input and a sequence prediction as output

These are called sequence-to-sequence prediction problems, or seq2seq for short. Note that that the length of the input and output sequences may differ. In fact, when there are multiple input time steps and multiple output time steps, this is called a *many-to-many type sequence prediction problem*. Unfortunately, seq2seq models can be sample-inefficient and perform poorly on various benchmarks.

EXAMPLES OF SEQ2SEQ MODELS

Sequence-to-Sequence (seq2seq) models have been utilized across a range of applications in Natural Language Processing (NLP) and other domains. The following are some examples of tasks and specific model implementations that leverage the seq2seq paradigm.

Machine Translation

Example: Google's Neural Machine Translation (GNMT) system
GNMT is a seq2seq model used by Google Translate. It employs multiple layers of LSTMs for both encoding and decoding. The model also integrates an attention mechanism to focus on relevant parts of the source sentence while generating the target sentence.

Text Summarization

Example: Pointer-generator networks

For abstractive text summarization, where the summary is not just extracted but can be a new text. The pointer-generator network combines the benefits of extractive and abstractive summarization. It can copy words from the source text through pointing and can also generate new words.

Conversational Agents (Chatbots)

Example: The initial versions of OpenAI's GPT-2 for dialogue generation.
By training on dialogue datasets, seq2seq models can be used to generate conversational responses.

Image Captioning

Example: Show and Tell model
This model uses a convolutional neural network (CNN) as an encoder to process the image and an RNN as a decoder to generate a descriptive caption. While the encoder here is not processing a sequence, the decoder is generating one, so the model still follows the seq2seq paradigm.

Speech Recognition

Example: Listen, Attend, and Spell (LAS)
LAS uses a seq2seq model to transcribe spoken language into text. The encoder processes the audio frames, and the decoder, with an attention mechanism, generates the corresponding textual transcription.

Video Captioning

Example: Video-to-Text models
Similar to image captioning, but the encoder processes a sequence of frames (video) to produce a textual description or captions for each frame or segment.

Molecular Design

Example: Models for drug discovery
Seq2seq models can be used to translate between different representations of molecules or predict molecular properties, aiding in drug discovery and design.

Time Series Forecasting

Example: Stock price prediction
Using past stock prices (sequence of prices) to predict future prices.

Program Translation

Example: Code translation models
Translating code from one programming language to another.

Music Generation

Example: Melody generation models
Given a sequence of musical notes, generate a continuation or a harmonizing sequence.

The preceding examples showcase the versatility of the seq2seq architecture, making it a foundational tool in many areas of machine learning and artificial intelligence.

WHAT ABOUT RNNs AND LSTMs?

The inputs for an RNN have the same length: shorter sentences are padded (either on the left or on the right) to a specified length, and sentences are truncated if they are longer than that specified length.

However, encoder/decoder models generate an encoding of the input *before* passing the encoding to a decoder for processing. As a result, there is no restriction on the length of an input sentence: an encoder/decoder model can process variable and different length input sentences and also generate sentences of different lengths as output.

The Encoder-Decoder LSTM architecture is comprised of two models: one model reads the input sequence and encodes that sequence into a fixed-length vector, followed by a second model that decodes the fixed-length vector and also outputs the predicted sequence. The Encoder-Decoder LSTM was developed for NLP problems where it achieved SOTA performance for text translation.

In an analogous fashion, an RNN Encoder-Decoder architecture is comprised of two RNNs whereby the encoder maps a variable-length source sequence to a fixed-length vector, and the decoder maps the vector representation back to a variable-length output sequence.

LSTMs and Their Final Layer

An LSTM-based model consists of multiple LSTM cells whereby the output of one LSTM cell is treated as a "context vector" that becomes the input for the next LSTM cell. However, the outputs of the intermediate hidden cells of an LSTM are discarded: only the output of the final cell (which is the "cell state") in a given LSTM is passed to the next LSTM.

Why does an LSTM discard those other intermediate outputs? One reason might be that the final cell state contains the cumulative information that is accrued from processing each of the preceding hidden layers, and therefore the contents of the final cell state is essentially a superset of all the preceding cells. In other words, everything is "rolled up" into the right-most final layer, so the preceding intermediate layers provide no additional information. Although the preceding logic is plausible, it is not actually true, as demonstrated clearly by the attention mechanism that takes into account the output from *all* the hidden layers.

Processing in an LSTM is sequential and *cannot* be performed in parallel because of the dependencies between adjacent hidden layers. By contrast, the attention mechanism *can* be parallelized because the similarity between each word in a sentence and every word in the sentence is computed, and therefore there are no sequential dependencies.

Hidden State in LSTMs Versus Transformer Architecture

For RNNs and LSTMs, a hidden state is produced as output in each layer of the RNN and LSTM. Moreover, only the *final* (i.e., rightmost) hidden state is passed to the next component (be it an RNN or an LSTM) in the sequence of components.

The preceding technique ignores the output of all-but-the-last-layer in an RNN or an LSTM. Although you might think that this technique ignores important information, it could be considered a reasonable design decision for the following reason: the final layer of each component has the information from the preceding layers "rolled up" into the final layer. Be that as it may, it turns out that the outputs for all the hidden states *is* useful, and capturing those outputs is a key aspect in the implementation of the attention mechanism.

Incidentally, you might be surprised to discover that early versions of TensorFlow 1.x had support for the attention mechanism, which preceded the popularity of the transformer architecture. However, by the time that people became aware of such support, the RNN and LSTM components of the transformer architecture were no longer considered necessary.

ENCODER/DECODER MODELS

Encoder-decoder models were designed to solve seq2seq tasks. Such models are the foundation for other models and architectures, such as attention models, transformers, BERT, and GPT models. Interestingly,

BERT is an encoder-only architecture: more details are provided in Chapter 5.

The encoder-decoder framework is a neural network design paradigm used for sequence-to-sequence tasks, where the input is a sequence, and the output is another sequence. This architecture comprises two main components: the encoder and the decoder.

The encoder processes the input sequence and compresses its information into a fixed-size context vector, often referred to as the "hidden state" or "context." In many models, this context represents the last hidden state of the encoder. Typically, RNNs or their variants like LSTM and GRU are used for this purpose. The decoder takes the context vector produced by the encoder and generates the output sequence from it. It is also typically an RNN, LSTM, or GRU, which produces the output sequence step-by-step, often conditioned on the previous step's output and the context from the encoder.

Attention mechanisms are often incorporated into the decoder to allow it to focus on different parts of the input sequence at each step of the output generation, improving performance, especially for longer sequences.

The Relationship Between seq2seq and Encoder/Decoder

The seq2seq model is essentially an implementation of the encoder-decoder architecture. The seq2seq framework is built on the encoder-decoder paradigm, where the encoder processes the source sequence and the decoder generates the target sequence.

When people refer to seq2seq models, they are often discussing models that use an encoder to process the source sequence and a decoder to generate the target sequence. When the term "seq2seq" is used, it typically refers to models that follow this encoder-decoder structure.

The following statement encapsulates the relationship between seq2seq models and encoder/decoder models: all seq2seq models are encoder-decoder models, but not all encoder-decoder models are necessarily used for seq2seq tasks (though most are).

Although all seq2seq models are built on the encoder-decoder architecture, the encoder-decoder framework can be used in tasks that are not strictly sequence-to-sequence. For example, image captioning uses an image as input (encoded by a CNN) and a sequence of words as output (generated by an RNN or LSTM), fitting the encoder-decoder mold but not the typical seq2seq paradigm where both input and output are sequences.

EXAMPLES OF ENCODER/DECODER MODELS

The encoder-decoder architecture is a foundational concept that underlies many models, especially in sequence-to-sequence tasks. Here are some examples of tasks and specific implementations that leverage the encoder-decoder framework.

Machine Translation

Example: Sequence-to-Sequence with Attention
This is one of the pioneering models in neural machine translation. The encoder processes the source language, and the decoder generates the target language. An attention mechanism allows the decoder to focus on different parts of the source sentence during translation.

Image Captioning

Example: Show Attend, and Tell
The encoder, typically a CNN, processes the image. The decoder, usually an RNN or LSTM, generates a caption. An attention mechanism allows the decoder to focus on different regions of the image while generating the caption.

Speech Recognition

Example: DeepSpeech 2 by Baidu
The encoder processes the audio signal, and the decoder produces the corresponding textual transcription.

Text Summarization

Example: Abstractive Summarization models
The encoder processes the original long text, and the decoder generates a concise summary. Many of these models also integrate attention mechanisms.

Video Captioning

Example: Sequence-to-Sequence Video-to-Text
The encoder processes sequences of video frames, and the decoder generates a description or caption for each frame or segment.

Named Entity Recognition (using seq2seq)

Example: Models that treat NER as a seq2seq task

The encoder processes a sequence of words, and the decoder generates a sequence of entity tags.

Image-to-Image Translation

Example: Pix2Pix

This model uses an encoder-decoder architecture for tasks such as converting satellite images to maps or black-and-white photos to color.

Music Translation

Example: Models translating one instrument's sound to another

Anomaly Detection in Time Series

Example: Autoencoder-based models for anomaly detection

The encoder processes a sequence of data points to create a compressed representation, and the decoder reconstructs the sequence. Large reconstruction errors can indicate anomalies.

Semantic Segmentation in Images

Example: U-Net architecture

Used for biomedical image segmentation, the encoder captures the context in the image, and the decoder then uses this context to produce a high-resolution segmentation map.

The preceding examples highlight the flexibility and wide applicability of the encoder-decoder architecture across various domains in machine learning and artificial intelligence. The encoder-decoder architecture is a foundational concept that underlies many models, especially in sequence-to-sequence tasks. In the following sections, there are some examples of tasks and specific implementations that leverage the encoder-decoder framework.

AUTOREGRESSIVE MODELS

Autoregressive models that are based on the transformer architecture are decoder-only architectures. Autoregressive models utilize previous predictions to generate a new prediction. Hence, training them involves a language modeling task: models have to learn a language and interdependencies between words and phrases, including semantics. Autoregressive models predict a value for the next time step in a sequence based on results from previous time steps.

Autoregressive models are pre-trained with an important constraint: they can only see tokens that precede the current token and are blocked from seeing subsequent tokens. This mechanism "forces" autoregressive models to predict the next token without the benefit of actually examining the next token. This constraint is achieved by setting the values in the upper triangular portion of the attention matrix to 0.

Autoregressive (AR) LLMs are well-suited for generative NLP tasks. Although AR LLMs can work with either forward context or backward context, they cannot use forward and backward context simultaneously.

As you will see in Chapter 6, the autoregressive model XLNet uses *permutative language modeling* during the pre-training phase, which enables XLNet to gather information from both sides of every token in a sequence. However, this type of model has two important limitations.

The first limitation pertains to word prediction during a given time step: an autoregressive model relies on the word that precedes and the word that follows the current word. The second limitation is the fact that the accuracy of a predicted word depends on the accuracy of predicting previous words in sequence.

Autoregressive Transformers

The "normal" transformer decoder is autoregressive at inference time and non-autoregressive at training time. Consequently, the transformer model is autoregressive because its decoder is autoregressive.

However, non-autoregressive variants of the transformer do exist: they are more research topics than out-of-the-box solutions. More information about such variants is available at *https://openreview.net/ forum?id=B1l8BtlCb*.

How to Speed Up Autoregressive Transformers

In the following article, the authors assert that they can make autoregressive transformer-based models two times faster than corresponding models on Hugging Face:

https://www.reddit.com/r/MachineLearning/comments/uwkpmt/p_ what_we_learned_by_making_t5large_2x_faster

The authors describe three techniques that doubled the performance of a T5 model:

1. Storing 2 computation graphs in a single Onnx file

2. Zero copy performed to retrieve output from Onnx Runtime

3. A generic tool to convert any model (whatever the architecture) to FP16

Keep in mind the following comments and recommendation, para-phrased from the preceding reddit article:

1. The double graph technique is only relevant for autoregressive models.

2. The fp16 technique is not useful on BERT-like models.

3. Use tensorrt on BERT-like and apply int8 quantization, which can result in a 5X to 10X increase in performance on moderately long sequences and very short sequences, respectively.

Recall that T5 is based on both the encoder and the decoder component of the transformer architecture, which means that T5 is also an autoregressive model.

The authors also provide a notebook (Onnx Runtime only):

https://github.com/ELS-RD/transformer-deploy/blob/main/demo/generative-model/t5.ipynb

There is a Github repository that contains the preceding notebook:

https://github.com/ELS-RD/transformer-deploy

The following website provides an nbviewer link to the same notebook:

https://nbviewer.jupyter.org/url/github.com/ELS-RD/transformer-deploy/blob/main/demo/generative-model/t5.ipynb

If you want to execute the code in the notebook, the following binder link will start a Jupyter server:

https://mybinder.org/v2/gh/ELS-RD/transformer-deploy/main?filepath=demo%2Fgenerative-model%2Ft5.ipynb

AUTOENCODING MODELS

Autoregressive models (discussed earlier in this chapter) are very good when the goal is to perform Natural Language Generation (NLG). However, Natural Language Understanding (NLU) tasks are not well-suited for autoregressive models, nor for seq2seq models; the latter are suitable for language translation. A better choice for NLU involves an autoencoding model.

Autoencoders learn a representation (i.e., an encoding) for a set of data, most often for the purpose of dimensionality reduction, such that the input layer and the final layer are the same. In simplified terms, autoencoding models are pre-trained by corrupting the input tokens in some fashion and then attempting to reconstruct the original sentence. For example, the BERT model "corrupts" input sequence by replacing a subset of the tokens with a [MASK] token.

To a certain extent, autoencoding models attempt to overcome limitations in autoregressive models. Autoencoding models are based on the original transformer and they examine two-sided dependencies of tokens in a sentence to obtain bidirectional context.

A limitation of autoencoder models is due to the MLM step that is performed during the pre-training step. Since MLM attempts to predict a masked token during MLM, a limitation arises when multiple masked tokens depend on each other during this prediction step.

A second limitation arises for models (such as BERT) that process sequence of fixed length with a maximum allowable length (which is 512 for BERT). Note that the MLM task and the BERT model are discussed in Chapter 6.

Autoencoders

An *autoencoder* is a fully connected simple neural network that is one type of encoder-decoder model in which the input layer and the output layer are the same, and typically one hidden layer between the input layer and the output layer that is smaller than the input and output layers. The purpose of the hidden layer is to perform dimensionality reduction: after the model has been trained, the contents of the hidden layer are retained for other downstream tasks (such as QnA), whereas the input and output layers are discarded.

Autoencoders are a type of neural network used primarily for unsupervised learning tasks, especially dimensionality reduction and feature learning. An autoencoder consists of two main parts: an encoder and a decoder. The encoder compresses the input into a latent-space representation, and the decoder reconstructs the input data from this representation. The primary goal of an autoencoder is to minimize the difference between the original input and its reconstruction, thereby learning a compact and efficient representation of the data in the process.

There are variations of this architecture that contain additional hidden layers, some of which are deeper than the input and output layers. Perform an online search with "image-autoencoders," and you will find a plethora of interesting types of autoencoders.

Autoencoding Transformers

An autoencoding transformer is a neural network that combines the unsupervised learning capabilities of autoencoders with the powerful sequence-processing abilities of transformers. It is designed to encode input sequences into latent representations using transformer mechanisms and then decode them back, aiming to minimize the reconstruction error. This architecture can learn compact and meaningful representations of sequence data, making it useful for a variety of tasks in NLP and beyond.

An autoencoding transformer combines the principles of both autoencoders and transformers. It uses the transformer architecture to encode the input data into a latent representation and then decode it back into its original form. An autoencoding transformer can be used for various tasks, such as

- Representation Learning: To learn meaningful representations of the input data
- Denoising: To reconstruct clean data from noisy input
- Anomaly Detection: Large reconstruction errors can indicate anomalies or outliers in the data

For example, the BERT (Bidirectional Encoder Representations from Transformers) model can be seen as a kind of autoencoding transformer. BERT is trained to predict masked portions of text, thereby encoding the surrounding context into its embeddings. Although it does not reconstruct the entire input like traditional autoencoders, its training principle is similar in that it learns representations based on reconstructing parts of the input.

Here is an important point: deciding between autoregressive models and autoencoding models depends on the task and training, not on the architecture. Moreover, it is possible to use a decoder for autoencoding, and it is possible to use an encoder for autoregressive tasks.

THE TRANSFORMER ARCHITECTURE: INTRODUCTION

The transformer architecture debuted in 2017, and it is designed as an encoder-decoder architecture that is a `seq2seq` model. The transformer has had a tremendous impact on language modeling, partly through its self-attention mechanism that tracks how tokens are related to each other.

The transformer architecture performs NLP-related tasks that fundamentally different from other architectures. In fact, the transformer architecture facilitated the development of various well-known large language models (LLMs), such as BERT, T5, GPT-2, and GPT-3.

The Original Transformer Architecture

You might be surprised to discover that the original transformer architecture was initially a seq2seq model that involves LSTMs. Someone discovered that the transformer architecture performed equally well without LSTMs because of the attention mechanism, which in turn led to the seminal paper "Attention is all you need," as mentioned earlier in this chapter (*https://www.topbots.com/leading-nlp-language-models-2020/*).

The interesting development of the transformer architecture is that there are several types of transformer architectures:

- An encoder-only architecture (such as BERT-based models)
- A decoder-only architecture (such as GPT-x)
- Both an encoder and a decoder architecture (such as T5 and BART)

Therefore, when you learn about transformer-based LLMs, one question to ask is which type of transformer architecture is used in the LLM. Examples of models that include both the encoder and the decoder are seq2seq models, BART, and the T5 model (Google) that can be fine-tuned to perform many tasks.

The word *encoder* is overloaded: an encoder can refer to the *entire* encoder component, or can it refer to one of the 6 (or 12) encoders that are inside the entire encoder component (similar comments apply to the decoder). Consequently, the following terms are used in this book to disambiguate the words encoder and decoder:

- A *component* is the full encoder or decoder of the original transformer architecture.
- A *block* contains the layers that perform attention, feed forward, and so forth.
- A *layer* is an element (in a block) that performs attention, feed forward, and so forth.

Transformer-based architectures typically have either 6 encoder blocks and 6 decoder blocks for the encoder component and the decoder component, respectively, or they have 12 encoder blocks for the encoder component and 12 decoder blocks for the decoder component (and other values are possible as well). Keep in mind that a *block* in the encoder component is just a synonym for a self-contained smaller encoder; similarly, a *block* in the decoder component is actually a self-contained smaller decoder. For now, make a mental note that every block in the encoder component contains *two* layers, whereas one block in the decoder component contains *three* layers.

As you will see in Chapter 6, BERT uses only the encoder component from the transformer, whereas GPT-2 involves only the decoder component from the transformer, and T5 utilizes the encoder as well as the decoder.

Order of Operations

If a transformer-based model consists of a single component, then all operations are performed in that component in a bottom-up fashion. If a transformer-based model comprises the encoder component as well as the decoder component, then operations are performed in a bottom-up fashion in the *encoder* component, after which its output is passed to the decoder component, where additional operations are performed in a bottom-up fashion. After all the processing has been completed, you can add another layer to the model for performing other tasks, as discussed in Chapter 6.

Independence from RNNs/LSTMs

Interestingly, the initial implementation of the transformer architecture included RNNs and LSTMs. At some point, someone discovered that comparable accuracy was possible *without* RNNs or LSTMs. This discovery led to the expression "Attention is all you need" in the seminal paper for the transformer architecture. In particular, the transformer architecture differs from other architectures in the following important ways:

- It relies on an attention mechanism.
- Model training can be parallelized.
- No CNN/RNN/LSTMs are required.

Note that the encoder-decoder model differs from a seq2seq model that often contain RNNs or LSTMs.

The independence from RNNs and LSTMs simplifies the architecture of the transformer, which relies on self-attention, which means that every word in a sentence is compared with every other word in the same sentence. This "global" approach to processing documents has demonstrated better results than other techniques that process "local" portions of a document. Moreover, the transformer architecture is better equipped for processing long-range dependencies in a corpus.

RNNs have been useful for solving a variety of tasks, including NLP-based tasks. In particular, machine translation systems that map sequences of words from a source language to a target language relied on RNNs. In fact, translation tasks can be handled by an encoder-decoder architecture as well as a seq2seq (sequence-to-sequence) architecture.

The transformer architecture was initially designed for machine translation models, so it was structured as an encoder/decoder architecture. In fact, the transformer architecture has been extremely effective for language models. After the initial transformer architecture was published, researchers developed architectures that are more efficient in terms of computation as well as memory consumption, both of which are especially important for small devices (such as cell phones) and for processing binary images.

Indeed, transformers involve significant computational complexity that exceeds the capacity of devices such as smart phones: *https://arxiv. org/abs/2201.03545*.

The Transformer Component Blocks

In general, we use the letter T to indicate the number of tokens that are passed into the initial embedding layer. The output of the initial embedding layer is a Txd matrix of values, where d is the input width of the model. The value of d is 512 in the transformer paper, and in other models d can equal 1,024 or 2,048. *The transformer blocks perform various operations without changing the shape of the data (i.e., Txd).*

Here is an important point: the positional encodings and the output from the transformer blocks in the encoder component or the decoder component have shape Txd (T and d are defined in the preceding paragraph)

The Main Transformer Components

As you learned in the previous section, the *complete* transformer architecture involves an attention mechanism (discussed in Chapter 1), positional encodings (discussed later), an encoder, and a decoder for the purpose of handling sequence-to-sequence tasks. The attention mechanism can consist of the following types:

- Attention in the encoder
- Masked attention in the decoder
- Attention between the encoder and the decoder

The first step involves embedding the input, which involves a matrix (called the *position embedding matrix*). Thus, the input consists of a vector with multiple tokens.

Yet another interesting detail regarding transformer-based models is that some of them use only the *encoder* (BERT), some use only the *decoder* (GPT-3), and some use both the encoder *and* the decoder (T5). Each of these three architectures are suited for different types of NLP tasks, which is discussed in more detail in Chapter 7.

Here is a summary of three important aspects of the transformer architecture, two of which are discussed in greater detail later in this chapter:

The *attention mechanism* (discussed in Chapter 1) is a sequence-to-sequence operation that takes a series of vectors as an input and produces a different sequence of vectors. Some attention calculations are just a weighted average of all the input vectors.

The *encoder* component contains six blocks, each of which contains several layers that in turn contains two sub-layers: the first sub-layer contains the self-attention mechanism and the second sub-layer consists of a feed forward network.

The *decoder* component includes six blocks, each of which contains several layers that in turn contain three sub-layers: two of those sub-layers are the same as their counterpart in the encoder, and the third layer is a multi-head attention layer for transforming the input of the encoder.

Make note of the fact that although the encoder and decoder are very similar components, the decoder block contains an extra sub-layer consisting of a multi-head attention layer.

THE TRANSFORMER IS AN ENCODER/DECODER MODEL

There are two important advantages that the transformer architecture has over other architectures:

- their lower computational complexity
- their higher connectivity, which is particularly advantageous in sequences that involve long-term dependencies

In addition, the encoder and the decoder are trained to minimize the conditional log-likelihood.

As you will see in Chapter 4, the encoder component in the original transformer paper (available in arxiv) has 6 identical layers. Moreover, some LLMs contain 12 identical layers instead of 6 identical layers. Each layer consists of the following elements:

- Multi-Head Attention
- Add & Normalization
- Feed Forward Network
- Add & Normalization

When discussing the encoder or the decoder, it is helpful to visualize the encoder as a vertical stack of encoder elements, situated to the left of the decoder component in the diagram of the transformer architecture, which in turn also consists of a vertical stack of decoder elements.

The decoder component resembles an enhancement of the encoder component that includes a third layer for the "masked attention," as listed here:

- Masked Multi-Head attention
- Add & Normalization
- Multi-Head Attention
- Add & Normalization
- Feed Forward Network
- Add & Normalization

The masked multi-head attention in the decoder component also performs masking to prevent "forward looking" into future tokens. The decoder component can also consist of 6 identical layers or 12 identical layers that match the number of elements in the encoder component.

Recall that in the case of a sequence of LSTM elements, the final hidden layer of a given LSTM is passed to only *one* LSTM, which is the next LSTM in the sequence. Hence, there is a one-to-one relationship between the output of one LSTM and the input for the next LSTM in the sequence.

Therein lies an important difference regarding the manner in which output is passed from one element to the next element in a sequence of elements. Unlike the LSTM-based sequence of elements, the output of the encoder component is passed to *every* masked attention layer in every element of the decoder.

Moreover, this third decoder layer accepts input not only from the output of the encoder component, but also from the lower decoder layer in the vertical stack of elements in the decoder component. Hence, if the encoder and decoder components each consist of N elements, then the output of the encoder is passed to *every* one of the N elements in the decoder. In a sense, the output from the encoder component to the decoder component is a one-to-many relationship. Chapter 4 contains more information regarding the transformer architecture.

THE TRANSFORMER FLOW AND ITS VARIANTS

The input to a transformer consists of a set of tokens whose maximum length is typically 512 or 1,024, and the length of associated input vectors is called the *context size*. Sentences that are longer than the maximum length must be truncated, which could result in a loss of accuracy if the truncated portions contain important information.

Importantly, the transformer encodes those vectors *in parallel* via a multi-head attention mechanism (discussed later). By contrast, RNNs and LSTMs process tokens sequentially.

After the tokens have been encoded as one-dimensional vectors and processed by the encoder component, the result is sent to the decoder to generate an output sequence. Note that the decoder processes inputs *sequentially* instead of processing inputs in a parallel manner. Later, you will learn about models use only the encoder (e.g., BERT), other models that use only the decoder (e.g., GPT-3), and some models that use both the encoder and decode (e.g., BART and T5). Here is a cumulative summary of what you have learned thus far about the transformer architecture:

- It relies on an attention mechanism.
- Model training can be parallelized.
- No CNN/RNN/LSTMs are required.
- Some models use only the encoder (e.g., BERT).
- Some models use only the decoder (e.g., GPT-3).
- Some models use the encoder and the decoder (e.g., BART and T5).
- The maximum input length is 512.

The transformer architecture has been used for tasks in other domains that are unrelated to NLP, such as chemistry, computer vision, image classification, and video (among others). Please read the following article on the transformer architecture: *https://arxiv.org/pdf/1706.03762.pdf.*

Transformer-based LLMs led to the development of pre-trained models that are trained on a large and unlabeled corpus. Moreover, such models can be fine-tuned for specialized "downstream" tasks by appending a task-specific layer to models and then performing additional training based on a relatively small number of labeled examples.

Three Variants of the Transformer Architecture

The previous section indicated that the transformer architecture involves a combination of self-attention, an encoder, and a decoder. Interestingly, there are models that implement different subsets (components) of the transformer architecture. Although all of them provide a self-attention mechanism, they vary in the following ways:

- Encoder only
- Decoder only
- Encoder and decoder (the original architecture)

As you learned earlier in this chapter, GPT uses only the decoder component of the transformer architecture, whereas BERT uses only the encoder component. The BART and T5 are two models that use both the encoder and the decoder of the transformer architecture. Additional details about the three different implementations of the transformer architecture are provided later in this chapter.

Transformer-Based NLP Models

In addition to having different combinations of the top-level components of the transformer architecture, transformer-based NLP models can be categorized as one of three main types, examples of which are provided in parentheses:

- Seq2seq (BART/T5)
- Autoencoding (BERT)
- Autoregressive (GPT)

The preceding transformer models were trained as language models on large amounts of text in a self-supervised fashion. In addition, XGLM is a family of large-scale multilingual autoregressive language models that achieve SOTA results on multilingual few-shot learning. XGLM from MetaAI is now available in Hugging Face transformers:

https://huggingface.co/spaces/valhalla/XGLM-zero-shot-COPA

Transformer Accelerator from NVidia

Now that transformer-based models have exceeded one trillion parameters, computational speed has become increasingly important for these models, as well as future models, which will be even larger. Although early speculation suggested that GPT-4 might reach 100 trillion parameters, GPT-4 appears to have 1.76 trillion parameters, based on 8 "components" that each have 220 billion parameters.

Currently, NVidia provides the A100 GPU chip, and the successor to the A100 GPU is the H100 GPU that can provides significantly faster computing power than the A100. Depending on the application, the H100 can provide between 8 and 30 times faster processing than the A100.

"Hopper" is the name of the chip design of the H100, which includes a transformer engine for improved performance. The H100 supports other techniques for improved performance: *https://www.nvidia.com/en-us/data-center/h100*.

Transformer-Based Architecture for Graphs

Although the original transformer architecture is well-suited for NLP-related tasks, an *enhanced* transformer architecture is also available for processing arbitrary graphs. In particular, this enhanced architecture modifies three existing aspects of the transformer as well as adding a new property:

- the attention mechanism
- the positional encoding
- the layer normalization
- edge feature representation

More information about this architecture is accessible online:

https://arxiv.org/pdf/2012.09699.pdf

THE TRANSFORMERS LIBRARY FROM HUGGING FACE

Hugging Face created a Python-based transformers library and an open-source repository to develop models based on the transformer architecture that is accessible at

https://github.com/huggingface/transformers.

The Hugging Face open source transformers library has three primary components:

- Model Classes
- Configuration Classes
- Tokenizer Classes

Model classes provide more than two dozen pre-trained transformer models.

Configuration classes provide various classes with the parameters that are necessary to instantiate a model.

Tokenizer classes are components that equip each model with a vocabulary and methods for encoding/decoding strings to manage token embeddings and indices. Later in this chapter, you will see

`Python`-based code samples that show you how to use a tokenizer class from Hugging Face.

The `transformers` Library and NLP Tasks

The `transformers` library provides pre-trained models for `NLU` and `NLG`. In fact, Hugging Face provides more than 30 pre-trained models for more than 100 languages, along with operability between `TensorFlow` 2 and `PyTorch`. Furthermore, Hugging Face supports `BERT`-related models, `GPT-2`/`GPT-3`, `XLNet`, and others. Here is a list of some of the models supported by Hugging Face:

- BART (from Facebook)
- BERT (from Google)
- Blenderbot (from Facebook)
- CamemBERT (from Inria/Facebook/Sorbonne)
- CTRL (from Salesforce)
- DeBERTa (from Microsoft Research)
- DistilBERT (from Hugging Face)
- ELECTRA (from Google Research/Stanford University)
- FlauBERT (from CNRS)
- GPT-2 (from OpenAI)
- Longformer (from AllenAI)
- LXMERT (from UNC Chapel Hill)
- Pegasus (from Google)
- Reformer (from Google Research)
- RoBERTa (from Facebook)
- SqueezeBert
- T5 (from Google AI)
- Transformer-XL (from Google/CMU)
- XLM-RoBERTa (from Facebook AI)
- XLNet (from Google/CMU)

Check the online documentation for more information regarding the models in the preceding bullet list.

These language models collectively support NLU and NLG to perform tasks like text classification, information extraction, and text generation.

The Transformer `pipeline` Class

The `transformers` library provides a standard interface to multiple models, which simplifies the task of integrating language models into custom applications. In particular, the `transformers` library supports `JAX`, `PyTorch`, and `TensorFlow`.

The `transformer` library also provides a `pipeline()` class that you can use in a pipeline-based mechanism. The following code block illustrates how to instantiate a transformer pipeline for various NLP tasks that are specified inside double quotes (complete code samples are discussed later):

```
from transformers import pipeline
classifier1 = pipeline("ner")
classifier2 = pipeline("token-classification")
classifier3 = pipeline("question-answering")
classifier4 = pipeline("sentiment-analysis")
classifier5 = pipeline("text-generation")
classifier6 = pipeline("feature-extraction")
classifier7 = pipeline("summarization")
classifier8 = pipeline("zero-shot-classification")
```

As you can see in the preceding code block, the `pipeline()` class supports NER, token classification, sentiment analysis, and so forth. In addition, the `transformers` library supports the preceding NLP tasks in more than 100 languages. The Hugging Face Hub contains numerous models:

https://huggingface.co/models

TRANSFORMER ARCHITECTURE COMPLEXITY

The complexity of the transformer architecture is the sum of the complexity of the attention mechanism and the complexity of various components of the transformer architecture. Matrix multiplication involves $O(N^2)$ complexity for each product to calculate the pairwise similarity between every pair of tokens.

The following list contains the complexity of several components of the transformer architecture:

- $O(N^2*D)$: complexity of self-attention
- $O(N*D^2)$: complexity of the query/key/value projection-layers
- $O(N*D^2)$: complexity of the feedforward layer

In most cases, the value of D is significantly larger than N. For instance, the value of D in GPT-3 is 12288, and N is much smaller than D. Another detail to consider is that bandwidth is usually a bottleneck for LLMs, which means that a reduction in compute time and memory resources in conjunction with the same bandwidth does not improve the overall performance.

Reducing Attention Complexity

The attention mechanism in the transformer architecture has $O(N^2)$ complexity, where N equals the number of tokens. Fortunately, the Performer architecture computes attention with complexity $O(N)$, and therefore the Performer architecture can support much wider-context windows. For example, the Flamingo LLM (not discussed in this book) uses the Perceiver model (not discussed in this book) due to the size of the images that are processed.

HUGGING FACE TRANSFORMER CODE SAMPLES

Before we delve into additional details regarding the transformer architecture, let's look at several Python-based code samples that illustrate how to use Hugging Face transformers to perform NLP-related tasks.

Although these code samples are very simple, they show you how to perform NER, QnA, and sentiment analysis using a Hugging Face transformer. In addition, code samples provide a concrete foundation from which you can increase your working knowledge of transformers and transformer-based language models.

Transformer and NER Tasks

Listing 3.1 displays the content of hf_transformer_ner.py that illustrates how to perform an NER task with the Hugging Face transformer.

Listing 3.1: hf_transformer_ner.py

```
from transformers import pipeline
import pandas as pd

nlp = pipeline('ner')
result = nlp("I am a UCSC instructor and my name is
Oswald")
print("result:",result)
print()
```

```
df = pd.DataFrame(result)
print("df:",df)
print()


nlp = pipeline('ner')
result = nlp("I Love Chicago Pizza and I Really
Like New York Bagels")
print("=> result:",result)
print()


df = pd.DataFrame(result)
print("df:",df)
```

Listing 3.1 starts with an `import` statement and then initializes the variable `nlp` as an instance of the `pipeline` function, with `ner` as a parameter. Next, the variable `nlp` is invoked with a hard-coded sample sentence. The output is assigned to the variable `result`, whose contents are then displayed. Launch the code in Listing 3.1 with the following command:

```
python3 hf_transformer_ner.py
```

The preceding command launches the version of `Python` that is installed on your machine. As you learned in the introduction to this chapter, `Hugging Face` currently supports `Python 3.7`, but in the future, it is likely that later versions of `Python` will also be supported. The preceding command will display the following output:

```
=> result: [{'word': 'UC', 'score':
0.9993938207626343, 'entity': 'I-ORG', 'index':
4}, {'word': '##SC', 'score': 0.9974051713943481,
'entity': 'I-ORG', 'index': 5}, {'word': 'Oswald',
'score': 0.9988114833831787, 'entity': 'I-PER',
'index': 11}]
```

```
df:    word      score  entity  index  start  end
0        UC   0.999394   I-ORG      4      7    9
1      ##SC   0.997405   I-ORG      5      9   11
2    Oswald   0.998811   I-PER     11     38   44
```

```
=> result: [{'word': 'Chicago', 'score':
0.962387204170227, 'entity': 'I-ORG', 'index': 3,
```

```
'start': 7, 'end': 14}, {'word': 'Pizza', 'score':
0.958823561668396, 'entity': 'I-ORG', 'index': 4,
'start': 15, 'end': 20}, {'word': 'New', 'score':
0.6438480615615845, 'entity': 'I-ORG', 'index': 9,
'start': 39, 'end': 42}, {'word': 'York', 'score':
0.8661817908287048, 'entity': 'I-ORG', 'index': 10,
'start': 43, 'end': 47}, {'word': 'Ba', 'score':
0.5761372447013855, 'entity': 'I-MISC', 'index':
11, 'start': 48, 'end': 50}, {'word': '##gel',
'score': 0.4892355501651764, 'entity': 'I-MISC',
'index': 12, 'start': 50, 'end': 53}]
```

```
df:      word      score   entity   index   start   end
0     Chicago   0.962387   I-ORG        3       7    14
1       Pizza   0.958824   I-ORG        4      15    20
2         New   0.643848   I-ORG        9      39    42
3        York   0.866182   I-ORG       10      43    47
4          Ba   0.576137   I-MISC      11      48    50
5      ##gel   0.489236   I-MISC      12      50    53
```

Transformer and QnA Tasks

Listing 3.2 displays the content of hf_transformer_qa.py that illustrates how to perform a question-and-answer task with the Hugging Face transformer.

Listing 3.2: hf_transformer_qa.py

```
from transformers import pipeline

nlp = pipeline('question-answering')

result = nlp({
  'question': "Do you know my name?",
  'context': "My name is Oswald"
})

print("result:",result)
```

Listing 3.2 starts with an import statement and then initializes the variable nlp as an instance of the pipeline function, with question-answering as a parameter. Next, the variable nlp is invoked with a question/context pair. The output is assigned to the variable `result`, whose contents are then displayed. Launch the code in Listing 3.2, and you will see the following output:

```
result: [{'word': 'UC', 'score':
0.9993938207626343, 'entity': 'I-ORG', 'index':
4}, {'word': '##SC', 'score': 0.9974051713943481,
'entity': 'I-ORG', 'index': 5}, {'word': 'Oswald',
'score': 0.9988114833831787, 'entity': 'I-PER',
'index': 11}]
```

Transformer and Text Summarization

Listing 3.3 displays the content of `hf_text_summarization.py` that illustrates how to perform text summarization with the Hugging Face transformer. Note that the block of text in this code sample is identical to the text in the introduction of this chapter.

Listing 3.3: hf_text_summarization.py

```
from transformers import pipeline

summarizer = pipeline("summarization")

text = """
This chapter is the first of two chapters that
discusses the transformer architecture, which is
the foundation for a plethora of language models,
such as BERT and its variants (discussed in
Chapters 4 and 5), as well as the GPT-x family from
OpenAI, various other LLMs (discussed in Chapters 6
and 7).

This chapter describes the main components of the
original transformer, along with Python-based
transformer code samples for various NLP tasks,
such as NER, QnA, and mask filling tasks. Please
read chapter one that discusses some topics that
are relevant to the material in this chapter.

The first part of this chapter introduces the
transformer architecture that was developed by
Google and released in late 2017. This section also
discusses some NLP Transformer models.
```

The second part of this chapter discusses the transformers library from Hugging Face, which is a company that provides a repository of more than 20,000 transformer-based models. This section also contains Python-based transformer code samples that perform various NLP tasks, such as NER, QnA, and mask filling tasks.

The third part of this chapter provides more details regarding the encoder component, along with additional details regarding the attention mechanism, as well as the decoder component, which is the other main component of the transformer architecture.

Before you read this chapter, keep in mind that there are cases of "forward referencing" concepts that are discussed in later chapters, which provide context for a given concept. Of course, if you are unfamiliar with a concept discussed in a later chapter, then it will also be challenging to fully understand the topic under discussion. As a result, you will probably need to read some topics more than once, after which concepts become easier to grasp when you understand the current context and the context of referenced material in later chapters (fortunately, this reading process is finite).
"""

```
result = summarizer(text)
#print("summary text:",result)
print("summary text:",result[0]['summary_text'])
```

Listing 3.3 starts with an `import` statement and then initializes the variable `summarizer` with the result of invoking the `pipeline` class with the `summarization` task. The next portion of Listing 3.3 initializes the string variable `text` with the contents of the introduction to this chapter. The final code block initializes the variable result with the output from `summarizer(text)` and then displays the contents of `summary_text`.

Launch the code in Listing 3.3, and you will see the following output when you launch the code for the first time:

```
Downloading: 100%|
          | 1.80k/1.80k [00:00<00:00, 283kB/s]
Downloading: 100%|
           | 1.22G/1.22G [00:27<00:00, 44.2MB/s]
Downloading: 100%|
          | 899k/899k [00:00<00:00, 1.55MB/s]
Downloading: 100%|
          | 456k/456k [00:00<00:00, 2.02MB/s]
Downloading: 100%|
          | 26.0/26.0 [00:00<00:00, 6.87kB/s]


summary text:  This chapter is the first of two
that discusses the transformer architecture, which
is the foundation for a plethora of language
models. This chapter describes the main components
of the original transformer, along with Python-
based transformer code samples for various NLP
tasks. The second part of this chapter discusses
the transformers library from HuggingFace,
which provides a repository of more than 20,000
transformer-based models.
```

During subsequent invocations of the `Python` code, the download section will be skipped because the LLM is already available on your machine. Compare the generated output with the contents of the variable `text` to determine whether the code provides an accurate summary.

Transformer and Text Translation

Listing 3.4 displays the content of `hf_text_translation.py` that shows you how to translate text from English to Italian with the `Hugging Face` transformer.

Listing 3.4: hf_text_translation.py

```
from transformers import pipeline


translator = pipeline("translation_en_to_
it",model="Helsinki-NLP/opus-mt-en-it")


input = "Today the weather was really nice and
sunny"
input = "I love Chicago deep dish pizza and a
bottle of stout"
```

```
results = translator(input, clean_up_tokenization_
spaces=True, min_length=50)
print("results[0]['translation_text']:")
print(results[0]['translation_text'])
```

Listing 3.4 starts with an `import` statement and then initializes the variable `translator` as an instance of the `pipeline function`, along with the parameter `translation_en_to_it` (i.e., English to Italian). Next, the variable `nlp` is invoked with a question/context pair. The output is assigned to the variable `result`, whose contents are then displayed. Notice that the suffix `en-it` (shown in bold) for the model name is a shorthand technique that specifies English-to-Italian translation. Launch the code in Listing 3.4, and you will see the following output:

```
Adoro la pizza a base di piatti profondi di Chicago
e una bottiglia di robusto... e un po' di roba...
e... e... un po' di roba...
```

TRANSFORMER AND MASK-RELATED TASKS

This section shows you how to perform mask-filling tasks with various sentences. You will also see an example of what happens when you specify more than one `<mask>` element in a sentence (answer: it will not work). Before you launch the code samples, please ensure that you are connected to the Internet, otherwise you will see this type of error message:

```
raise ValueError(
ValueError: Connection error, and we cannot find
the requested files in the cached path. Please try
again or make sure your Internet connection is on.
```

Listing 3.5 displays the content of `hf_fill_mask1.py` that illustrates how to perform a mask-filling task with the `Hugging Face` transformer.

Listing 3.5: hf_fill_mask1.py

```
from transformers import pipeline

mlm = pipeline("fill-mask")
prompt = "The dog <mask> over the fence"
```

```
result = mlm(prompt)
print("prompt:",prompt)
print("result:",result)
print("--------------")

mlm = pipeline("fill-mask")
prompt = "The dog <mask> over the pool"
result = mlm(prompt)
print("prompt:",prompt)
print("result:",result)
print("--------------")

mlm = pipeline("fill-mask")
prompt = "The horse <mask> over the wall"
result = mlm(prompt)
print("prompt:",prompt)
print("result:",result)
```

Listing 3.5 starts with an `import` statement and then initializes the variable `nlp` as an instance of the `pipeline` function that takes `fill-mask` as a parameter. Next, the variable `nlp` is invoked with a hard-coded text string. The output is assigned to the variable `result`, whose contents are then displayed. Launch the code in Listing 3.5, and you will see the following output:

```
prompt: The dog <mask> over the fence
result: [{'sequence': '<s>The dog jumps over the
fence</s>', 'score': 0.27710869908332825, 'token':
13855, 'token_str': 'Ġjumps'}, {'sequence':
'<s>The dog leaps over the fence</s>', 'score':
0.1510920524597168, 'token': 32564, 'token_str':
'Ġleaps'}, {'sequence': '<s>The dog jumped over the
fence</s>', 'score': 0.06851337850093842, 'token':
4262, 'token_str': 'Ġjumped'}, {'sequence':
'<s>The dog climbs over the fence</s>', 'score':
0.04117066413164139, 'token': 30318, 'token_str':
'Ġclimbs'}, {'sequence': '<s>The dog walks over the
fence</s>', 'score': 0.03938476741313934, 'token':
5792, 'token_str': 'Ġwalks'}]

--------------
```

```
prompt: The dog <mask> over the pool
```

result: [{'sequence': '<s>The dog jumps over the pool</s>', 'score': 0.1273069977760315, 'token': 13855, 'token_str': 'Ġjumps'}, {'sequence': '<s>The dog walks over the pool</s>', 'score': 0.106533944606781, 'token': 5792, 'token_str': 'Ġwalks'}, {'sequence': '<s>The dog runs over the pool</s>', 'score': 0.06851048767566681, 'token': 1237, 'token_str': 'Ġruns'}, {'sequence': '<s>The dog leaps over the pool</s>', 'score': 0.05455796793103218, 'token': 32564, 'token_str': 'Ġleaps'}, {'sequence': '<s>The dog leaping over the pool</s>', 'score': 0.03309628739953041, 'token': 33189, 'token_str': 'Ġleaping'}]

```
prompt: The horse <mask> over the wall
```

result: [{'sequence': '<s>The horse jumps over the wall</s>', 'score': 0.05724393203854561, 'token': 13855, 'token_str': 'Ġjumps'}, {'sequence': '<s>The horse rode over the wall</s>', 'score': 0.056807991117239, 'token': 12783, 'token_str': 'Ġrode'}, {'sequence': '<s>The horse leaps over the wall</s>', 'score': 0.04696424677968025, 'token': 32564, 'token_str': 'Ġleaps'}, {'sequence': '<s>The horse climbs over the wall</s>', 'score': 0.04176592454314232, 'token': 30318, 'token_str': 'Ġclimbs'}, {'sequence': '<s>The horse rides over the wall</s>', 'score': 0.04105382785201073, 'token': 9668, 'token_str': 'Ġrides'}]

Listing 3.6 displays the content of hf_fill_two_masks.py that shows you what happens when you specify more than one <mask> element in the same sentence.

Listing 3.6: hf_fill_two_masks.py

```
from transformers import pipeline

mlm = pipeline("fill-mask")
prompt = "The horse <mask> over the fence and the <mask> ate the pizza"
result = mlm(prompt)
print("prompt:",prompt)
print("result:",result)
```

Launch the code in Listing 3.6, and you will see the following output:

```
raise PipelineException(
transformers.pipelines.base.PipelineException: More
than one mask_token (<mask>) is not supported
```

Prompt and Fill Task

Listing 3.7 displays the content of hf_prompt_fill.py that illustrates how to specify a prompt and then perform a fill-mask task with the Hugging Face transformer.

Listing 3.7: hf_prompt_fill.py

```
from transformers import pipeline


pipe = pipeline("fill-mask", model="bert-base-
uncased")


# => part 1:
movie_desc = "the main characters of the movie
matrix are neo, morpheus, and trinity."
prompt = "The movie is about [MASK]."
output = pipe(movie_desc + prompt)


print("desc:  ",movie_desc)
print("prompt:",prompt)
for element in output:
  print(f"Token {element['token_str']}:
  \t{element['score']:.3f}%")
print("-------------\n\n")


# => part 2:
movie_desc = "In the movie transformers aliens can
morph into a wide range of vehicles."
prompt = "The movie is about [MASK]."
output = pipe(movie_desc + prompt,
targets=["animals","cars"])
```

```
print("desc:   ",movie_desc)
print("prompt:",prompt)
for element in output:
  print(f"Token {element['token_str']}:
    \t{element['score']:.3f}%")
```

Listing 3.7 starts with an `import` statement and then initializes the variable `nlp` as an instance of the `pipeline function` that takes `fill-mask` as a parameter. Next, the variable `nlp` is invoked with a hard-coded text string. The output is assigned to the variable `result`, whose contents are then displayed. Launch the code in Listing 3.7, and you will see the following output:

```
desc:    the main characters of the movie matrix are
neo, morpheus, and trinity.
prompt: The movie is about [MASK].
Token trinity:   0.058%
Token neo:       0.053%
Token love:      0.050%
Token dreams:    0.028%
Token fate:      0.024%
-------------


desc:    In the movie transformers aliens can morph
into a wide range of vehicles.
prompt: The movie is about [MASK].
Token cars:      0.139%
Token animals:   0.006%
```

SUMMARY

This chapter started with an introduction to the transformer architecture, followed by a description of three variations of the transformer architecture: encoder only (BERT), decoder only (GPT), and both encoder and decoder (BART and T5).

Next, you learned about the `transformers` library from Hugging Face, which is a company that provides a huge repository of transformer-based models. Then you saw code samples that use transformer-based models to perform various NLP tasks, such as NER, QnA, and mask-filling tasks.

In addition, you learned about the details of the encoder component and the decoder component, which are the two main components of the transformer architecture. You also saw how the encoder and decoder have similar structures, with an additional masked self-attention layer in the decoder.

## CHAPTER 4

TRANSFORMER ARCHITECTURE IN GREATER DEPTH

This chapter is the second of two chapters on the transformer architecture, which is the foundation for a plethora of language models, such as BERT and its variants (Chapters 5 and 6), followed by the GPT-x family and its competitors (Chapters 7 and 8).

The first part of this chapter discusses positional encoding, which involve the `sine()` and `cosine()` functions for the transformer architecture. You will also learn about three types of positional encoding in this section.

The second part of this chapter discusses additional details about the encoder component of the transformer architecture, along with an overview of the decoder component. This section also provides information about how to determine whether to use an encoder, a decoder, or both encoder and decoder in an LLM.

The third part of this chapter discusses `Auto` classes, such as `Auto-Model`, `AutoConfig`, and `AutoTokenizer`. You will learn about LLMs that provide improvements over the original transformer architecture, such as the Reformer, Longformer, and the Switch transformer, which consists of one trillion parameters.

The final part of this chapter contains an example of loading a Japanese dataset, followed by an example of sentiment analysis.

Now that you have seen some `Python`-based transformer code samples, let's delve into the internal structure of the transformer.

AN OVERVIEW OF THE ENCODER

As you have learned, there are LLMs that are encoder-only, LLMs that are encoder and decoder, and LLMs that are decoder-only. This section pertains to the first two types of LLMs, and a subsequent section discusses LLMs that contain a decoder.

After word embeddings are created from input tokens, a *positional encoding* vector is created for each token. This topic is discussed in a subsequent section that explains how to use the `sine()` and `cosine()` functions to generate a positional vector for each token.

The next step involves the attention mechanism, which is a crucial part of the transformer architecture: an encoder *without* an attention mechanism exposes only the *final* state of the encoder to the decoder. Consequently, the previous states of the encoder are not available to the decoder, which results in an information bottleneck, whereby everything regarding the input must be encoded in a single output from the encoder. Indeed, the preceding scenario applies to RNNs and LSTMs: both of these architectures provide only the output of the final layer of the current component to the next component (such as another RNN or another LSTM component).

By contrast, an encoder that uses an attention mechanism will enable a decoder to access *all* the other hidden states of an encoder, thereby avoiding the information bottleneck problem.

The Number of Encoder Layers

Although the diagram for the transformer architecture ("Attention is All You Need") displays only one encoder layer (and only one decoder layer), the encoder component for the transformer architecture typically has six or twelve concatenated encoder components. Each encoder component consists of elements that have *two* layers: the output of the first layer becomes the input for the second layer (like a miniature pipeline). The final output of the sixth (or in some cases, the twelfth) encoder component is then passed to *every* decoder element in the decoder component.

Similarly, the decoder component also has six (sometimes more) concatenated decoder components whereby the output of one element (in a single component) becomes the input for the next element. However, notice that each encoder element has *two* sub-elements, whereas each decoder element consists of *three* sub-elements, one of which is the output from the encoder.

The LLMs that contain an encoder and a decoder involve of an encoder block consisting of multiple identical components, as well as a decoder block with multiple identical components. Each block in the encoder and the decoder is loosely analogous to filter elements in a convolutional neural network (CNN).

How Does the Encoder Work?

As mentioned in the previous section, the encoder component of the transformer is actually a vertical stack of encoder blocks. The original paper pertaining to the attention mechanism specifies one encoder with six components, but it is possible to specify a larger number of blocks.

Each encoder processes its input and generates encoded output that is passed upward to the next component in the current encoder block. The final (top-most) encoder in the stack of encoder blocks contains the representation of the initial input sentence. The encoded result is passed to *every* component of the decoder block for additional processing steps.

Now that we discussed the flow of word embeddings through the encoder component, we can delve into the process for converting the tokens in an input sentence to word embeddings, which is the topic of the next section.

The Initial Word Embedding for an Encoder

Machine learning models (which includes transformer-based models) cannot process string-based input tokens. Instead, the tokens of a corpus must be converted to a set of word embeddings. Different algorithms use different techniques for generating word embeddings. For example, word2vec performs this task via a shallow neural network (i.e., a single hidden layer).

However, the transformer architecture involves several steps. The first step creates a "token encoding" for each token, which consists of one-hot vectors (search online if you need more details about one-hot encodings). The size of the token encodings varies because it depends on the size of the tokenizer's vocabulary: the latter can be as small as 20,000 unique tokens and as large as 200,000 unique tokens.

The second step involves projecting the one-hot vectors to a lower dimensional space. At this point, they are ready to be processed by the initial layer encoder of the transformer architecture's encoder. Consequently, the encoder layer generates a hidden or "masked" state for the input tokens, after which another layer predicts the correct value for the masked token. (Ensure you understand the difference between fine-tuning and pre-training a model.)

At this point we can proceed in two directions, depending on the specific task at hand. If the objective is pre-training, the hidden states generated from the initial encoder layers are further processed by subsequent layers to make predictions regarding the masked tokens, not the "hidden states" themselves.

On the other hand, if the task is classification, a classification layer is utilized, replacing the language modeling layer used in pre-training. In both scenarios, the processing continues through the remaining encoder blocks that constitute the encoder component of the transformer architecture.

Let's reiterate an important detail: word embeddings for transformer architectures involve an attention mechanism in which *every* word embedding is based on all the word embeddings of all the tokens in a given sentence. Consequently, there is a crucial difference between word embeddings that are generated by the `word2vec` algorithm compared to those that are generated via an attention mechanism: the latter generates *different* embeddings for the same word that appears in multiple sentences, whereas `word2vec` generates a *single* word embedding for a given word, regardless of the context for that word.

Hence, given a sentence with n tokens, the construction of each word embedding involves the remaining `(n-1)` words. Therefore, the attention-based mechanism has the order `O(N^2)`, where `N` is the number of unique tokens in the corpus.

WHAT ARE POSITIONAL ENCODINGS?

Positional encodings are added to the embeddings of tokens in a sequence to provide the model with information about the positions of the tokens within the sequence. Since transformer models, which are based on self-attention mechanisms, do not inherently have a sense of order or position, positional encodings are crucial to enable the model to consider the order of tokens when making predictions.

Positional encodings inject information about the relative or absolute position of the tokens in the sequence. This information is essential for sequence-to-sequence tasks such as translation, summarization, and so forth, where the order of words is vital.

Positional encodings have the same dimension as the word embeddings, which enables us to add them to the word embeddings. Moreover, the positional encodings are added to the word embeddings before the embeddings are passed into the transformer model.

Furthermore, positional encodings allows a model to work with sequences consisting of variable lengths, and also enables parallel processing of sequences, which is a significant advantage of transformer models over recurrent neural networks (RNNs).

The actual construction of positional encodings is based on a combination of the trigonometric `sine()` and `cosine()` functions, which is described in more detail in the next section.

The sine() and cosine() Functions for Positional Encodings

Positional encodings are calculated via the trigonometric `sine()` and `cosine()` functions, after which they are added to every word embedding. As a simplified explanation, consider a vertically aligned set of graphs for the following set of `sine()` functions, whose frequencies are in the set {1, 2, 3, . . . , k}, where k is an arbitrary large positive integer, and each graph has its own vertical y-axis that range between -1 and 1:

```
{sine(x), sine(2x), . . . ., sine(kx)}
```

Now draw a vertical line at any location on the horizontal x-axis: that line will intersect the k `sine()` functions in k *different* positions that are between -1 and 1. Let s equal the value of the intersection of the vertical line and the `sine()` function. Then, we can construct the vector S = [s1, s2, . . . , sk], which contains pair-wise distinct values.

In an analogous manner, consider a vertically aligned set of graphs for the following set of `cosine()` functions:

```
{cosine(x), cosine(2x), . . . ., cosine(kx) }
```

If you draw a vertical line that intersects the horizontal x-axis at any location, that line will intersect the k `cosine()` functions in k positions. Since each `cosine()` function is drawn with its own vertical y-axis that ranges between -1 and 1, then the y-coordinate of each intersection point is also a value between -1 and 1, which consists of the set of values C = [c1, c2, . . . , ck]. The values in the preceding list are unique values because the k `cosine()` functions have different frequencies.

The preceding sets of values S and C are the basis for positional encodings, where a vector is constructed from sine-based values for even index positions and cosine-based values for odd index positions. Specifically, a positional encoding vector has this form:

```
P = [s1, c1, s2, c2, . . . , sk, ck]
```

However, the `si` and `ci` values are calculated via the following formulas (which differ from the sine and cosine values calculated previously for S and C):

```
si = sin(pos/[10000]**di]
ci = sin(pos/[10000]**di]
```

The value of `di` equals `(2*i)/dk`, where `i` is the current index value in the positional encoding vector and `dk` is the input dimensionality. Note that the index `i` starts from 0, which means the sine-based terms are in positions with an even index whereas the cosine-based terms are in positions with an odd index.

As a reminder, the constructed vector has the same shape as the word embedding, and therefore we can add positional encoding vectors to word embeddings to obtain new vectors with the same shape as the word embeddings.

The new vectors (i.e., the sum of the embedding vectors and the positional encodings) are passed to the first encoder block in the encoder component.

As a result, we can identify the original location of each token in the embeddings. We can now summarize positional encodings as having the following properties:

- They are based on the position of tokens.
- They contain unique values.
- They are bounded above by 1.

The vector-based sum of the word context and its positional encoding equal the embedding with context:

```
Embedding with context = word context + positional
encoding
```

In addition, a language model generally does not require labels for its pre-training.

Three Types of Positional Encodings

The previous section discussed positional encoding, which is one type of encoding. However, there are at least three different techniques that produce position-related information, as shown here:

- position embedding
- position encoding
- relative positions

Transformer-based language models can use different encoding techniques. For example, BERT uses position embeddings instead of position encoding.

OTHER DETAILS REGARDING ENCODERS

The preceding sections described the initial portions of an encoder as well as the purpose of positional encodings. If you look at the encoder in the transformer architecture, you will notice that there is a multi-head attention block and a feedforward network in each layer, along with an add-and-normalize step. These aspects of the encoder are discussed in the following subsections.

The Multi-Head Attention Block in an Encoder

The Multi-Head Attention block in the encoder of a transformer model serves several critical purposes in enhancing the model's ability to process and analyze sequences of data:

- Parallelized Attention Mechanisms
- Improved Representation Learning
- Enhanced Focus on Different Positions
- Scalability and Efficiency

The Multi-Head Attention block involves several parallel attention heads, each working independently to compute attention scores and outputs. In addition, the presence of multiple heads enables the model to learn different representations of the data simultaneously, capturing various aspects of the relationships between tokens.

The Feed Forward Network in an Encoder

The feedforward neural network (FFNN) in the encoder of a transformer model plays a pivotal role in processing the information obtained from the previous layers and mapping it to a potentially more complex space to capture intricate patterns in the data.

Specifically, the FFNN involves the ReLU (Rectified Linear Unit) or GELU (Gaussian Error Linear Unit) non-linear activation functions. In fact, the FFNN typically consists of one or more linear layers followed by non-linear activation functions.

Unlike the attention layers, which consider relationships between different tokens, the FFNN processes each token independently. This enables the FFNN to focus on extracting features from individual tokens without being influenced by other tokens in the sequence.

Regularization techniques like dropout can be applied in the FFNN to prevent overfitting and encourage the learning of robust representations.

In concise terms, the FFNN in the encoder of a transformer model serves to introduce non-linear transformations, extract features from individual tokens, add depth to the model, and enhance the learning of complex, hierarchical representations of the data. It works in tandem with the multi-head attention layer to process and analyze sequences effectively, playing a crucial role in the success of transformer models in a wide range of NLP tasks.

What is Add and Normalize?

As described previously, the add-and-normalize step combines the input to a component with the output from a component, after which that combination undergoes normalization. This step is performed on the multi-head attention layer as well as the feed forward layer.

The purpose of the addition step is somewhat analogous to a repeater in a network that essentially "boosts" a (weakened) signal. The purpose of the normalization step is to ensure that the resulting values are in the same range (i.e., no outliers or other unusually large values), which in turn can result in faster computation time.

We can now represent the elements of the encoder component of the transformer architecture as follows (each ENC is an encoder block):

```
Input embedding > positional encoding > ENC1 >
ENC2 > . . . ENCn
```

The number of encoder blocks n is typically 6 or 12, and sometimes 24 (and can potentially be a larger number). The input INP to the first encoder ENC1 is the sum of the input embedding and the positional encoding, and the content of each encoder block ENC is shown here:

```
MHA(out)+INP > ADD+Norm > FF > ADD+Norm > next
encoder block
```

Now that you have an understanding of how initial word embeddings are created for tokens from a given corpus, let's look at the self-attention mechanism in an encoder in greater detail.

AN OVERVIEW OF THE DECODER

The decoder component is very similar to the encoder component, and it consists of the following:

- Multiple decoder blocks
- Positional encoding
- Output embedding

The output embedding is the bottom-most element of each decoder block (which typically involves 6 or 12 such blocks), and its counterpart is the input embedding in the encoder component. Above this element is the positional encoding, which is the counterpart to the positional encoding in the encoder component. Above the positional encoding is a collection of one or more decoder blocks.

You can think of the decoder component as a superset of the encoder component: while encoder blocks contain two sublayers, decoder blocks those same sublayers, as well as a third sub-layer, which is called the *masked multi-head attention* layer.

The masked multi-head attention (MMHA) layer ensures that only "backward looking" (right-to-left) attention can be performed. The BERT model is trained as a *bidirectional* model, which means that it can see the preceding token as well as the next token of any given token in a sequence of tokens.

Hence, BERT does not need to predict the next token in a sequence because it actually *knows* the next token. The MMHA layer effectively disables any LLM from looking at the next token, which in turn means that the next token must be predicted. Incidentally, LLMs that can only perform backward-looking attention are called *autoregressive* models.

How Does the Decoder Component Work?

The decoder component works in a similar fashion as the encoder component, along with the addition of the MMHA that is described in the preceding section. The decoder component contains decoder blocks, where the first decoder block decodes the input that is provided from the encoder component. The output from the first decoder block (and subsequent decoder blocks) is passed to the next decoder block (in a bottom-up fashion) in the decoder component. Moreover, the output from the encoder component is accessible to every decoder block in the decoder component.

*Every decoder block in the decoder component receives the output from the prior decoder block **as well as** the output from the encoder component (ingested by the multi-head attention layer) as its input.*

Self-Attention in a Decoder

The encoder block and decoder block both contain a multi-head attention element. In addition, the decoder block contains a component with a *masked* multi-head attention element.

The masked multi-head element prevents the decoder from examining the next token in the sequence, thereby "forcing" the decoder to generate the next word.

The preceding is accomplished by setting the values in the upper-right matrix equal to negative infinity, after which the `softmax()` function replaces these values with the value 0, thereby ensuring that the next token is unavailable.

Generating the Output Sequence

This step is performed in a sequential fashion that involves a loop-like sequence of operations:

1. Start with the start token <SOS> as the initial input to the decoder.

2. Pass this token through the output embedding layer to obtain the corresponding embedding.

3. Use this embedding along with the encoder's output (or context vector) as input to the decoder component to generate a hidden state.

4. The hidden state is used to generate a probability distribution over the vocabulary for the next output token.

5. Sample or select the most probable token from the distribution as the output token.

6. Append this output token to the previously generated list of output tokens.

7. Use the list of output tokens generated so far (including the most recent output token) as the new input to the decoder in the next step, along with the encoder's output.

8. Repeat steps #2 to #7 until an end token <EOS> is generated or a maximum sequence length is reached.

As an example, consider the sentence S that equals "I love Chicago pizza." Input Sentence: "I love Chicago pizza."

Encoder Output: (A representation of the input sentence in a high-dimensional space, obtained after processing the input sentence through the encoder.)

The sequence of decoder steps is shown below:

1. Start with the start token <SOS> as the initial input to the decoder.

   Current Input Token: <SOS>

2. Pass this token through the output embedding layer to obtain the corresponding embedding.

   Embedding of <SOS>: [0.1, 0.3, ..., 0.5] (hypothetical embedding vector)

3. Use this embedding along with the encoder's output as input to the decoder component to generate a hidden state.

   Hidden State: [0.4, 0.2, ..., 0.9] (hypothetical hidden state vector)

4. The hidden state is used to generate a probability distribution over the vocabulary for the next output token.

   Probability Distribution: {"J": 0.7, "aime": 0.1, "Chicago": 0.05, "pizza": 0.05, ..., "<EOS>": 0.01} (hypothetical distribution over a French vocabulary)

5. Sample or select the most probable token from the distribution as the output token.

   Selected Output Token: "J" (hypothetically the most probable token according to the distribution)

6. Append this output token to the previously generated list of output tokens.

   Output Tokens So Far: [<SOS>, "J"]

7. Use the list of output tokens generated so far (including the most recent output token) as the new input to the decoder in the next step, along with the encoder's output.

   New Input to Decoder: [<SOS>, "J"]

8. Repeat steps #2 to #7 until an end token <EOS> is generated or a maximum sequence length is reached.

   Repeat the process, and in subsequent iterations, we might generate the tokens "aime", "la", "pizza", "de", "Chicago", and finally "<EOS>", resulting in the French sentence: "J'aime la pizza de Chicago."

ENCODER, DECODER, OR BOTH: HOW TO DECIDE?

There are three main implementations of the transformer architecture:

- encoder-only (for classification)
- decoder-only (for language modeling)
- encoder-decoder (for machine translation)

Encoder-only models are well-suited for tasks that require an understanding of the input, such as sentence classification and named entity recognition. Examples of encoder-only models include `BERT`, `alBERT`, `DistilBERT`, `RoBERTa`, and `ELECTRA`.

Encoders are well-suited for tasks such as token classification. Another task is extractive question-answering, where we predict the start and end token of a passage of text from a document that best answers a question. The encoder block is well-suited for these tasks is because the encoder maps an input sequence to an output sequence of the same dimensionality. The encoder contextualizes the token embedding vectors that are provided to the system, *not* to generate new sequences of a different length.

Decoder-only models are autoregressive models that are well-suited for generative tasks such as text generation. Examples of encoder-only models include `GPT`, `GPT-2`, and `TransformerXL`. Given word the attention layers can only access the words positioned before it in the sentence. Interestingly, decoder-only models are sometimes preferred over encoder-decoder models for language generation capabilities.

Encoder-decoder models (also called *sequence-to-sequence* models) are well-suited for generative tasks that require an input, such as machine translation where we encode sequences from one source language, and then a decoder produces a sequence of possibly different length in a target language.

Another type of encoder-decoder architecture is a multimodal transformer architecture (for example, vision-to-text). Encoder-decoder models are often referred to as `seq2seq` and they are capable of producing an output sequence of a different length than the input sequence.

An example of an encoder-decoder model is `BART`, which is an acronym for Bidirectional and Autoregressive Transformer. The encoder component of `BART` works the same way as the encoder component of `BERT`: it processes and contextualizes the input. However, the encoder component of `BART` also provides the key and value vectors from its last attention layer to the attention layers of the decoder. The decoder component generates its output auto-regressively.

There are transformer-based models that contain both components of the transformer architecture and also perform NLP-related tasks that require only one transformer component. To clarify, the T5 architecture performs classification tasks that only require an encoder, and yet T5 uses the encoder *and* the decoder of the transformer architecture. In addition, recall from the transformer architecture that attention appears in several ways:

- self-attention in the encoder
- self-attention in the decoder
- cross-attention in the encoder-decoder

The cross-attention mechanism enables the decoder to consume information from the encoder. As a result, the self-attention mechanism can differ in these architectures, as described in the next section.

Causal Self-Attention

Causal self-attention indicates that tokens can only access past tokens that also belong to the same text string (sentence). This is the mechanism that prevents decoders from "seeing" all the tokens in an input sequence (more details below). In some transformer architectures, self-attention *must* be causally dependent on previous tokens, whereas other transformer architectures do not impose this restriction.

Specifically, self-attention in encoder-based architectures is *not* required to be causally dependent on current and past tokens. By contrast, encoder-decoder-based architectures *require* causal self-attention in the decoder because each autoregressive decoding step must depend only on previous tokens. Finally, in decoder-based architectures, self-attention *must* be causal as well.

The technique for enforcing causal or "masked" attention involves setting the upper-triangular values of the `nxn` attention-based matrix equal to `-oo`, after which the `softmax()` function applied to this matrix sets all the values in the upper-triangular portion equal to negative infinity, whose `softmax()` value is 0. As a result, tokens can only access previous tokens.

Unidirectional and Bidirectional Embeddings

A *unidirectional* context of a token examines the token in one direction to create embeddings, which typically involves the previous tokens. Since we write text in a single direction (often left-to-right and sometimes right-to-left), it is meaningful that text generation is well-suited for unidirectional embeddings.

A *bidirectional* context of a token examines the previous tokens and the successive tokens from a given token to generate embeddings. Bidirectional embeddings are useful for sentence-level tasks such as rewriting or summarization.

Keep in mind the following point: the transformer architecture supports bidirectional encoder blocks and unidirectional decoder blocks. Moreover, autoregressive models work with unidirectional embeddings.

DELVING DEEPER INTO THE TRANSFORMER ARCHITECTURE

Earlier, you learned about several aspects of the transformer architecture, such as the flow of data through the encoder component and the decoder component. This section briefly describes additional details regarding the transformer, some of which are listed here:

- Encoder-decoder architecture
- Weight matrix and multi-head attention
- Key, query, and values are not hyper parameters
- The scaling factor `dk`
- Length of input sequence
- The forward pass
- Residual connections
- Layer Normalization
- The Dropout Rate
- Transformers and Backprop
- Language Translation and Word Order
- Segment Embedding
- The Compressive Transformer

First, the multi-head attention that is a layer in the decoder component is implemented with a single weight matrix. In addition, the `Q`, `K`, and `V` values are the input to the multi-head attention, and their initial values are identical.

Interestingly, the dimensions of the key, query, and value vectors that are created by the attention mechanism cannot be modified programmatically, which means that their dimensions are *not* hyperparameters.

Although the scaling factor `d` in the term `Q*Kt/d` might seem unusual, this term was determined empirically. Its purpose is to ensure that the inner product will produce "reasonable" values.

The transformer architecture, RNNs, and LSTMs all have a limit placed on the length of an input sequence. If a text sequence is too long, you can employ the usual techniques (e.g., truncation and chunking) for handling such text sequences with transformer-based models.

An interesting difference pertains to the forward pass during the training phase as well as the inference phase: during the former, a single forward pass is performed for the entire *sequence*, whereas during the latter, a decoder forward pass is performed for every *token*.

Residual Connections

A *residual connection* (also known as a *skip connection*) was introduced in the ResNet (Residual Network) model for computer vision, after which it was implemented in AlphaZero, AlphaFold, and in the transformer architecture.

The rationale for a residual connection is because the performance of a neural network can degrade as more layers are added to the neural network. A residual connection involves adding the initial input to every *other* layer in a neural network, which effectively increases the processed output. A residual connection is somewhat analogous to a repeater that boosts an attenuated signal in a network.

Perhaps the following details can clarify how to use a residual connection in a neural network. Suppose that x is an input for a neural network, and F is a function that processes x as it goes through the first layer, so the output becomes x1 = F(x). The next layer also uses F to process x1, and its output becomes x2 = F(x1). Continuing in this fashion, we have a sequence of values {x, x1, x2, ..., xn}.

A *residual connection* simply adds the input x to the subsequent outputs, which creates the sequence {x, x+F(x), x + F(x1), x + F(x2), ..., x + F(xn)}. Note that there are variations whereby alternating values are updated to produce the following sequence:

```
{x, F(x), x+F(x1), F(x2), x+F(x3), ..., x+F(xn)}
```

Layer Normalization

Layer normalization (LN) appears immediately after the multi-head attention layer and also immediately after the feedforward network (discussed later). Thus, the left-to-right execution sequence is as follows:

```
Multi-Head Attention > LN > FeedForward > LN
```

Layer normalization bears some similarity to batch normalization: the latter normalizes across the *samples* in a batch, whereas the former normalizes across the *features*. Specifically, normalization subtracts the mean and then divides by the standard deviation for all the feature values. Note that this transformation is called standardization in other situations outside of layer normalization (yes, it is confusing). Here is the complete formula:

```
h = g * (x-mean)/sigma + b (g = adaptive gain and
b = bias)
```

The following link contains information about layer normalization and residual connections in transformers:

https://deepai.org/publication/on-layer-normalizations-and-residual-connections-in-transformers

The following links provide more details regarding the use of layer normalization versus batch normalization in NLP:

https://stats.stackexchange.com/questions/346680/why-are-batch-normalization-techniques-less-popular-in-natural-language-applicat
https://paperswithcode.com/method/layer-normalization

The Dropout Rate

The concept of a dropout rate in the transformer architecture is the same as the concept of a dropout rate for CNNs, which is a concept that was originally proposed by Geoffrey Hinton. Apparently, Hinton thought of this idea when he was standing in line at a bank; he considered it as a way to prevent (or at least reduce) the possibility of collusion between customers and bank tellers.

The idea for the dropout rate in CNNs is simple, clever, and surprisingly effective: the dropout rate is a number between 0 and 1, and it is the percentage of the number of neurons that are ignored during each pass through the neural network. For example, if the dropout rate is 0.20, the 20% of the neurons in a hidden layer are ignored during forward propagation (and they are ignored during backdrop, as well). Each time a new data point (i.e., vector of numbers) is processed by the neural network, a randomly selected set of neurons consisting of 20% of the given layer are ignored. This concept reduced overfitting, with the intent of making the model more generalizable.

In the case of the transformer architecture, the dropout rate is applied to the self/cross multi-head attention layers, as well as the position-wise feedforward networks.

Transformers and Backward Error Propagation

Transformer-based models undergo "backprop" (backward error propagation), just like other deep learning models (such as CNNs). The interesting aspect is that backprop is performed throughout the model:

- the FF (feedforward) sub-layers
- the weight matrices Q, K, and V
- the encoder weights
- the decoder weights
- the embeddings

In addition to self-attention, the decoder also contains cross-attention layers that attend to the encoder outputs. The weights in these layers are also updated during backpropagation.

The preceding list applies to encoder-only models, decoder-only models, and encoder-decoder models. To learn more about the aspects of backprop in transformer-based models, please read the following paper:

https://aclanthology.org/2020.emnlp-main.463.pdf

Language Translation and Word Order

Google Translate is an online tool that uses transformers to perform language translation, and its accuracy is very impressive, as is its ability to generate sentences with a grammatically correct word order. If you have translated between languages that have a different word order (e.g., English and German), you might be wondering how this is actually performed. For example, here is an English sentence and its translation into German:

I **have read** the book.

Ich **habe** das Buch **gelesen**.

The compound English verb "have read" is translated as "habe gelesen" in German, and the past participle "gelesen" appears *after* the German noun "Buch."

Segment Embedding

Segment embedding is a technique for concatenating multiple sentences, an example of which is shown below:

```
"I love pizza"
"Chicago pizza is my favorite"
```

The two sentences are combined as follows:

```
tokens = [ [CLS], I, love, pizza, [SEP], Chicago,
pizza, is, my, favorite, [SEP]]
```

As you can see, the token [CLS] is the first token, and the [SEP] token is used for separating sentences, as well as the final token.

Now you are in a position to understand how to construct the sequence that is passed into an encoder:

```
INPUT = token embeddings + sequence embeddings +
positional embeddings
```

The Compressive Transformer

DeepMind created the Compressive Transformer as an extension of the transformer that provides an improved architecture for long-range memory, along with a new dataset for memory reasoning in language models.

The compressive transformer performs a reduction: it maps past hidden activations (memories) to a smaller set of compressed representations (compressed memories). The Compressive Transformer uses the same attention mechanism over its set of memories and compressed memories, learning to query its short-term granular and long-term coarse memories.

In essence, the Compressive Transformer keeps a fine-grained memory of past activations, which are then compressed into coarser compressed memories.

AUTOENCODING TRANSFORMERS

There are two main types of transformer-based models: autoencoding models and auto regressive models. The primary differentiator between autoencoding models and autoregressive models is not their architecture: the difference is based on the tasks and training that are performed. In particular, autoencoder models learn encodings, whereas autoregressive models can be used for fine-tuning tasks.

Perhaps the most well-known autoencoding model is BERT, which performs two pre-training tasks: MLM (masked layer modeling) and NSP (next sentence prediction). MLM replaces approximately 15% of the input tokens with a [MASK] token and then attempts to predict the original inputs.

The NSP task involves determining whether a pair of sentences appear in this exact order in a corpus. BERT learns an encoding that can be processed by tasks such as question-answering. Keep in mind that BERT-style models perform pre-training on *unsupervised* datasets.

Interestingly, the *decoder* component of the original transformer can be used for autoencoding as well as auto regressive tasks; this is similar for the encoder component and autoregressive tasks. The following list describes some of the functionality of autoencoding, autoregressive, and seq2seq models:

- autoencoding models encode the inputs based on masked elements
- autoregressive models use all previous predictions for future predictions
- seq2seq models transform sequences without altering semantics

THE "AUTO" CLASSES

Hugging Face `AutoClasses` are convenience classes that retrieve the appropriate model from the name and path that is specified as a parameter value. The simplest of this set of classes is the `AutoModel` class, which is essentially a base class. In fact, the `transformers` package provides various class that have an `Auto` prefix, and they are primarily in the following groups:

*   `AutoModel`
*   `AutoConfig`
*   `AutoTokenizer`

The `transformers` package from Hugging Face provides the `AutoModel` classes that you can import into your code with the following code snippets:

*   `from transformers import AutoModel`
*   `from transformers import AutoModelForSequenceClassification`
*   `from transformers import AutoModelForTokenClassification`

For example, the following code snippet creates an instance of the `BertModel` via the `AutoModel` class:

```
model = AutoModel.from_pretrained('bert-base-cased')
```

The `AutoModelForSequenceClassification` class extends the functionality of the `AutoModel` class by adding one more classification layer on top of the pre-trained model outputs.

The `AutoModelForTokenClassification` class extends the functionality of the `AutoModel` class by providing a classification layer on top of an existing model. In addition, this class is required to perform an NER (named entity recognition) task.

The following three classes are counterparts to the three classes in the list at the beginning of this section, and the `TF` prefix indicates that they are for TensorFlow:

*   `from transformers import TFAutoModel`
*   `from transformers import TFAutoModelForSequenceClassification`
*   `from transformers import TFAutoModelForTokenClassification`

An instance of `AutoConfig` creates an instance of a class of the appropriate architecture (i.e., for configuration), and an instance of `AutoTokenizer` creates an instance of a class of the appropriate architecture.

IMPROVED ARCHITECTURES

The architectures in this section provide improvements over the original transformer architecture:

* Reformer
* Longformer
* Switch
* ELECTRA

Reformer

The Reformer architecture is more efficient than the original transformer architecture and provides larger context windows. The Reformer architecture achieves its efficiency largely by means of two techniques:

* Locality-sensitive-hashing (LSH)
* Reversible residual layers

LSH reduces the complexity in processing long sequences, whereas reversible residual layers are more efficient in terms of memory usage. More information about the Reformer architecture is accessible at:

https://ai.googleblog.com/2020/01/reformer-efficient-transformer.html

Longformer

The Longformer model is a modification of the transformer architecture that is well-suited for processing long documents. Calculating attention values has `O(N^2)` complexity (where `N` is the sequence length) in the original transformer architecture.

By contrast, the Longformer model has reduced the complexity for calculating attention to `O(N)`. More information regarding the Longformer model is accessible online:

https://arxiv.org/abs/2004.05150
https://towardsdatascience.com/longformer-the-long-document-transformer-cdfeefe81e89

The Switch Transformer: One Trillion Parameters

Google researchers created the Switch LLM that contains one trillion parameters, which is almost six times as large as GPT-3 (175 billion parameters). This model is one of the largest models ever created, and as much as four times faster than T5-XXL (a previous LLM from Google). This following article discusses how to the "switch" mechanism works in a modified version of the transformer architecture:

https://towardsdatascience.com/understanding-googles-switch-transformer-904b8bf29f66

The researchers combined a simple architecture with large data-sets and parameter counts. Since large-scale training is computationally intensive, they adopted a "Switch transformer," which is a technique that uses only a subset of the parameters of a model. In addition to the model's sparseness, the Switch transformer adroitly takes advantage of GPUs and TPUs for intense matrix multiplication operations.

ELECTRA

ELECTRA is an acronym for Efficiently Learning an Encoder that Classifies Token Replacements Accurately; it uses self-supervised learning. ELECTRA can pre-train transformer networks in a computationally efficient manner. ELECTRA involves pre-training text encoders as discriminators rather than generators.

HUGGING FACE PIPELINES AND HOW THEY WORK

There are three main steps required to perform various NLP-related tasks using Hugging Face:

- Import the Hugging Face `pipeline` function.
- Load a pre-trained model from Hugging Face.
- Specify a sentence (or string) to the pre-trained model for processing.

The Hugging Face `pipeline(task-name)` function that is specified as the first step in the preceding list provides an intuitive mechanism to use an NLP model for inference. A pipeline can abstract most of the code from the library and provide a dedicated API for a variety of tasks, some of which are given here:

- AutomaticSpeechRecognitionPipeline
- QuestionAnsweringPipeline
- TranslationPipeline

In addition, the Hugging Face `pipeline` function is a high-level abstraction that is designed to perform the following tasks:

- tokenizing the text in a corpus
- converting text into integers
- passing those integers through the model

As you can see from the preceding list, the tasks that you might have performed programmatically are performed by the `pipeline` function in Hugging Face. By contrast, TensorFlow 2 requires you to perform explicitly some of the preceding tasks with the appropriate code.

In addition to the pre-trained model, the `pipeline` object can specify the tokenizer, the feature extractor, and the underlying framework.

The first step involves an `import` statement for the `transformers` library, as shown here:

```
from transformers import pipeline
```

The second step involves specifying a string that indicates the task that you want to perform. For example, the next code snippet is for sentiment analysis:

```
nlp = pipeline('sentiment-analysis')
```

The preceding code snippet 1) selects a pre-trained model that 2) has been fine-tuned for sentiment analysis and 3) is in English. If you want to see a simple and complete code sample that shows you how to obtain the sentiment (either positive or negative), look at the code sample in Chapter 8. Keep in mind that the score is a number between 0 and 1 for positive sentiment as well as negative sentiment, and you can also process an array of sentences instead of using a loop to iterate through each sentence.

After the classifier object is instantiated, which is called `nlp` in the preceding code snippet, the model is downloaded and stored in a location where it can be accessed for subsequent invocations of Python scripts that reference the model (i.e., a one-time download is performed). However, if you modify the model, then the original model will be downloaded again.

There are three main steps involved when you pass some text to a pipeline:

- The text is preprocessed into a format the model can understand.
- The preprocessed inputs are passed to the model.
- The predictions of the model are post-processed, so you can make sense of them.

Available Pipelines from Hugging Face

Earlier, you saw a list of the NLP tasks that transformers can perform, and they are reproduced here for your convenience:

- feature extraction (get the vector representation of a text)
- fill mask
- NER
- question-answering
- sentiment analysis
- summarization
- text generation
- translation
- zero-shot-classification

HUGGING FACE DATASETS

This section contains Python code samples that show you how to list all the available Hugging Face datasets and how to load a specific dataset.

Listing 4.1 displays the content of `hf_datasets.py` that shows you how to display the list of available Hugging Face datasets.

Listing 4.1: hf_datasets.py

```
from datasets import list_datasets, load_dataset
from pprint import pprint

datasets_list = list_datasets()
print(f"HuggingFace provides {len(datasets_list)}
datasets")
print()

print("=> FIRST FIVE DATASETS:")
print(f"{datasets_list[:5]}")
print()

"""
print("=> LIST OF DATASETS:")
pprint(datasets_list,compact=True)
print()
```

```
print("=> DETAILS OF EACH DATASET:")
# this list contains details of each dataset:
datasets_list = list_datasets(with_details=True)
pprint(datasets_list)
"""
```

Listing 4.1 imports two classes from `datasets` and then initializes the variable `datasets_list`. This results in invoking the `list_datasets()` API, and then displays the contents of the datasets in this variable. Launch the code in Listing 4.1 with Python 3.7, and you will see a partial list of the more than 600 datasets in Hugging Face.

```
HuggingFace provides 3753 datasets


=> FIRST FIVE DATASETS:
['acronym_identification', 'ade_corpus_v2',
'adversarial_qa', 'aeslc', 'afrikaans_ner_corpus']


=> DETAILS OF EACH DATASET:
[datasets.ObjectInfo(
        id='acronym_identification',
        description='Acronym identification
training and development sets for the acronym
identification task at SDU@AAAI-21.',
        files=None
),
 datasets.ObjectInfo(
        id='ade_corpus_v2',
        description=' ADE-Corpus-V2  Dataset:
Adverse Drug Reaction Data. This is a dataset for
Classification if a sentence is ADE-related (True)
or not (False) and Relation Extraction between
Adverse Drug Event and Drug. DRUG-AE.rel provides
relations between drugs and adverse effects. DRUG-
DOSE.rel provides relations between drugs and
dosages. ADE-NEG.txt provides all sentences in the
ADE corpus that DO NOT contain any drug-related
adverse effects.',
        files=None
),
// details omitted for brevity
```

```
datasets.ObjectInfo(
        id='ncoop57/csnc_human_judgement',
        description='This new dataset is designed
to solve this great NLP task and is crafted with a
lot of care.',
        files=None
)]
```

Loading the Iris Dataset

Listing 4.2 shows you how to load the `cifar10` dataset in Hugging Face and display some of its contents.

Listing 4.2: hf_load_dataset.py

```
from datasets import load_dataset
train_ds, test_ds = load_dataset('cifar10',
split=['train[:4000]', 'test[:1000]'])

#display one column:
#print("=> train_ds['label']:")
#print(train_ds['label'])
#print()
"""

partial output:
[6, 9, 9, 4, 1, 1, 2, 7, 8, 3, 4, 7, 7, 2, 9, 9, 9,
3, 2, 6, 4, 3, 6, 6, 2, 6, 3, 5, 4, 0, 0, 9, 1, 3,
4, 0, 3, 7, 3, 3, 5, 2, 2, 7, 1, 1, 1, 2, 2, 0, 9,
5, 7, 9, 2, 2, 5, 2, 4, 3, 1, 1, 8, 2, 1, 1, 4

...

7, 3, 0, 8, 6, 7, 7, 0, 0, 1, 4, 1, 1, 6, 6, 6, 1,
3, 6, 0, 1, 3, 8, 5, 0, 1, 6, 5, 5, 4, 3, 9, 8, 6,
0, 5, 4, 9, 2, 8, 4, 8, 8, 2, 1, 4, 8, 6, 7, 3, 1,
3, 4, 9, 4, 8, 4, 5, 0, 9, 1, 3, 8, 7, 5, 4, 6]

"""

#display one row:
print("=> train_ds[7]['img'][0][0]:")
#print(train_ds[7]['img'][0][0])
# => output: [28, 35, 39]
```

```
print("train_ds[7]['img'][0]:")
print(train_ds[7]['img'][0])
# => output:
#[[28, 35, 39], [30, 34, 44], [33, 44, 47], [62,
83, 72], [63, 84, 72], [31, 49, 46], [29, 47, 50],
[42, 62, 63], [55, 77, 71], [67, 83, 74], [92, 108,
98], [76, 96, 85], [57, 80, 68], [75, 99, 88], [69,
82, 79], [57, 59, 60], [74, 72, 73], [98, 103,
100], [86, 99, 92], [71, 80, 73], [59, 67, 62],
[62, 67, 66], [57, 60, 63], [42, 46, 48], [51, 63,
57], [46, 60, 52], [41, 55, 47], [38, 53, 44], [37,
51, 41], [43, 56, 45], [52, 64, 53], [46, 58, 47]]

# approximately 46K output:
#print(train_ds[7])

# approximately 46K output:
#print(train_ds[7]['img'])

#display a batch of rows:
#print("=> train_ds[3:6]:")
#print(train_ds[3:6])
```

Listing 4.2 starts with an import statement and then initializes the variables `train_ds` and `test_ds` with the result of invoking the `load_datasets()` API. Launch the code in Listing 4.2, and you will see the following output, which includes download details when you launch this code for the first time:

```
Downloading: 3.77kB [00:00, 1.44MB/s]
Downloading: 1.50kB [00:00, 401kB/s]
Downloading and preparing dataset cifar10/plain_
text (download: 162.60 MiB, generated: 418.17 MiB,
post-processed: Unknown size, total: 580.77 MiB) to
/Users/oswaldcampesato/.cache/huggingface/datasets/
cifar10/plain_text/1.0.0/951e017399fa3b30edfca5646
8a9
1ac6a03c9167c0b3f79367e777d1f9a0cf7e...
Downloading:   10%|                      | 17.6M/170M
Dataset cifar10 downloaded and prepared to /Users/
oswaldcampesato/.cache/huggingface/datasets/
cifar10/plain_text/1.0.0/951e017399fa3b30edfca56468
a91ac6a03c9167c0b3f79367e777d1f9a0cf7e.
```

```
Subsequent calls will reuse this data.
[00:14<05:30, 462kB/s]
```

Loading a Japanese Dataset

Listing 4.3 shows you how to load one of the Japanese datasets in Hugging Face and display some of its contents.

Listing 4.3: hf_load_japanese.py

```
"""
Datasets involving japanese:
  'covid_qa_ucsd', 'covid_tweets_japanese',
'covost2', 'cppe-5',
  'snli', 'snow_simplified_japanese_corpus',
'so_stacksample',
  'Atsushi/fungi_diagnostic_chars_comparison_
japanese',
  'Atsushi/fungi_indexed_mycological_papers_
japanese',
"""

from datasets import load_dataset
snli = load_dataset('snli')
print("=> snli shape:",snli.shape)
print()

print("=> snli:")
print(snli)
print()

# split into train and test data:
train_ds, test_ds = load_dataset('snli',
split=['train[:4000]', 'test[:1000]'])

print("=> train_ds.column_names:")
print(train_ds.column_names)
print()
```

```
print("=> train_ds.features:")
print(train_ds.features)
print()

for idx in range(0,5):
  print("row",idx,"premise:    ",train_ds[idx]
['premise'])
  print("row",idx,"hypothesis:",train_ds[idx]
['hypothesis'])
  print("row",idx,"label:      ",train_ds[idx]
['label'])
  print()
print()

"""
sample output:
{'premise': 'A person on a horse jumps over a
broken down airplane.', 'hypothesis': 'A person is
training his horse for a competition.', 'label': 1}
"""
```

Listing 4.3 starts with an `import` statement and then initializes the variable `snli` as an instance of the `snli` dataset. The next block of code displays the shape and some metadata for the `snli` dataset.

The next portion of Listing 4.3 performs a train-test split of the data, which is a standard step for machine learning models. Next, the columns of `train_ds` (the training portion of the dataset) are displayed, which is followed by the display of the features of `train_ds`.

The final portion of Listing 4.3 contains a loop that displays the values for the premise, hypothesis, and label for the first five rows in the `train_ds`. Launch the code in Listing 4.3, and you will see the following output:

```
=> snli shape: {'test': (10000, 3), 'train':
(550152, 3), 'validation': (10000, 3)}

=> snli:
DatasetDict({
    test: Dataset({
        features: ['premise', 'hypothesis',
'label'],
```

```
        num_rows: 10000
    })
    train: Dataset({
        features: ['premise', 'hypothesis',
'label'],
        num_rows: 550152
    })
    validation: Dataset({
        features: ['premise', 'hypothesis',
'label'],
        num_rows: 10000
    })
})

=> train_ds.column_names:
['premise', 'hypothesis', 'label']

=> train_ds.features:
{'premise': Value(dtype='string', id=None),
'hypothesis': Value(dtype='string',
id=None), 'label': ClassLabel(num_classes=3,
names=['entailment', 'neutral', 'contradiction'],
names_file=None, id=None)}

row 0 premise:    A person on a horse jumps over a
broken down airplane.
row 0 hypothesis: A person is training his horse
for a competition.
row 0 label:      1

row 1 premise:    A person on a horse jumps over a
broken down airplane.
row 1 hypothesis: A person is at a diner, ordering
an omelette.
row 1 label:      2
```

```
row 2 premise:      A person on a horse jumps over a
broken down airplane.
row 2 hypothesis: A person is outdoors, on a horse.
row 2 label:        0

row 3 premise:      Children smiling and waving at
camera
row 3 hypothesis: They are smiling at their parents
row 3 label:        1

row 4 premise:      Children smiling and waving at
camera
row 4 hypothesis: There are children present
row 4 label:        0
```

TRANSFORMERS AND SENTIMENT ANALYSIS

Sentiment analysis can be used to ascertain a customer's sentiment regarding a particular product or event. Consider the following pair of sentences, where the sentiment for the first sentence below is clearly positive and the sentiment for the second sentence is obviously negative:

1. "I really liked the pizza."

2. "I don't enjoy driving every day."

Now consider the following sentence that consists of a positive sentiment followed by a negative sentiment:

3. "The movie was great, but the ticket prices were too high."

If we assign -1, 0, and +1 to phrases or sentences that are negative, neutral, or positive, respectively, then that might suggest assigning the values +1, 0, and -1 to three preceding sentences. However, it is not meaningful to assign 0 to sentence 3) because the sum of +1 and -1 "cancel out" and yield the value 0.

SOURCE CODE FOR TRANSFORMER-BASED MODELS

Hugging Face provides the following Github repository that contains the open source code for many transformer-based models:

https://github.com/huggingface/transformers/blob/main/src/
transformers/models/

A partial list of the transformer-based models, some of which are discussed in later chapters, is shown here:

- albert
- bart
- bert
- bert_generation
- bert_japanese
- bertweet
- big_bird
- deberta
- distilbert
- flaubert
- gpt2
- gpt_neo
- longformer
- megatron_bert
- megatron_gpt2
- pegasus
- perceiver
- reformer
- roberta
- squeezebert
- t5
- visual_bert
- xlm
- xml_roberta

SUMMARY

This chapter started with a description of positional encoding in the Transformer architecture, which involve the `sine()` and `cosine()` functions, as well as three types of positional encoding.

Then you obtained additional insight regarding the encoder component of the transformer architecture, and then an overview of the decoder component. Moreover, you learned how to decide whether to use an encoder, a decoder, or both encoder and decoder in an LLM.

In addition, you learned the Reformer, Longformer, and Switch transformers that provide improvements over the original transformer architecture.

Finally, you saw how work with Hugging Face datasets as well as how to load a Japanese dataset.

## CHAPTER 5

THE BERT FAMILY INTRODUCTION

This chapter provides information about the transformer-based BERT model, along with several other models in the "BERT family," as well as a description of some of the differences in these LLMs.

The first part of this chapter discusses various aspects of prompt engineering, along with various aspects of LLM development.

The second part of this chapter introduces BERT and some of its features, after which you will learn how BERT is trained and the BERT models that are available. In addition, you will learn how BERT differs from pre-BERT NLP models.

The third part of this chapter discusses BERT from the standpoint of the transformer architecture, and then how to perform NER tasks with BERT. This section includes BERTopic and topic modeling. The fourth part of this chapter discusses BERT and data cleaning tasks, such as normalization and how regular expressions are relevant for data cleaning in BERT.

The fifth part of this chapter delves into BERT embedding layers, as well as types of embeddings, such as token embeddings, segment embeddings, and position embeddings. You will also learn how to create, train, and save a BERT model.

The sixth part of this chapter pertains to the inner workings of BERT, such as MLM, NSP, and special BERT tokens. You will also learn about alternatives to MLM (e.g., PLM and MLNET) as well as an alternative to NSP (e.g., SOP). This section also includes a discussion of techniques such as subword tokenization, BPE, WordPiece, and SentencePiece.

The seventh part of this chapter discusses sentence similarity in BERT and word context, followed by examples of generating BERT tokens.

The eighth part of this chapter contains a list of several BERT-based trained models, along with brief description of their functionality. In addition, the code samples currently require Python 3.7, which you can download from the Internet.

The final section briefly introduces you to an assortment of BERT-based models, some of which might be interesting enough to delve more deeply into those models through other online resources.

WHAT IS PROMPT ENGINEERING?

You might have already heard about text generators, such as GPT-3, as well as text-to-image generators such as DALL-E 2 from OpenAI, Jurassic from AI21, Midjourney from Midjourney Inc., and Stable Diffusion from Stability AI. *Prompt engineering* refers to devising text-based prompts that enable AI-based systems to generate output that more closely matches whatever users want to "retrieve" from the AI. By way of analogy, think of prompts as similar to the role of coaches: they offer advice and suggestions to help people perform better in their given tasks.

Since prompts are based on words, the challenge involves learning how different words can affect the generated output. Moreover, it is difficult to predict how systems respond to a given prompt. For instance, if you want to generate a landscape, the difference between a dark landscape and a bright landscape is intuitive. However, if you want a beautiful landscape, how would an AI system generate a corresponding image? As you can surmise, "concrete" words are easier than abstract or subjective words for AI systems that generate images from text. Let us consider the previous example: how would you visualize the following?

- A beautiful landscape
- A beautiful song
- A beautiful movie

Although prompt engineering started with text-to-image generation, there are other types of prompt engineering, such as audio-based prompts that interpret emphasized text and emotions that are detected in speech, and sketch-based prompts that generate images from drawings. The most recent focus of attention involves text-based prompts for generating videos, which presents exciting opportunities for artists and designers. An example of image-to-image processing is accessible here:

https://huggingface.co/spaces/fffiloni/stable-diffusion-color-sketch

Prompts and Completions

A *prompt* is a text string that users provide to LLMs, and a *completion* is the text that users receive from LLMs. Prompts assist LLMs in completing a request (task), and they can vary in length. Although prompts can be any text string, including a random string, the quality and structure of prompts affects the quality of completions.

Think of prompts as a mechanism for giving "guidance" to LLMs, or even as a way to "coach" LLMs into providing desired answers. The number of tokens in a prompt plus the number of tokens in the completion can be at most 2,048 tokens. In Chapter 8 you will see a Python-based code sample of invoking the `completion()` API in GPT-3.

Types of Prompts

The following list contains well-known types prompts for LLMs:

- zero-shot prompts
- one-shot prompts
- few-shot prompts
- instruction prompts

A *zero-shot prompt* contains a description of a task, whereas a *one-shot prompt* consists of a single example for completing a task. As you can probably surmise, *few-shot prompts* consist of multiple examples (typically between 10 and 100). In all cases, a clear description of the task or tasks is recommended: more tasks provide GPT-3 with more information, which in turn can lead to more accurate completions.

T0 (for "zero shot") is an interesting LLM: although T0 is 16 times smaller (11 GB) than GPT-3 (175 GB), T0 has outperformed GPT-3 on language-related tasks. T0 can perform well on unseen NLP tasks (i.e., tasks that are new to T0) because it was trained on a dataset containing multiple tasks.

The following Web page provides the Github repository for T0, a site for training T0 directly in a browser, as well as more details about T0 and a 3GB version of T0:

https://github.com/bigscience-workshop/t-zero

As you can probably surmise, T0++ is based on T0, and it was trained with extra tasks beyond the set of tasks on which T0 was trained.

Another important detail is the first three prompts in the preceding list are also called zero-shot learning, one-shot learning, and few-shot learning, respectively.

Instruction Prompts

Instruction prompts are used for fine tuning LLMs, and they specify a format (determined by you) for the manner in which the LLM is expected to conform in its responses. You can prepare your own instruction prompts or you can access prompt template libraries that contain different templates for different tasks, along with different data-sets. Various prompt instruction templates are publicly available, such as the following links that provides prompt templates (see subsequent section for an example) for Llama (which is discussed in Chapter 9):

https://github.com/devbrones/llama-prompts
https://pub.towardsai.net/llama-gpt4all-simplified-local-chatgpt-ab7d28d34923

Reverse Prompts

Another technique uses a reverse order: input prompts are answers and the response are the questions associated with the answers (similar to a popular game show). For example, given a French sentence, you might ask the model, "What English text might have resulted in this French translation?"

System Prompts Versus Agent Prompts

The distinction between a system prompt and an agent prompt often comes up in the context of conversational AI systems and chatbot design.

A *system prompt* is typically an initial message or cue given by the system to guide the user on what they can do or to set expectations about the interaction. It often serves as an introduction or a way to guide users on how to proceed. Here are several examples of system prompts:

- "Welcome to ChatBotX! You can ask me questions about weather, news, or sports. How can I assist you today?"
- "Hello! For account details, press 1. For technical support, press 2."
- "Greetings! Type 'order' to track your package or 'help' for assistance."

By contrast, an *agent prompt* is a message generated by the AI model or agent in response to a user's input during the course of an interaction. It is a part of the back-and-forth exchange within the conversation. The agent prompt guides the user to provide more information, clarifies ambiguity, or nudges the user toward a specific action. Here are some examples of agent prompts:

```
User: "I'm looking for shoes."
Agent Prompt: "Great! Are you looking for men's or
women's shoes?"
User: "I can't log in."
```

```
Agent Prompt: "I'm sorry to hear that. Can you
specify if you are having trouble with your
password or username?"
User: "Tell me a joke."
Agent Prompt: "Why did the chicken join a band?
Because it had the drumsticks!"
```

The fundamental difference between the two is their purpose and placement in the interaction. A system prompt is often at the beginning of an interaction, setting the stage for the conversation. An agent prompt occurs during the conversation, steering the direction of the dialogue based on user input.

Both types of prompts are crucial for creating a fluid and intuitive conversational experience for users. They guide the user and help ensure that the system understands and addresses the user's needs effectively.

Prompt Templates

Prompt templates are predefined formats or structures used to instruct a model or system to perform a specific task. They serve as a foundation for generating prompts, where certain parts of the template can be filled in or customized to produce a variety of specific prompts. By way of analogy, prompt templates are the counterpart to macros that you can define in some text editors.

Prompt templates are especially useful when working with language models, as they provide a consistent way to query the model across multiple tasks or data points. In particular, prompt templates can make it easier to

- ensure consistency when querying a model multiple times
- facilitate batch processing or automation.
- reduce errors and variations in how questions are posed to the model

As an example, suppose you are working with an LLM and you want to translate English sentences into French. An associated prompt template could be the following:

"Translate the following English sentence into French: {sentence}"

Note that {sentence} is a placeholder that you can replace with any English sentence.

You can use the preceding prompt template to generate specific prompts:

- "Translate the following English sentence into French: 'Hello, how are you?'"

- "Translate the following English sentence into French: 'I love ice cream.'"

As you can see, prompt templates enable you to easily generate a variety of prompts for different sentences without having to rewrite the entire instruction each time. In fact, this concept can be extended to more complex tasks and can incorporate multiple placeholders or more intricate structures, depending on the application.

Prompts for Different LLMs

GPT-3, ChatGPT, and GPT-4 are LLMs that are all based on the transformer architecture and are fundamentally similar in their underlying mechanics. ChatGPT is essentially a version of the GPT model fine-tuned specifically for conversational interactions. GPT-4 is an evolution or improvement over GPT-3 in terms of scale and capabilities.

The differences in prompts for these models mainly arise from the specific use case and context, rather than inherent differences between the models. Here are some prompting differences that are based on use cases.

GPT-3 can be used for a wide range of tasks beyond just conversation, from content generation to code writing. Here are two examples of prompts for GPT-3:

- "Translate the following English text to French: 'Hello, how are you?'"
- "Write a Python function that calculates the factorial of a number."

ChatGPT is specifically fine-tuned for conversational interactions. Here are some examples of prompts for two different conversations with ChatGPT:

- User: "Can you help me with my homework?"
  ChatGPT: "Of course! What subject or topic do you need help with?"

- User: "Tell me a joke."
- ChatGPT: "Why did the chicken cross the playground? To get to the other slide!"

GPT-4 provides a larger scale and refinements, so the prompts would be similar in nature to GPT-3, but might yield more accurate or nuanced outputs. Here are two examples of prompts for GPT-4:

- "Provide a detailed analysis of quantum mechanics in relation to general relativity."

- "Generate a short story based on a post-apocalyptic world with a theme of hope."

These three models accept natural language prompts and produce natural language outputs. The fundamental way you interact with them remains consistent.

The main difference comes from the context in which the model is being used and any fine-tuning that has been applied. ChatGPT, for instance, is designed to be more conversational, so while you can use GPT-3 for chats, ChatGPT might produce more contextually relevant conversational outputs.

When directly interacting with these models, especially through an API, you might also have control over parameters like "temperature" (controlling randomness) and "max tokens" (controlling response length). Adjusting these can shape the responses, regardless of which GPT variant you are using.

In essence, while the underlying models have differences in scale and specific training/fine-tuning, the way you prompt them remains largely consistent: clear, specific natural language prompts yield the best results.

Poorly-Worded Prompts

When crafting prompts, be as clear and specific as possible to guide the response in the desired direction. Ambiguous or vague prompts can lead to a wide range of responses, many of which might not be useful or relevant to the user's actual intent.

Poorly-worded prompts are often vague, ambiguous, or too broad, and they can lead to confusion, misunderstanding, or non-specific responses from AI models. Here are some examples of poorly worded prompts, along with explanations:

"Tell me about that thing."
Problem: Too vague. What "thing" is being referred to?

"Why did it happen?"
Problem: No context. What event or situation is being discussed?

"Explain stuff."
Problem: Too broad. What specific "stuff" should be explained?

"Do what is needful."
Problem: Ambiguous. What specific action is required?

"I want information."
Problem: Not specific enough. What type of information is desired?

"Can you get me the thing from the place?"
Problem: Both "thing" and "place" are unclear.

"Where can I buy what's-his-name's book?"
Problem: Ambiguous reference. Who is "what's-his-name"?

"How do you do the process?"
Problem: Which "process" is being referred to?

"Describe the importance of the topic."
Problem: The "topic" is not specified.

"Why is it bad or good?"
Problem: No context. What is "it"?

"Help with the issue."
Problem: Vague. What specific issue requires assistance?

"Things to consider for the task."
Problem: Ambiguous. What "task" is being discussed?

"How does this work?"
Problem: Lack of specificity. What is "this"?

ASPECTS OF LLM DEVELOPMENT

If you have read the preceding chapters, you have an understanding of the architecture of encoder-only LLMs, decoder-only LLMs, and LLMs that are based on an encoder as well as a decoder. For your convenience, this section provides a list of language models that belong to each of these three types of models. Note that decoder-only models, such as the GPT-x family of LLMs, are discussed in Chapters 7 and 8.

With the preceding points in mind, some of the better-known encoder-based LLMs include the following:

· AlBERT
· BERT
· DistilBERT
· ELECTRA
· RoBERTa

The preceding LLMs are well-suited for performing NLP tasks such as NER and extractive question-answering tasks. In addition to encoder-only LLMs, there are several well-known decoder-based LLMs that include the following:

- CTRL
- GPT/GPT-2
- Transformer XK

The preceding LLMs perform text *generation*, which can also perform next word *prediction*. Finally, some of the well-known encoder/decoder-based LLMs include the following:

- BART
- mBART
- Marian
- T5

The preceding LLMs perform summarization, translation, and generate question-answering.

A recent trend has been the use of fine-tuning, zero/one/few-shot training, and prompt-based learning with respect to LLMs. Fine-tuning is typically accompanied by a fine-tuning dataset, and if the latter is not available (or infeasible), few-shot training might be an acceptable alternative.

One outcome from training the Jurassic-1 LLM is that wider and shallower is better than narrower and deeper with respect to performance because a wider context allows for more calculations to be performed in parallel.

Another result from Chinchilla is that smaller models that are trained on a corpus with a very large number of tokens can be more performant than larger models that are trained on a more modest number of tokens.

The success of the GlaM and Switch LLMs (both from Google) suggests that sparse transformers, in conjunction with MoE (Mixture of Experts), is also an interesting direction, potentially leading to even better results in the future.

In addition, there is the possibility of the "over curation" of data, which is to say that performing *very* detailed data curation to remove spurious-looking tokens does not guarantee that models will produce better results on those curated datasets.

The use of prompts has revealed an interesting detail: the results of similar yet different prompts can lead to substantively different responses. Thus, the goal is to create well-crafted prompts, which are inexpensive and yet can be a somewhat elusive task.

Another area of development pertains to the continued need for benchmarks that leverage better and more complex datasets, especially when LLMs exceed human performance. Specifically, a benchmark becomes outdated when all modern LLMs can pass the suite of tests in that benchmark. Two such benchmarks are XNLI and BigBench ("Beyond the Imitation Game Benchmark").

The following Web page provides a fairly extensive list of general NLP benchmarks as well as language-specific NLP benchmarks:

https://mr-nlp.github.io/posts/2021/05/benchmarks-in-nlp/

The following Web page provides a list of monolingual transformer-based pre-trained language models:

https://mr-nlp.github.io/posts/2021/05/tptlms-list/

LLM Size Versus Performance

Let us consider the size-versus-performance question: although larger models such as GPT-3 can perform better than smaller models, it is not always the case. In particular, models that are variants of GPT-3 have mixed results: some smaller variants perform almost as well as GPT-3, and some larger models perform only marginally better than GPT-3.

A recent trend involves developing models that are based on the decoder component of the transformer architecture. Such models are frequently measured by their performance via zero-shot, one-shot, and few-shot training in comparison to other LLMs. This trend, as well as the development of ever-larger LLMs, is likely to continue for the foreseeable future.

Interestingly, decoder-only LLMs can perform tasks such as token prediction and can slightly out-perform encoder-only models on benchmarks such as SuperGLUE. However, such decoder-based models tend to be significantly larger than encoder-based models, and the latter tend to be more efficient than the former.

Hardware is another consideration in terms of optimizing model performance, which can incur a greater cost, and hence might be limited to only a handful of companies. Due to the high cost of hardware, another initiative involves training LLMs on the Jean Zay supercomputer in France:

https://venturebeat.com/2022/01/10/inside-bigscience-the-quest-to-build-a-powerful-open-language-model/

Emergent Abilities of LLMs

The *emergent abilities* of LLMs refers to abilities that are present in larger models that do not exist in smaller models. In simplified terms, as models increase in size, there is a discontinuous "jump" whereby abilities manifest themselves in a larger model with no apparent or clear-cut reason.

The interesting aspect of emergent abilities is the possibility of expanding capabilities of language models through additional scaling. More detailed information is accessible in the following paper ("Emergent Abilities of Large Language Models"):

https://arxiv.org/abs/2206.07682

The Nobel-Prize-winning physicist Philip Anderson made the following statement in his 1972 essay called "More Is Different:"

> "Emergence is when quantitative changes in a system result in qualitative changes in behavior."

Interestingly, a scenario is described in which few-shot prompting is considered emergent (quoted from the preceding arXiv paper):

> "The ability to perform a task via few-shot prompting is emergent when a model has random performance until a certain scale, after which performance increases to well-above random."

(Be sure to examine Table 1 in the paper, which provides details regarding "few-shot prompting abilities" (e.g., truthfulness, the MMLU Benchmark) as well as "augmented prompting abilities" (e.g., chain of thought and instruction following).)

Note that emergent abilities *cannot* be predicted by extrapolation of the behavior of smaller models because (by definition) emergent abilities are not present in smaller models. No doubt there will be more research that explores the extent to which further model scaling can lead to more emergent abilities in LLMs.

KAPLAN AND UNDER-TRAINED MODELS

Kaplan et al. provided (empirical) power laws regarding the performance of language models, which they assert depends on the following:

- model size
- dataset size
- amount of compute for training

Kaplan et al. asserted that changing the network width or depth have minimal effects. They also claimed that optimal training of very large models involves a relatively modest amount of data. The paper with the relevant details is accessible online:

https://arxiv.org/abs/2001.08361

However, Chinchilla is a 70 B LLM that was trained on a dataset that is much larger than the size that is recommended by Kaplan et al. In fact, Chinchilla achieved SOTA status that has surpassed the performance of the following LLMs, all of which are between 2 and 7 times larger than Chinchilla:

- `Gopher (280B)`
- `GPT-3 (175B)`
- `J1-Jumbo (178B)`
- `LaMDA (137B)`
- `MT-NLG (530B)`

In addition, the creators of the Chinchilla LLM wrote the paper "Scaling Laws for Neural Language Models," which includes the suggested number of tokens for various models sizes to be fully trained instead of under trained (see Table 3 in that document). For example, the suggested training set sizes for models that have 175B, 520B, and 1 trillion parameters is 3.7 trillion tokens, 11.0 trillion tokens, and 21.2 trillion tokens, respectively. The largest entry in the same table is LMMs with 10 trillion parameters, with a recommended training set size of 216.2 trillion parameters.

Obviously, an LLM that exceeds 1 trillion parameters faces a significant challenge creating datasets of the recommended size, as described in the paper from the authors of Chinchilla. One interesting possibility involves ASR (not discussed in this book), which might enable the generation of datasets that are larger than 10 trillion tokens by transcribing audio to text. Indeed, some speculation suggests that GPT-4 might leverage ASR to create such a dataset.

WHAT IS BERT?

BERT is an acronym for Bidirectional Encoder Representations from transformers. BERT pre-trains deep bidirectional representations from unlabeled text in such a way that a pre-trained BERT model can be fine-tuned to create a SOTA model via the inclusion of one additional output layer for a wide range of NLP tasks. In fact, BERT achieved new SOTA results on eleven natural language processing tasks.

BERT achieved SOTA results in tasks such as question-answering (QnA) and language inference, with only some minor changes in its architecture. At the same time, BERT is computationally expensive: determining a pair of sentences that have the greatest similarity in a corpus of 10,000 sentences involves more than 60 hours of computation involving about 50 million inference computations.

BERT Training

BERT was pre-trained on a large set of unlabeled data from Wikipedia, and in addition to performing NLP-related tasks, BERT can be fine-tuned for other tasks. BERT uses the attention mechanism to generate word embeddings that involve the context of words that precede as well as the words that follow a given word. By contrast, algorithms such as word2vec are context-free, so word embeddings do not have any contextual information.

Note that the fine-tuning step for BERT differs from the pre-training step for BERT: the former involves labeled data whereas the latter involves unlabeled data.

BERT Models

The two most well-known versions of BERT are called BERT-Base and BERT-Large. BERT-Base consists of 12 layers, 12 attention heads, and 110 million parameters. BERT-Large is a larger pre-trained model that consists of 24 layers, 16 attention heads, and 340 million parameters. However, there are also several smaller BERT-based models, as shown in the following list:

```
BERT-medium  L=8 and H=512
BERT-small   L=4 and H=512
BERT-mini    L=4 and H=256
BERT-tiny    L=2 and H=128
```

BERT can be used in conjunction with the Hugging Face `trans-formers` library, which provides classes to perform various tasks, such as question-answering and sequence classification.

Since BERT does not utilize the decoder component, BERT is not suitable for text generation. Moreover, BERT is not suitable for unsupervised tasks (e.g., clustering) or for semantic similarity.

The BERT Architecture

BERT is based on the transformer architecture that was developed in 2017 by Google. BERT only requires the encoder portion of the transformer architecture to generate a language representation model. BERT has a vocabulary size of approximately 30,000 words, and each word embedding in BERT has 768 features, which means that each word embedding is a 1x768 vector of floating-point numbers.

The BERT model consists of the encoder component of the transformer architecture, which means that it is an encoder-only architecture. The main portion of BERT is a very large 12-layer neural network that processes text. However, you can replace the final classifier in BERT with a task-specific model, which enables you to leverage all of BERT's knowledge.

This final training step is referred to as "fine tuning," because the amount of training required to adapt BERT to your own task is very small compared to what it took Google to pre-train BERT. The fine-tuning step is a proportionately smaller task that can still involve a significant amount of computation.

BERT Features

BERT has a set of approximately 30,000 learned raw vectors. Moreover, approximately 80% of those raw vectors correspond to "normal" words (i.e., they exist in an English dictionary). The remaining 20% are subwords that are created by WordPiece: these subwords have the form "##s" or "##ed." The latter subwords are useful for detecting the past tense of a verb in a sentence. In addition, the BERT vocabulary consists of 45% uppercase and 25% lowercase terms (approximately).

Limitations of BERT

Although BERT can perform text-related tasks, interpret text, and make predictions, BERT cannot perform the following tasks:

- generate new text
- translate text between languages
- generate a response to questions

The reason for the preceding limitations is that BERT is based *only* on the encoder component of the transformer architecture. By contrast, LLMs that are based on the decoder component, such as GPT-based models, are able to perform all the tasks in the preceding list.

However, the original transformer model was trained on manually created translation examples, whereas BERT is pre-trained model that used a significantly larger dataset consisting of unlabeled text.

How is BERT Trained?

BERT is trained by first performing a pre-training step based on task-specific data, followed by a fine-tuning step. For example, if you want to perform sentiment analysis using BERT, you need a corpus of labeled data that specifies whether a sentence has positive or negative sentiment. In addition, the dataset is split into a training portion and a test portion, just as you have seen in code samples in previous chapters. It is also typical of machine learning algorithms that involve supervised learning, such as linear regression and classification algorithms.

Before the training step, BERT performs MLM, which involves 1) replacing approximately 15% of the tokens with a [MASK] token, and 2) an additional randomly selected set of words are replaced with a different (i.e., incorrect) set. The actual training step involves training BERT on a randomly selected sequences of 512 tokens, and the goal is for BERT to make predictions for *all* the input tokens.

In addition to MLM, BERT performs next sentence prediction (NSP). This task involves concatenating pairs of sentences: some pairs are adjacent sentences and other pairs consist of sentences from random locations. The goal of this task is for BERT to correctly predict whether the pairs of sentences are contiguous.

After the pre-training step has completed, the fine-tuning step involves training the model on a set of sample tasks. For example, if you want to train BERT to perform a question-answering task, then fine tune a pre-trained model (that was trained on a related task) on a corpus of question/answer data.

BERT-Base and BERT-Large

BERT-Base consists of 12 encoder layers, each stacked one on top of the other. All the encoders use 12 attention heads. The feedforward network in the encoder consists of 768 hidden units, so the size of the representation obtained from BERT base will also be 768.

By comparison, BERT-Large consists of 24 vertically stacked encoder layers, each of which have 16 attention heads. The feedforward network in each encoder layer consists of 1,024 hidden units. Thus, the size of the representation obtained from BERT-Large will be 1,024. In addition, the BERT-Large model contains 340 million parameters.

BERT Versus Earlier NLP Models

There are several important aspects of BERT that differentiate BERT from models that rely on algorithms (such as word2vec). First, BERT does not perform a stemming operation: instead, BERT performs subword tokenization via WordPiece. The primary difference is that stemming discards suffixes, whereas WordPiece does not discard the suffixes.

Second, BERT creates *contextual* word embeddings whereas word2vec creates *distributional* word embeddings. Specifically, BERT uses all the words in a sentence to generate a word embedding for each word in a given sentence, *and each word embedding is specific to the sentence in which the word appears*. As a result, a word that appears in multiple sentences has different word embeddings, whereas word2vec uses bigrams to calculate a single word embedding for words in sentences.

Third, BERT does not use cosine similarity (not directly, that is) to determine the extent to which two words are similar to each other. However, it is possible to use BERT with cosine similarities, provided that you fine tune BERT on suitable data, such as the data and code samples in the following repository:

https://github.com/UKPLab/sentence-transformers

BERT Self-Attention

In Chapter 1, we discussed the attention mechanism in transformer-base models. Different types of LLMs use different types of self-attention. Specifically, encoder-based models, such as BERT, use bidirectional self-attention. Decoder-based LLMs such as GPT use one-sided self-attention, which means that each token only attends to the context on its left side (but not its right side).

How BERT Processes Input Embeddings

Unlike RNNs and LSTMs that process word tokens in a sequential fashion, BERT processes a set of input embeddings in parallel to generate an embedding that consists of 768 floating point numbers for each input embedding.

BERT can also process variable length sentences because BERT generates a single weighted vector through deep bidirectional transformations that consider the contextual relationships between words in a sentence, rather than simply averaging the word embeddings.

Note that while the transformer architecture does allow for parallel processing of words in a sentence, this is a feature of the self-attention mechanism, not a parallel calculation of weighted averages.

The input representation for BERT is either a single text sentence or a pair of text sentences. In the case of two sentences, each token in the first sentence receives embedding A, and each token in the second sentence receives embedding B, and the sentences are separated by the token [SEP]. Input sequences for BERT can have a maximum length of 512 tokens: other models support a maximum input sequence length of 1,024 tokens.

By default, BERT supports two pre-training tasks, MLM and NSP, which were briefly discussed earlier in this section and will also be discussed later in this chapter.

Pyramid-BERT

Amazon created Pyramid-BERT, which is a technique that reduces various aspects of BERT-based models, with only a small reduction of 1.5% in accuracy:

- reduced training time
- reduced inference time
- reduced memory footprint

In addition to the preceding improvements, BERT models can process longer text sequences. Pyramid-BERT achieves its improvement by processing intermediate layers to remove some individual word embeddings. Specifically, Pyramid-BERT removes the redundancy that exists in the [CLS] token after the tokens have been processed by the final encoder.

BERTScore

BERTScore compares the meaning of what has been generated with what was meant to be generated. Given a sentence and a generated sentence, the BERTScore is calculated as follows:

- Pass both sentences through the pre-trained BERT model.
- Generate contextual embedding for each word.
- Perform an n-squared computation.
- Calculate the similarity of each reference word with each candidate word.
- Select the reference word that is most similar to the candidate word.
- Calculate the precision, recall, and f-score.

BERT AND NLP TASKS

NLP models can perform a variety of tasks, with varying degrees of accuracy, some of which are listed here:

- Document Classification
- Question-Answering
- Domain-specific text
- Non-English applications
- Named Entity Recognition
- Combining text with other feature types

Note that document classification can involve multi-class classification and multi-label label classification (i.e., a data point has more than one label).

BERT has achieved success in numerous tasks, such as content-based recommendations, question-answering (QnA), and video processing. During the unsupervised pre-training phase, BERT can process very large unlabeled datasets, followed by the fine-tuning phase that involves only a limited amount of labeled data. Hence, BERT-based language models are highly desirable because they achieve SOTA accuracy.

Since processing an extremely large corpus is time-consuming, a reduction in training time is possible via a technique known as "data-parallel model training," which involves partitioning the training dataset into multiple subsets, each of which is processed by means of a model replica.

Furthermore, the calculated gradients are mean-reduced in all model replicas during each optimization step, thereby ensuring that the weight updates as well as the model state are identical in all the model replicas.

BERT Vocabulary and Out-of-Vocabulary Words

The original BERT model has a fixed vocabulary size of about 30,000 tokens total. Between three-fifths and four-fifths of these are actually entire words, and the remaining set of words consists of subwords or "word pieces." BERT represents a given input token using a combination of embeddings that indicate the corresponding token, segment, and position.

When BERT encounters an out-of-vocabulary (OOV) word, its tokenizer uses WordPiece to decomposes the word into a set of subwords.

BERT and Word Order

BERT does not have retain information regarding word order: it can be applied to the words in any order (or all at once in parallel, as we do in practice). By contrast, RNNs and LSTMs can maintain word order because words are inputted in a sequential fashion. A given word is processed by combining the current word with the output from a previously processed word.

BERT considers word order through the use of positional embeddings, which are designed to give the model information about the position of each word in a sequence. BERT has a distinct positional embedding for each possible position in a sequence up to its maximum length (512 for BERT).

BERT and "Too Long" Sentences

BERT-Base can process a maximum of 512 input tokens, because this is the maximum length imposed by the PE on the length of the input sequence. If input sentences exceed this maximum, you have the following options:

1. Use a larger BERT model that handles input sequences of 2,048 tokens.

2. Truncate the input sentences that are longer than 512 tokens.

3. Discard sentences whose length exceeds 512 (not recommended).

4. Partition each sentence into chunks of 512 tokens.

Option #3 is the least recommended approach: it is analogous to dealing with outliers by discarding them. Although Option #4 is appealing, there may be logically-related dependencies between chunks that would not be captured by this technique.

Padding Sentences

BERT can be applied to any sentence length up to 512 tokens. However, to support parallel processing of multiple text samples at once, implementations of BERT require that you specify a single fixed length for all input text.

For the sake of parallelization, all input text sequences are padded out or truncated to a single fixed length, and

- a shorter fixed-length will make training and evaluating BERT faster
- BERT has a hard upper limit of 512 tokens

Padding Versus Truncation

Padding is required when input sentences or documents have different lengths. The padding character can be the value 0 or some other value that is specific to an algorithm. Left-padding prepends padding characters to a sentence or document, whereas post-padding appends padding characters to a sentence or document.

In addition, there are several ways to determine the number of padding characters that are required, some of which are listed here:

- Pad documents dynamically on a per-batch basis.
- Pad every document to the length of the longest document.
- Pad every document to the average length of the documents.

The first option involves padding documents dynamically so that the padding length is based on the current batch of documents.

Padding based on the longest document is inadvisable when there are outliers with respect to document lengths. For example, perhaps one document contains 50 K tokens, whereas every other document contains, at most, 1 K tokens.

Truncation involves specifying a maximum document length and then simply discarding tokens whose positions in documents exceed the specified maximum length. Unfortunately, this technique can lose valuable information that is contained in the discarded tokens.

A modified form of truncation involves padding shorter documents to a specified length (such as 1 K), and then splitting the document with 50 K tokens into a set of 50 shorter documents that contain 1 K tokens. However, splitting a document in this fashion could result in a loss of *contextual* information in the first few tokens that are referenced toward the end of the set of partial documents.

If you use the average document length as the value for the maximum document length, you can also encounter loss of information due to discarding tokens.

Another important detail: truncation of documents does not affect tasks such as sentiment analysis and spam detection because their predictions consist of a single value. However, machine translation and NER can be adversely affected by truncating documents.

BERT has a limit of 512 input tokens, whereas GPT-2 has a limit of 1,024 input tokens, which means that you must abide by these limits (and those of other language models) with respect to the length of input documents.

BERT AND THE TRANSFORMER ARCHITECTURE

BERT is one of the well-known early pre-trained language models based on the Transformer architecture, an event that has been called the "ImageNet moment for NLP."

The BERT architecture consists of an encoder-only component that contains multiple vertically stacked encoder layers. BERT was trained in a self-supervised manner on massive datasets. BERT gained a statistical understanding of language and could function as a language model.

There are many variants of pre-trained BERT models that are pre-trained on different types of datasets (such as legal, biomedical, scientific, and so forth). Many of those model variants have improved performance characteristics (such as RoBERTa, ALBERT, and DistilBERT), and they were pre-trained by large organizations that then made those models available for general use. Since pre-training is an expensive and time-consuming process, the availability of a plethora of pre-trained models is a great benefit to the community.

Interestingly, the first GPT model from OpenAI (discussed in Chapter 7) preceded BERT and was also influential in the development of BERT. OpenAI used language modeling, which is an unsupervised learning task that predicts the next word in a given sentence.

BERT and Bidirectionality

As its name indicates, BERT supports bidirectionality to process input sequence. In particular, BERT processes input sequences as entire sentences instead of individual tokens, to obtain context from both left-to-right and right-to-left directions of the input text.

Other models, such as ELMo and GPT, both use a unidirectional technique. ELMo actually supports a two-pass mechanism: a model is trained in a left-to-right fashion, and another model is trained in a right-to-left fashion, and the two models are concatenated to create a single model. Nevertheless, the bidirectionality of BERT is superior to the two-phase approach of ELMo.

BERT AND TEXT PROCESSING

This section and several subsections discuss how BERT performs the following NLP tasks:

- Token Classification
- NER (Named Entity Recognition)
- Text Classification

Token Classification

Token-level tasks involve making a prediction on each token in the input. BERT takes in a set of word embeddings and produces a set of better word embeddings, so token-level tasks are the most "natural" application.

BERT and NER

The BERT-based language models can be fine-tuned for downstream tasks such as NER and RE for specialized domains. Recall from Chapter 4 that every token in the input sequence is a combination of three vectors: the word embedding, the segment embedding, and the position embedding. You can use BERT to perform NER by adding a dense classification layer on top of the BERT model. The size of this layer matches the number of named entity categories you want to recognize (e.g., PERSON, ORGANIZATION, and LOCATION, plus the "O" label for tokens that are not part of any named entity).

Now you can fine-tune the model on the NER dataset. For each token in the input, use the BERT tokenizer to produce a contextualized embedding. This embedding is passed through the classification layer to produce a prediction for that token. The model is then trained to minimize the difference between its predictions and the true NER labels.

You might be wondering how predictions for subwords are processed: after all, these can be word pieces that do not have any meaning by themselves. As a result, some post-processing steps are required to combine predictions for subwords that belong to the same word and ensure coherent entity recognition.

Text Classification

BERT can be applied to traditional NLP tasks, such as text classification. Since BERT produces a collection of embeddings, we can perform some processing (such as averaging their values) and then forward the result to a classifier.

Next, a dense classification layer is added on top of the BERT model. This layer's size corresponds to the number of classes in the classification task. Only the representation of the [CLS] token (from the last layer of BERT) is used as the aggregate representation of the sequence and is passed to the classification layer. In other words, BERT processes the entire sequence and then uses the contextualized representation of the [CLS] token to make the classification.

BERT AND DATA CLEANING TASKS

Data cleaning is a fundamental machine learning process whose steps depend on the type of data and model. For example, classification algorithms such as kNN and SVM involve handling missing and incorrect data as data cleaning tasks, whereas NLP-related datasets can involve normalization.

Specifically, the following list contains data cleaning tasks that are relevant to datasets for BERT-based models:

- Remove stopwords.
- Perform Normalization.
- Use Regular Expressions.
- No stemming.
- Perform Lemmatization.

However, the first three bullet items are "conditional" tasks for the following reasons.

1. Removing stopwords can sometimes help to reduce noise and focus on the most informative words in the text. However, BERT is designed to work with raw text data, and removing stopwords might sometimes remove important contextual information that BERT could leverage.

2. Performing Normalization can involve tasks such as converting all text to lowercase or correcting typos, which can be beneficial in standardizing the text data. However, BERT is pre-trained on large corpora without extensive normalization to retain the nuances of the natural language, so extensive normalization is not always necessary.

3. Using regular expressions can be useful for cleaning and structuring text data, such as removing unwanted characters or patterns. However, it should be used judiciously to avoid removing important information.

After you have cleaned a dataset, the next step involves splitting a dataset into train and test subsets, typically with the Scikit-learn `train_test_split()` function.

Normalization

Normalization is the process of scaling numeric columns in a dataset so that they have a common scale. In addition, the scaling is performed as follows:

1. scaling values to the range [0,1]

2. without losing information

3. without distorting any differences that exist in the ranges of values.

You can perform data normalization via the `MinMaxScaler` class in the `scikit-learn` library.

After you have cleaned a dataset, you need to perform other tasks, such as splitting a dataset into train and test subsets, typically with the `scikit-learn` function `train_test_split()`. Next, you typically perform tokenization, which is discussed later in this chapter.

Regular Expressions

Regular expressions provide powerful functionality for searching and replacing text in a text string, document, or corpus. Since the focus of this book is transformer-based architectures and models, code samples for regular expressions are omitted. If you want to be comfortable with regular expressions, or perhaps become proficient in their use, there are free online resources available.

THREE BERT EMBEDDING LAYERS

BERT has three types of embedding layers:

- token embeddings
- segment embeddings
- position embeddings

Word embeddings for BERT consists of a one-dimensional vector with 768 floating point numbers for each token, which are created by the component-wise sum of three floating point vectors, as described in the next paragraph.

Each token embedding has the shape (1, 768), which are just vector representations of a word. Each segment embedding has the shape (1, 768), which is a vector representation to help BERT distinguish between paired input sequences. Each position embedding has the shape (1, 768), which enables BERT to keep track of the position of tokens in the input sequence. The three preceding vectors are added to form another vector that is passed to the encoder layer for BERT.

Three Types of Positional Embeddings

BERT can process input sequences that have a maximum length of 512. Since BERT works with fixed-length sequences, you need to determine the maximum length of a set of variable length input sequences, which must be truncated to 512. Sentences that have fewer than 512 tokens can be padded so that they have a length of 512.

The next step involves calculating a compatible vector that contains the positional information for each token. Specifically, the embedding layer can be represented via a (512,768) table such that the ith row contains the vector representation of words in the ith position.

BERT also has a special token, [CLS], for the first position and the [SEP] token for the separator between consecutive sentences. The generated output consists of the component-based sum of three vectors: the vector with token embeddings, the vector with segment embeddings, and the vector position embeddings.

As a reminder, *causal attention* means that tokens can only access past tokens that are part of the same text string, whereas non-causal attention do not have this restriction. Furthermore, there are the following types of position-related encoding techniques:

- position embedding
- position encoding
- relative positions

The main points regarding BERT involve the following architectural and training-related details:

- **non-causal** attention (contrast with GPT-2)
- position embedding
- unsupervised pre-training
- supervised fine tuning

CREATING A BERT MODEL

The Hugging Face `transformers` package contains the `AutoModel` class that enables you to instantiate a model from a checkpoint. This class is a wrapper class that is designed in such a way that the correct model can be determined for a given checkpoint. Alternatively, you can specify the explicit class if you have advance knowledge of the model that you require. Let's take a look at how this works with a BERT model.

Listing 5.1 displays the content of `bert_model.py` that illustrates how to create a BERT model.

Listing 5.1: bert_model.py

```
from transformers import BertConfig, BertModel

# 1) initialize the config object
config = BertConfig()

# 2) initialize a BERT model:
model = BertModel(config)

# display the contents of the configuration object:
print(config)
```

Listing 5.1 starts with an import statement and then initializes the variable config as an instance of the BertModel class. Next, the variable model is initialized as an instance of BertModel, along with the config variable. The final code snippet displays the contents of the config variable. Launch the code in Listing 5.1, and you will see the following output:

```
BertConfig {
    "attention_probs_dropout_prob": 0.1,
    "classifier_dropout": null,
    "gradient_checkpointing": false,
    "hidden_act": "gelu",
    "hidden_dropout_prob": 0.1,
    "hidden_size": 768,
    "initializer_range": 0.02,
    "intermediate_size": 3072,
    "layer_norm_eps": 1e-12,
    "max_position_embeddings": 512,
    "model_type": "bert",
    "num_attention_heads": 12,
    "num_hidden_layers": 12,
    "pad_token_id": 0,
    "position_embedding_type": "absolute",
    "transformers_version": "4.10.3",
    "type_vocab_size": 2,
    "use_cache": true,
    "vocab_size": 30522
}
```

TRAINING AND SAVING A BERT MODEL

The previous section showed you how to create a BERT model, and this section shows you how to save a BERT model. Listing 5.2 displays the content that illustrates how to create a BERT model and then save that model on your machine.

Listing 5.2: save_bert_model.py

```
from transformers import BertConfig, BertModel
from transformers import BertConfig, BertModel

# initialize the config object
config = BertConfig()

# BERT model initialized with random values:
model = BertModel(config)

#model.save_pretrained(a_directory_location)
model.save_pretrained("/tmp")
```

Listing 5.2 starts by importing several classes from the transform-ers library, and then initializes the variables config and model, just as you saw in Listing 5.1. The final code snippet saves the pertained model in the /tmp directory, which you can save in a different location. Launch the code in Listing 5.2, and you will see the following output in the /tmp directory:

```
-rw-r--r-- 1 618 Nov 4 13:15 config.json
-rw-r--r-- 1 438013119 Nov 4 13:15 pytorch_model.
bin
```

The file pytorch_model.bin is called the "state dictionary," which is a large file because it contains all the weights of the model. The file config.json contains attributes for the architecture of the model.

THE INNER WORKINGS OF BERT

BERT implements a number of interesting techniques, some of which are listed here:

- MLM (Masked Language Model)
- NSP (Next Sentence Prediction)

- Special tokens ([CLS] and [SEP])
- Language mask
- Wordpiece (subword tokenization is used in BERT)
- SentencePiece (used in ALBERT)

Each topic in the preceding list is discussed briefly in the following subsections, along with PLM and MLNET (both are alternatives to MLM) and SOP (an alternative to NSP).

What is MLM?

The *masked language model* (MLM) is a BERT unsupervised pre-training task on unlabeled data, during which BERT processed the contents of Wikipedia as well as BookCorpus. In this task, approximately 15% of the words were replaced with the [MASK] token, and then BERT would predict the missing words. Note that this task was performed on "chunks" of data that were submitted to BERT. Another pre-training task is next sentence prediction (NSP).

Many words in Wikipedia involve dates, names of people, and names of locations, some of which were replaced by the [MASK] token. During the training process, BERT ascertained the missing tokens correctly. Note that the appendix contains some information regarding transfer learning, pre-training, and fine-tuning language models.

PLM and MPNet: Alternatives to MLM

In the previous section you learned about MLM, which is a technique that selects 15% of the tokens from a corpus and replaces approximately 80% of them with [MASK]. Models such as BERT attempt to discover the correct tokens during their pre-training step.

Another technique is *permuted language modeling* (PLM), which examines the dependency among predicted tokens. Unlike BERT, which does not perform PLM, XLNet does support PLM to determine those dependencies. Although XLNet introduces a permutation operation that can potentially alter the original positions of the tokens, it still maintains positional information through the use of transformer architecture which inherently considers positional encodings. However, the permutation operation can indeed introduce complexities in learning the true positional relationships between tokens.

A third technique is *MPNet*, which is a pre-training method that provides the advantages of BERT and XLNet while avoiding their limitations. The code and the pre-trained models using MPNet are available at *https://github.com/microsoft/MPNet*.

What is NSP?

Next sentence prediction (NSP) is an out-of-the-box pre-training task that is performed by BERT (the other pre-training task is MLM). NSP combines pairs of sentences in the following way:

· The second sentence is logically related to the first sentence in 50% of the pairs.
· The second sentence is *not* logically related to the first sentence in 50% of the pairs.

The purpose of NSP is to identify which pairs of sentences are correct and which pairs of sentences are incorrect.

One other point needs to be mentioned. NSP is typically described in terms of "sentence pairs," which can be further clarified as follows:

· A "sentence" is a "span of text."
· A "span of text" can be longer than a sentence.
· A "span of text" can be shorter than a sentence.
· The length of the pair must be <= 512 tokens.

NSP Versus SOP

Although NSP is a worthwhile pre-training task, there are alternatives. *Sentence Order Prediction* (SOP) is an example that bears some resemblance to NSP. An interesting detail regarding SOP is that sometimes two passages of text are presented in reverse order instead of in the "normal" order.

In fact, the architects of RoBERTa and XLNet replaced NSP with SOP because the latter led to better results than NSP on their models. In addition, SOP is a task that is more challenging than NSP because NSP can be circumvented by comparing the topic of the two passages: if they differ, then it is unlikely that the second passage followed the first.

NSP Versus Language Modeling

BERT is designed for bidirectional encodings, which means that BERT can process sentences in both directions: in a left-to-right fashion as well as a right-to-left fashion (i.e., analogous to bidirectional LSTMs).

Hence, in MLM and NSP tasks, you can give BERT the entire input sequence at once, and BERT gets to factor in all of the words in the text into its predictions.

By contrast, if you perform language modeling on GPT-based models, those models can only process sentences in a left-to-right fashion. The masked attention element in the decoder component prevents a model from *looking* at the next word in a sentence, and forces the model to *predict* the next word.

Real-Time Processing of Input Tokens

BERT has a bidirectional capability that can be advantageous when you process entire input sentences. However, there are situations where you probably need to process input sequences in a sequential fashion instead of processing a complete input sequence.

For example, speech recognition is generally performed on a token-by-token basis, albeit with at least one caveat. Specifically, the German language structure places auxiliary verbs in the final position of a clause or sentence, and Japanese has a language structure whereby human translators listen to entire sentences before providing a translation into another language such as English.

Another use-case involves autocompletion of a string or next-word prediction. In a sense, GPT-3 performs "autocompletion" on a much larger scale: given a text-based input prompt, GPT-3 can generate entire sentences, paragraphs, or even articles.

SUMMARY

This chapter started with an introduction to the BERT model and some of its features. You saw how BERT is trained and some of the BERT models that are available. Next, you learned how BERT differs from earlier NLP models.

In addition, you learned how to perform NER with BERT, along with BERTopic and topic modeling. Then you saw how to perform data cleaning tasks with BERT, such as normalization and how regular expressions are relevant for data cleaning in BERT.

Next you learned about BERT embedding layers, along with token embeddings, segment embeddings, and position embeddings. You saw a Python-based code sample that explained how to create, train, and save a BERT model.

Then, we discussed some of the inner workings of BERT, such as MLM, NSP, and special BERT tokens. You learned about subword tokenization, BPE, WordPiece, and SentencePiece.

In addition, you learned about sentence similarity in BERT, word context, and then Python code samples that generate BERT tokens.

## CHAPTER 6

THE *BERT* FAMILY IN GREATER DEPTH

This chapter continues the discussion of the transformer-based BERT model, with topics such as a BERT specific tokenizer, sentence similarity, generating BERT tokens, and the BERT family of LLMs.

The first part of this chapter contains a Python-based code sample for special BERT tokens, followed by a discussion about a BERT tokenizer and a DistilBERT tokenizer. This section also shows you how to perform sentiment analysis with BERT. The second part of this chapter describes the sequence of steps that are involved in BERT encoding. Then you will learn about sentence similarity in BERT as well as Sentence-BERT. You will also see how to generate BERT tokens.

The third part of this chapter provides a list of LLMs that are part of the BERT family, such as ALBERT, BART, and DistilBERT. This section also provides a ink to a short Python-based code sample for training a BERT model on your laptop, along with information regarding the RoBERTa LLM. The fourth part of this chapter contains an assortment of topics, such as translation into Italian and Japanese, Web-based tools for BERT, topic modeling with BERT, and Google PaLM.

A CODE SAMPLE FOR SPECIAL BERT TOKENS

BERT uses the special token [CLS] to indicate the start of a text string and the special token [SEP] to separate sentences. For example, consider the following sentence:

```
Pizza with four toppings and trimmings.
```

The BERT tokenization of the preceding sentence is here:

```
['[CLS]', 'pizza', 'with', 'four', 'topping',
'##s', 'and', 'trim', '##ming', '##s', '.',
'[SEP]']
```

Listing 6.1 displays the content of bert_special_tokens.py that illustrates how to display the special tokens in BERT.

Listing 6.1: bert_special_tokens.py

```
import transformers
import numpy as np

# instantiate a BERT tokenizer and model:
print("creating tokenizer...")
tokenizer = transformers.BertTokenizer.from_
pretrained('bert-base-uncased', do_lower_case=True)

print("creating model...")
nlp = transformers.TFBertModel.from_pretrained
('bert-base-uncased')

# hidden layer with embeddings:
text1      = "cell phone"
input_ids1 = np.array(tokenizer.encode(text1))
[None, :]
embedding1 = nlp(input_ids1)

print("input_ids1:")
print(input_ids1)
print()

print("tokenizer.sep_token:    ",tokenizer.sep_
token)
print("tokenizer.sep_token_id:",tokenizer.sep_
token_id)
print("tokenizer.cls_token:    ",tokenizer.cls_
token)
print("tokenizer.cls_token_id:",tokenizer.cls_
token_id)
```

```
print("tokenizer.pad_token:    ",tokenizer.pad_
token)
print("tokenizer.pad_token_id:",tokenizer.pad_
token_id)
print("tokenizer.unk_token:    ",tokenizer.unk_
token)
print("tokenizer.unk_token_id:",tokenizer.unk_
token_id)
print()
```

Listing 6.1 starts with two `import` statements and then initializes the variable `tokenizer` as an instance from a pre-trained model. Next, the variable `nlp` is initialized as an instance of a pre-trained model.

The next portion of Listing 6.1 initializes the variable `text1` as a two-word string, followed by the variable `input-ids1` that consists of the tokens for the two words, along with two special tokens.

The final code block consists of a set of `print()` statements that display several special tokens and their `token_id` values. Launch the code in Listing 6.1, and you will see the following output:

```
creating tokenizer...
creating model...
input_ids1:
[[ 101 3526 3042   102]]

tokenizer.sep_token:     [SEP]
tokenizer.sep_token_id: 102
tokenizer.cls_token:     [CLS]
tokenizer.cls_token_id: 101
tokenizer.pad_token:     [PAD]
tokenizer.pad_token_id: 0
tokenizer.unk_token:     [UNK]
tokenizer.unk_token_id: 100
```

BERT-BASED TOKENIZERS

Although BERT-based models have considerable similarity, there are differences among their tokenizers. The following subsections identify the differences for the BERT tokenizer and the DistilBERT tokenizer.

The BERT Tokenizer

Listing 6.2 displays the content of `bert_tokenizer.py` that shows you how BERT tokenizes an English sentence.

Listing 6.2: bert_tokenizer.py

```
from transformers import BertTokenizer


tokenizer = BertTokenizer.from_pretrained
('bert-base-uncased')
sentence = "I love Chicago pizza"
encoding = tokenizer.encode(sentence)


print("=> sentence:",sentence)
print("=> encoding:",encoding)
print("=> tokens: ",tokenizer.convert_ids_to_tokens
(encoding))
print()


sentence = 'My favorite word is syzygy'
encoding = tokenizer.encode(sentence)


print("=> sentence:",sentence)
print("=> encoding:",encoding)
print("=> tokens: ",tokenizer.convert_ids_to_tokens
(encoding))
```

Listing 6.2 starts with an `import` statement and then initializes the variable `tokenizer` as an instance from a pre-trained model. Next, the variable `sentence` is initialized as a text string (sentence), and the variable encoding is initialized with the result of invoking the `encode()` method of the tokenizer. The values of all three variables are then displayed.

The next portion of Listing 6.2 initializes `sentence` as another text string, and encoding is reinitialized by invoking the `encode()` method a second time. Once again, the values of the three variables are displayed. Launch the code in Listing 6.2, and you will see the following output:

```
=> sentence: I love Chicago pizza
=> encoding: [101, 1045, 2293, 3190, 10733, 102]
```

```
=> tokens:    ['[CLS]', 'i', 'love', 'chicago',
'pizza', '[SEP]']


=> sentence: My favorite word is syzygy
=> encoding: [101, 2026, 5440, 2773, 2003, 25353,
9096, 6292, 102]
=> tokens:    ['[CLS]', 'my', 'favorite', 'word',
'is', 'sy', '##zy', '##gy', '[SEP]']
```

The DistilBERT Tokenizer

Every variant of BERT has a specific input type and can use different parameters. For example, DistilBERT *does* use the same special tokens as BERT, but DistilBERT does *not* use token_type_ids.

Listing 6.3 displays the content of distilbert_tokenizer.py that shows you that DistilBERT tokenizes an English sentence in the same manner as BERT.

Listing 6.3: distilbert_tokenizer.py

```
from transformers import DistilBertTokenizer

tokenizer = DistilBertTokenizer.from_pretrained
('distilbert-base-uncased')
sentence = "I love Chicago pizza"
encoding = tokenizer.encode(sentence)

print("=> sentence:",sentence)
print("=> encoding:",encoding)
print("=> tokens: ",tokenizer.convert_ids_to_tokens
(encoding))
print()


sentence = 'My favorite word is syzygy'
encoding = tokenizer.encode(sentence)

print("=> sentence:",sentence)
print("=> encoding:",encoding)
print("=> tokens: ",tokenizer.convert_ids_to_tokens
(encoding))
```

Listing 6.3 differs from Listing 6.2 in the first two lines, which replace `BERT` with `DistilBERT` and `bert-base-uncased` is replaced with `distilbert-base-uncased`. Launch the code in Listing 6.3, and you will see the following output, which is identical to the output for Listing 6.2:

```
=> sentence: I love Chicago pizza
=> encoding: [101, 1045, 2293, 3190, 10733, 102]
=> tokens:   ['[CLS]', 'i', 'love', 'chicago',
'pizza', '[SEP]']

=> sentence: My favorite word is syzygy
=> encoding: [101, 2026, 5440, 2773, 2003, 25353,
9096, 6292, 102]
=> tokens:   ['[CLS]', 'my', 'favorite', 'word',
'is', 'sy', '##zy', '##gy', '[SEP]']
```

SENTIMENT ANALYSIS WITH DISTILBERT

In Chapter 2, you learned how to work with tokenizers and the DistilBERT model. In this section, you will see how to perform text classification with DistilBERT.

The `pipeline` class in the code sample "abstracts away" many of the details, making it easier to run inference, but less flexible than manually setting up the model and tokenizer. If you are looking to fine tune the model on custom data, you will need a more detailed setup than what `pipeline` provides. In addition, the code sample uses the default sentiment analysis configuration of DistilBERT. If you have a custom-trained model, replace `distilbert-base-uncased` with the path to your model.

Listing 6.4 displays the content of `distilbert_sentiment_anal-ysis.py` that shows you how to perform sentiment analysis.

Listing 6.4: distilbert_sentiment_analysis.py

```
from transformers import
pipeline, DistilBertTokenizer,
DistilBertForSequenceClassification

# Load DistilBERT tokenizer and model
tokenizer = DistilBertTokenizer.from_pretrained
('distilbert-base-uncased')
```

```
model = DistilBertForSequenceClassification.from_
pretrained('distilbert-base-uncased')

# Create the sentiment analysis pipeline
classifier = pipeline('sentiment-analysis',
model=model, tokenizer=tokenizer)

# Test the classifier
sentences = ["This is an amazing product!",
"I don't really like this movie."]
predictions = classifier(sentences)

for text, prediction in zip(sentences,
predictions):
   label = prediction['label']
   score = prediction['score']
   print(f"'{text}' is classified as {label} with
a score of {score:.4f}")
```

Listing 6.4 starts with an `import` statement and then initializes the variable `tokenizer` and the variable `model` from the second and third imported classes. Next, the variable `classifier` is initialized by invoking `pipeline()` and specifying the `sentiment_analysis` task, as well as referencing the previously defined `model` and `tokenizer`.

The next portion of Listing 6.4 defines the variable sentences as a list of strings (short sentences), and then initializes the variable predictions with the result of invoking the classifier with the variable sentences.

The final portion of Listing 6.4 contains a loop that iterates through the sentences and their corresponding predictions. During each iteration, the variables `label` and `score` are initialized and then printed. Launch the code in Listing 6.13, and you will see the following output:

```
'This is an amazing product!' is classified as
LABEL_0 with a score of 0.5325
'I don't really like this movie.' is classified as
LABEL_0 with a score of 0.5307
```

The interesting aspect of the preceding output is the value LABEL_0 for the label, which suggests that DistilBERT is displaying an internal variable. In fact, DistilBERT reports very similar scores for other sentences that are clearly highly positive or highly negative.

However, DistilBERT is primarily a pre-trained language representation model that is trained to predict masked tokens in a sentence, and out-of-the-box DistilBERT is not specifically fine-tuned for sentiment analysis. It is more of a general-purpose representation that captures the semantics of the English language (or other languages, depending on the specific model variant). For specific tasks like sentiment analysis, you would typically take the pre-trained DistilBERT model and fine tune it on a sentiment analysis dataset.

BERT ENCODING: SEQUENCE OF STEPS

BERT performs the following sequence of steps, all of which have been illustrate via code snippets in previous sections:

Step 1: Tokenize the text.

Step 2: Map the tokens to their IDs.

Step 3: Add the special [CLS] and [SEP] tokens.

As a simple example, the sentence "I got a book" has a total of six tokens (four word tokens, and the start and end tokens), along with the following indices:

[CLS]	**101**
i	1,045
got	2,288
a	1,037
book	2,338
[SEP]	**101**

Listing 6.5 displays the content of `bert_encoding_plus.py` that illustrates how to display the special tokens in BERT.

Listing 6.5: bert_encoding_plus.py

```
import transformers
import numpy as np
# instantiate a BERT tokenizer and model:
print("creating tokenizer...")
tokenizer = transformers.BertTokenizer.from_
pretrained('bert-base-uncased', do_lower_case=True)
print("creating model...")
nlp = transformers.TFBertModel.from_pretrained
('bert-base-uncased')
```

```
text="When were you last outside? I have been
inside for 2 weeks."
encoding = tokenizer.encode_plus(
    text,
    max_length=32,
    add_special_tokens=True, # Add '[CLS]' and
'[SEP]'
    return_token_type_ids=False,
    pad_to_max_length=True,
    return_attention_mask=True,
    return_tensors='pt',  # Return PyTorch tensors
)

print("encoding.keys():")
print(encoding.keys())
print()

print("len(encoding['input_ids'][0]):")
print(len(encoding['input_ids'][0]))
print()

print("encoding['input_ids'][0]:")
print(encoding['input_ids'])
print()

print("len(encoding['attention_mask'][0]):")
print(len(encoding['attention_mask'][0]))
print()

print("encoding['attention_mask']:")
print(encoding['attention_mask'])
print()

print("tokenizer.convert_ids_to_tokens
(encoding['input_ids'][0]):")
print(tokenizer.convert_ids_to_tokens
(encoding['input_ids'][0]))
print()
```

Listing 6.5 starts with two `import` statements and then initializes the variables tokenizer and `nlp` in the same fashion as previous code samples. Next, the variable `text` is initialized as a text string, followed by the variable `encoding` that acts as a configuration-like "holder" of parameters and their values.

The final portion of Listing 6.5 consists of six pairs of `print()` statements, each of which displays a parameter/value pair that is defined in the `encoding` variable. Launch the code in Listing 6.5, and you will see the following output:

```
creating tokenizer...
creating model...

encoding.keys():
dict_keys(['input_ids', 'attention_mask'])

len(encoding['input_ids'][0]):
32

encoding['input_ids'][0]:
tensor([[ 101, 2043, 2020, 2017, 2197, 2648,
1029, 1045, 2031, 2042, 2503, 2005, 1016, 3134,
1012,  102,    0,    0,    0,    0,    0,    0,
   0,    0,    0,    0,    0,    0,    0,    0,
   0,    0]])

len(encoding['attention_mask'][0]):
32

encoding['attention_mask']:
tensor([[1, 1, 1, 1, 1, 1, 1, 1, 1, 1, 1, 1, 1, 1,
1, 1, 0, 0, 0, 0, 0, 0, 0, 0, 0, 0, 0, 0, 0, 0, 0,
0]])

tokenizer.convert_ids_to_tokens(encoding['input_
ids'][0]):
['[CLS]', 'when', 'were', 'you', 'last', 'outside',
'?', 'i', 'have', 'been', 'inside', 'for', '2',
'weeks', '.', '[SEP]', '[PAD]', '[PAD]', '[PAD]',
'[PAD]', '[PAD]', '[PAD]', '[PAD]', '[PAD]',
```

```
'[PAD]', '[PAD]', '[PAD]', '[PAD]', '[PAD]',
'[PAD]', '[PAD]', '[PAD]']
```

SENTENCE SIMILARITY IN BERT

Word2vec and GloVe use word embeddings to find the semantic similarity between two words. However, sentences contain additional information as well as relationships between multiple words. A well-known example that clearly shows the need for contextual awareness is illustrated in the following pair of sentences:

- The dog did not cross the street because it was too narrow.
- The dog did not cross the street because it was too tired.

One technique for sentence similarity involves computing the average of the word embeddings of the words in each sentence and then computing the cosine similarity of the resulting pair of word embeddings. This method is simple and computationally efficient, but it may not always capture the nuances of sentence semantics as effectively as more sophisticated methods, because it does not take into account the order of the words and the relationships between them. It essentially treats the sentence as a "bag of words." However, despite its simplicity, it can still provide reasonably good results in many cases, especially when used with high-quality word embeddings.

Keep in mind that while many word embedding techniques, including Word2Vec and GloVe, are trained in an unsupervised manner using large corpora, it is not inherently necessary for all word embedding techniques to be unsupervised. There are supervised and semi-supervised word embedding techniques as well.

Word Context in BERT

Listing 6.6 displays the content of `bert_context.py` that illustrates how BERT generates a different word vector for the same word that is used in a different context.

To launch the code in Listing 6.6, make sure that you have installed the `transformers` library by typing the following command in a command shell:

```
pip3 install transformers
```

Note: This code downloads a 536 M BERT model.

Listing 6.6: bert_context.py

```
import transformers

text1 = "cell phone"

# instantiate a BERT tokenizer and model:
tokenizer = transformers.BertTokenizer.from_
pretrained('bert-base-uncased', do_lower_case=True)

nlp = transformers.TFBertModel.from_pretrained
('bert-base-uncased')

# hidden layer with embeddings:
input_ids1 = np.array(tokenizer.encode(text1))
[None,:]
embedding1 = nlp(input_ids1)

# display text1 and its context:
print("text1:",text1)
print("embedding1[0][0]:")
print(embedding1[0][0])
print()

text2 = "cell mate"
# hidden layer with embeddings:
input_ids2 = np.array(tokenizer.encode(text2))
[None,:]
embedding2 = nlp(input_ids2)

# display text2 and its context:
print("text2:",text2)
print("embedding2[0][0]:")
print(embedding2[0][0])
```

Listing 6.6 starts with `import` statements and then initializes the variables `tokenizer`, `nlp`, `input_ids1`, and `embedding1` in exactly the same manner that you have seen in previous code samples. The next block of code displays the values of `text1` and `embedding1[0][0]`.

The next portion of Listing 6.6 is virtually the same as the previous code block, based on the replacement of `text1` with `text2`. The output of Listing 6.6 is here:

```
text1: cell phone
embedding1[0][0]:
tf.Tensor(
[[-0.30501425  0.14509355 -0.18064171 ...
-0.3127299  -0.12173399
  -0.09033043]
 [ 0.80547976 -0.15233847  0.61319923 ...
-0.7498784   0.00167803
  -0.11698578]
 [ 1.0339862  -0.66511637 -0.17642722 ...
-0.24407595  0.03978422
  -0.8694502 ]
 [ 0.87851435  0.10932285 -0.27658027 ...
0.18180653 -0.5829581
  -0.34113947]], shape=(4, 768), dtype=float32)


text2: cell mate
embedding2[0][0]:
tf.Tensor(
[[-0.24141303  0.1146469  -0.13710016 ...
-0.2908613  -0.04577148
   0.2965925 ]
 [ 0.05608664 -1.0035615   0.12738925 ...
-0.30271983  0.17530476
   0.7245784 ]
 [ 0.2818157  -0.28047347 -0.6547173  ...
0.04996978  0.01698243
   0.03285426]
 [ 1.039136    0.12364347 -0.2661501  ...
0.09439699 -0.7794917
  -0.24966209]], shape=(4, 768), dtype=float32)
```

Listing 6.6 also generates the following informative message:

```
Some weights of the model checkpoint at bert-
base-uncased were not used when initializing
TFBertModel: ['nsp___cls', 'mlm___cls']
```

```
- This IS expected if you are initializing
TFBertModel from the checkpoint of a model trained
on another task or with another architecture
(e.g. initializing a BertForSequenceClassification
model from a BertForPretraining model).
- This IS NOT expected if you are initializing
TFBertModel from the checkpoint of a model that
you expect to be exactly identical (initializing
a BertForSequenceClassification model from a
BertForSequenceClassification model).
All the weights of TFBertModel were initialized
from the model checkpoint at bert-base-uncased.
If your task is similar to the task the model of
the ckeckpoint was trained on, you can already
use TFBertModel for predictions without further
training.
```

What is Sentence-BERT?

Sentence-BERT is a pre-trained LLM that is based on the BERT LLM, which performs sentence BERT-Networks that modify BERT and RoBERTa architectures. Then, output is a fixed size sentence embedding that is generated with the following techniques:

1. Add a pooling operation to the output of the transformers.

2. Compute the mean of all output vectors.

3. Compute a max-over-time of the output vectors.

There are several pre-trained Sentence-BERT models available that are downloadable:

https://public.ukp.informatik.tu-darmstadt.de/reimers/sentence-transformers/v0.2/

Now that you have seen an example where BERT generates a different word vector for a word that is used in a different context, let's look at BERT tokens, which is the topic of the next section.

GENERATING BERT TOKENS (1)

Listing 6.7 displays the content of `bert_tokens1.py` that illustrates how to convert a text string to a BERT-compatible string and then tokenize the latter string into BERT tokens.

Listing 6.7: bert_tokens1.py

```
from transformers import BertTokenizer, BertModel

tokenizer = BertTokenizer.from_pretrained
('bert-base-uncased')

text1 = "Pizza with four toppings and trimmings."
marked_text1 = "[CLS] " + text1 + " [SEP]"
tokenized_text1 = tokenizer.tokenize(marked_text1)

print("input sentence #1:")
print(text1)
print()

print("Tokens from input sentence #1:")
print(tokenized_text1)
print()

print("Some tokens in BERT:")
print(list(tokenizer.vocab.keys())[1000:1020])
print()
```

Listing 6.7 imports `BertTokenizer` and `BertModel`, and uses the former to initialize the variable `tokenizer`. Next, the variable `text1` is initialized to a text string, and `marked_text1` prepends `[CLS]` to `text1` and then appends `[SEP]` to `text1`. The last variable that is initialized is `tokenized_text1`, which is assigned the result of invoking the `tokenizer()` method on the variable `marked_text1`.

The next three blocks of `print()` statements display the contents of `text1`, `tokenized_text1`, and a range of 20 BERT tokens, respectively. Launch the code in Listing 6.7, and you will see the following output:

```
input sentence #1:
Pizza with four toppings and trimmings.

Tokens from input sentence #1:
['[CLS]', 'pizza', 'with', 'four', 'topping',
'##s', 'and', 'trim', '##ming', '##s', '.',
'[SEP]']
```

Some tokens in BERT:
```
['"', '#', '$', '%', '&', "'", '(', ')', '*', '+',
',', '-', '.', '/', '0', '1', '2', '3', '4', '5']
```

GENERATING BERT TOKENS (2)

Listing 6.8 displays the content of `bert_tokens2.py` that illustrates how to convert a text string to a BERT-compatible string and then tokenize the latter string into BERT tokens.

Listing 6.8: bert_tokens2.py

```
from transformers import BertTokenizer, BertModel

tokenizer = BertTokenizer.from_pretrained
('bert-base-uncased')

text2 = "I got a book and after I book for an hour,
it's time to book it."
marked_text2 = "[CLS] " + text2 + " [SEP]"
tokenized_text2 = tokenizer.tokenize(marked_text2)

print("input sentence #2:")
print(text2)
print()

print("Tokens from input sentence #2:")
print(tokenized_text2)
print()

# Map token strings to their vocabulary indices:
indexed_tokens2 = tokenizer.convert_tokens_to_ids
(tokenized_text2)

# Display the words with their indices:
for pair in zip(tokenized_text2, indexed_tokens2):
    print('{:<12} {:>6,}'.format(pair[0], pair))
```

The first half of Listing 6.8 is almost identical to the first half of Listing 6.2, using the variable `text2` instead of `text1`.

The next portion of Listing 6.8 contains two blocks of `print()` statements that display the contents of `text2` and `tokenized_text2`, respectively. The next code snippet initializes the variable `indexed_ tokens2` to the result of converting the tokens in `tokenized_text2` to `id` values.

The final portion of Listing 6.8 contains a loop that displays tokens and their associated `id` values. The output of Listing 6.8 is here:

```
input sentence #2:
I got a book and after I book for an hour, it's
time to book it.


Tokens from input sentence #2:
['[CLS]', 'i', 'got', 'a', 'book', 'and', 'after',
'i', 'book', 'for', 'an', 'hour', ',', 'it', "'",
's', 'time', 'to', 'book', 'it', '.', '[SEP]']


[CLS]              101
i                1,045
got              2,288
a                1,037
book             2,338
and              1,998
after            2,044
i                1,045
book             2,338
for              2,005
an               2,019
hour             3,178
,                1,010
it               2,009
'                1,005
s                1,055
time             2,051
to               2,000
book             2,338
it               2,009
.                1,012
[SEP]              102
```

THE BERT FAMILY

BERT (from Google) has spawned a remarkable set of variations of the original BERT model, each of which provides some interesting features. Some of those variations are listed here:

- ALBERT (Google)
- Bidirectional and Autoregressive Transformers (BART)
- BERT (Google)
- BIO BERT
- Clinical BERT
- DeBERTa (Microsoft)
- DistilBERT (Hugging Face)
- DOC BERT
- KeyBERT
- Google SMITH
- SBERT
- TinyBERT
- VisualBERT
- XLM-R
- XLNET

Some of the models in the preceding list are discussed in the following subsections, and you can perform an online search for more information regarding the models that are not discussed in this chapter. In addition, RoBERTa is discussed in a subsequent section.

ALBERT

ALBERT (from Google Research and Toyota Technological Institute) is an acronym for A Lite BERT for Self-Supervised Learning of Language Representations. ALBERT and RoBERTa are significantly smaller than BERT, and far more capable than BERT.

The primary motivation for ALBERT is to outperform BERT's accuracy on the benchmarks. This typically means increasing the size of the model and making modifications to the training process to scale well: that is, to allow the model to increase in accuracy without over-fitting.

Recall that BERT word embeddings are 1x768 vectors of floating point numbers. By contrast, the initial word embeddings in ALBERT only have 128 features (1x128 vectors). Interestingly, ALBERT also contains a matrix that scales the 1x128 word embeddings to 1x768 word embeddings. Moreover, ALBERT has 12 layers and a hidden size of 4,096, which is half the depth and four times the width of BERT-Large.

According to the Github repository for ALBERT (*https://github.com/google-research/ALBERT*),

> "ALBERT uses parameter-reduction techniques that allow for large-scale configurations, overcome previous memory limitations, and achieve better behavior with respect to model degradation."

Specifically, ALBERT (unlike BERT) shares its parameters in *all* layers, which reduces the number of parameters, but has no effect on the training and inference time. In addition, ALBERT uses embedding matrix factorization, which further reduces the number of parameters.

There are several details to keep in mind regarding the parameter sharing technique adopted by ALBERT. First, although parameter sharing *does* reduce the number of unique parameters, the *execution time* during the training step or the inference (prediction) step is still comparable to BERT. Second, although parameter sharing results in lower accuracy, the accuracy is actually still quite good. Third, parameter reduction allows for greater scalability in terms of depth (i.e., the number of subcomponents in the encoder component) and the width of the embeddings.

Another distinction regarding ALBERT is its use of SOP, which is an improvement over the NSP that is used in BERT. Finally, ALBERT does not use a dropout rate, which further increases the model capacity.

ALBERT uses both whole-word masking and "n-gram masking," where the latter refers to masking multiple sequential words. Here is a code snippet for ALBERT:

```
from transformers import AlbertForMaskedLM,
AlbertTokenizer

model1 = AlbertForMaskedLM.from_pretrained
('albert-xxlarge-v1')
tokenizer = AlbertTokenizer.from_pretrained
('albert-xxlarge-v1')

model2 = AlbertForMaskedLM.from_pretrained
('albert-xxlarge-v2')
tokenizer = AlbertTokenizer.from_pretrained
('albert-xxlarge-v2')
```

ALBERT achieves higher benchmark scores than BERT, XLNet, and RoBERTa, but *only* for its largest size ALBERT-xxlarge, whereas

ALBERT-Base generally has comparable performance with BERT-Base. As an interesting aside, here are the dates when ALBERT, XLNet, and RoBERTa were released in 2019:

- ALBERT: 09/26/2019 (Google)
- XLNet: 06/19/2019 (Google + CMU)
- RoBERTa: 07/26/2019 (U of W + Facebook)

BART

BART is a model that has three main components: encoder (12 layers), decoder (12 layers), and `lm_head` (a Linear Layer). BART is well-suited for the task of text generation: it can reconstruct text containing `[MASK]` tokens, so it is similar to an autoencoder. Moreover, its performance is similar to RoBERTa.

You can also access sections of the BART model by making programmatic invocations such as `model.model.encoder`, `model.model.decoder`, and `model.lm_head`. However, Hugging Face has built-in functions to access the encoder and decoder with additional flexibility.

By way of comparison, BART can also outperform GPT-2. BART can be used for abstractive text summarization, which is a task that is more difficult than extractive summarization. In fact, at one point in time BART was the SOTA model for text summarization. If you are unfamiliar with text summarization, it is described in more detail at

https://pub.towardsai.net/a-full-introduction-on-text-summarization-using-deep-learning-with-sample-code-ft-huggingface-d21e0336f50c

BioBERT

BioBERT is a BERT-based model that was pre-trained on biomedical data, which can be fine-tuned on various biomedical-specific tasks, such as NER and question answering (among others). Two well-known datasets for pre-training BioBERT are PubMed and PubMed Central that contain an extensive set of citations and biomedical articles, respectively. BioBERT can be fine-tuned to perform biomedical-specific tasks, such as NER (which is also the case for ClinicalBERT). You can download BioBERT here: *https://github.com/naver/biobert-pre-trained*.

ClinicalBERT

ClinicalBERT is a BERT-based model that was pre-trained on a clinical corpus that contains detailed information regarding patients. For example, the model contains information regarding patient symptoms, patient diagnosis, activities, and treatments. Since clinical documents contain nomenclature ("jargon") that is industry-specific. ClinicalBERT was pre-trained on a set of clinical documents called MIMIC-III. Furthermore, ClinicalBERT can be fine-tuned on a variety of tasks, such as prediction-related tasks.

deBERTa (Surpassing Human Accuracy)

The deBERTa model from Microsoft actually surpassed human accuracy:

https://www.microsoft.com/en-us/research/blog/microsoft-deberta-surpasses-human-performance-on-the-superglue-benchmark/

The architecture for this model comprises 48 transformer layers with 1.5 billion parameters. This model has a GLUE score of 90.8, and a SuperGLUE score of 89.9, which manages to exceed the human performance score of 89.8. If need be, you can perform an online search for details regarding GLUE and SuperGLUE.

Microsoft also announced its intent to integrate DeBERTa with the Turing natural language representation model Turing NLRv4 (also from Microsoft). The Turing models are ubiquitous in the Microsoft ecosystem, including products such as Bing and Azure Cognitive Services.

DistilBERT

DistilBERT is a smaller variant of BERT that contains 66 million parameters, which is 40% of the number of parameters of BERT-Base (which has 110 million parameters). DistilBERT uses a technique known as *distillation* (i.e., training a smaller model to approximate a larger model) to approximate BERT. Even so, DistilBERT achieves over 95% of BERT accuracy and is 60% faster than BERT-Base, which makes DistilBERT useful for transfer learning. Recent advances from Neural Magic that use sparse-based techniques have made BERT-large faster than DistilBERT with no reduction in accuracy. Details regarding Neural Magic and the sparse-based technique are accessible online:

https://neuralmagic.com/

https://arxiv.org/abs/2111.05754

Knowledge distillation involves a small model (called the "student") that is trained to mimic a larger model or an ensemble of models (called the "teacher"). DistilBERT is an example of a distilled network: it contains half the number of layers of BERT. In addition, DistilBERT initializes the student's layers from the teacher's layers as described here:

https://towardsdatascience.com/distillation-of-bert-like-models-the-theory-32e19a02641f

As an illustration, here is an example of instantiating a DistilBERT tokenizer:

```
import transformers
tokenizer = transformers.AutoTokenizer.from_
pretrained('distilbert-base-uncased',
do_lower_case=True)
```

Here is another technique for instantiating a DistilBERT tokenizer:

```
from transformers import DistilBertTokenizer:
tokenizer = DistilBertTokenizer.from.
pretrained('distilbert-base-uncased')
```

Google SMITH

The SMITH model from Google is a model for analyzing documents. In a very simplified description, the SMITH model is trained to understand passages within the context of the entire document. By contrast, BERT is trained to understand words within the context of sentences. However, the SMITH model (which outperforms BERT) supplements BERT by performing major operations that are not possible in BERT.

TinyBERT

TinyBERT is based on distillation, and utilizes a new two-stage learning framework that performs transformer distillation during pre-training as well as the task-specific learning stages. As a result, TinyBERT captures the general-domain and the task-specific knowledge in BERT. Here are some details regarding TinyBERT:

- contains only 4 layers
- performance is greater than 96% of BERT-Base
- 7.5x smaller than BERT-Base
- 9.4x faster than BERT-Base on inference

More details regarding TinyBERT are at *https://paperswithcode.com/paper/190910351*.

VideoBERT

VideoBERT is a BERT-based model for processing videos, which involves generating language tokens and visual tokens. Language tokens can be extracted via ASR (automatic speech recognition), and visual tokens can be created by first sampling image frames of a video and then converting those frames into visual tokens.

Next, the language tokens and visual tokens are combined into sentences with BERT-specific special tokens such as `[CLS]`, `[MASK]`, and `[SEP]`, after which MLM is performed. However, instead of NSP (next sentence prediction), VideoBERT performs an alignment check, which determines whether a given text string and the adjacent video make meaningful sense.

VisualBERT

VisualBERT is an interesting BERT-based model that combines images and text. This model uses attention to detect "alignment" between image regions and text. This model is discussed at *https://arxiv.org/ abs/1908.03557v1.*

There are several community-based implementations of Visual BERT, and the one with the highest number of Github stars is at *https:// github.com/uclanlp/visualbert.*

XLNET

XLNet is an autoregressive pre-trained model that outperforms BERT on numerous tasks. XLNet uses *permutative language modeling* (PLM) to overcome the limitations of the MLM task that is performed by BERT. Unlike BERT, XLNet does not have any input constraints. XLNet also contains an attention mask that enables XLNet to understand word order, as well as two-stream self-attention that is explained online:

h t t p s : / / t o w a r d s d a t a s c i e n c e . c o m / what-is-two-stream-self-attention-in-xlnet-ebfe013a0cf3

In high-level terms, given an input sequence S consisting of N tokens, XLNet calculates the probability that the ith token in S occurs in the first i tokens of S, which is denoted by P(xi|x<i). This probability is performed for *all* possible permutations of the tokens in the sequence S. Recall that there are N! possible permutations of a sequence of N tokens (see the disadvantages section below).

Note: For any given sentence with N tokens, XLNet processes the N! sentences that are permutations of the given sentence.

Disadvantages of XLNet

The first disadvantage of XLNet is due to its computational complexity, which requires longer training time in comparison to BERT.

Second, XLNet can underperform on smaller/shorter input sentences. The pre-training step of XLNet focuses on long input sequences and permutative language modeling is designed to capture long-term dependencies.

Third, while XLNet does leverage positional information, it's performed in a different manner compared to traditional approaches. In the PLM approach, the model learns to predict tokens in various orders, not just the original order in the sentence, which can potentially lead to a kind of "discrepancy" in how positional information is used. However, it still uses positional encodings to retain some sense of positional information, and it is designed to learn bidirectional context, which can help it understand the relationships between different positions in a sequence.

How to Select a BERT-Based Model

There are various criteria that you need to consider when deciding which model to use in your environment, some of which are listed here:

- hardware availability and cost
- train "from scratch" versus fine-tuning
- the type of downstream tasks
- availability of public models

BERT is a good choice if you do not have high priority requirements. However, if you need faster inference speed, and you can also sacrifice some accuracy on prediction metrics, then consider DistilBERT as a starting point. By contrast, if you need the best prediction metrics, then RoBERTA (from Facebook) would be a better choice. Yet another option is XLNet, which can provide better longer-run results.

WORKING WITH ROBERTA

RoBERTa (from Facebook) is an acronym for A Robustly Optimized BERT Pre-training Approach. The architects of RoBERTa made the following improvements to BERT to create RoBERTa:

- discarded NSP (Next Sentence Prediction)
- uses the GPT-2 "variant" of BPE (not the original BPE)
- performed dynamic masking instead of static masking

- performed training on longer sequences.
- used 160 GB of training data instead of 16 GB (BERT)
- text samples use complete sentences (not spans of text)
- applying a mask to randomly selected sets of tokens during each iteration
- a different tokenization scheme

RoBERTa leverages BERT's language masking strategy, along with some modifications to some of BERT's hyper parameters. Note that RoBERTa was trained on a corpus that is at least 10 times larger than the corpus for BERT.

Unlike BERT, RoBERTa does *not* perform an NSP task, which actually improves the training procedure. Instead, RoBERTa uses a technique called *dynamic masking*, whereby different tokens are masked in different training iterations during the training process. As a result, RoBERTa outperforms both BERT and XLNet on GLUE benchmark results.

ITALIAN AND JAPANESE LANGUAGE TRANSLATION

This section contains a code sample that translates an English sentence into Italian and Japanese.

Listing 6.9 displays the content of `bert_translate.py` that illustrates how to translate a text string from English into Italian.

Listing 6.9: bert_translate.py

```
from transformers import AutoTokenizer,
AutoModelForSeq2SeqLM

# English to Italian:
tokenizer = AutoTokenizer.from_pretrained
("Helsinki-NLP/opus-mt-en-it")
model = AutoModelForSeq2SeqLM.from_
pretrained("Helsinki-NLP/opus-mt-en-it")
text = "I love deep dish pizza!"
tokenized_text = tokenizer.prepare_seq2seq_batch
([text], return_tensors='pt')

# Perform translation and decode the output
translation = model.generate(**tokenized_text)
```

```
translated_text = tokenizer.batch_decode
(translation, skip_special_tokens=True) [0]

# Print translation from English to Italian:
print("Initial English text:", text)
print("Italian translation: ", translated_text)

# English to Japanese:
tokenizer = AutoTokenizer.from_pretrained
("Helsinki-NLP/opus-mt-en-jap")
model = AutoModelForSeq2SeqLM.from_pretrained
("Helsinki-NLP/opus-mt-en-jap")
text = "I love deep dish pizza!"
tokenized_text = tokenizer.prepare_seq2seq_batch
([text], return_tensors='pt')

# Perform translation and decode the output
translation = model.generate(**tokenized_text)
translated_text = tokenizer.batch_decode
(translation, skip_special_tokens=True) [0]

# Print translation from English to Japanese:
print("Japanese translation:", translated_text)
```

Listing 6.9 starts with an import statement and then initializes the variables tokenizer and model to instances of a tokenizer and model, respectively. Next, the variable text is initialized as a test string and the variable tokenized_text is initialized with the result of tokenizing the contents of the variable text.

The next portion of Listing 6.9 performs the translation into Italian, after which the translated text is displayed. Another block of text performs a similar operation whereby the initial English text is translated into Japanese, and then the result is displayed. Launch the code in Listing 6.9, and you will see the following output:

```
Initial English text: I love deep dish pizza!
Italian translation:  Adoro la pizza dei piatti
profondi!
Japanese translation: わたし は 深 い 偽り の 板 を いだ き,
```

Now that you have seen an example of translating text between a pair of languages, let's look at LLMs that provide multilingual support, which is the topic of the next section.

MULTILINGUAL LANGUAGE MODELS

Multilingual support in LLMs has become increasingly important, which can sometimes involve additional challenges. For example, English has a vast set of available tokens, whereas there are multiple languages that have a low data availability. How can we train a language model with a limited number of tokens? Several techniques are discussed in the next section.

Training Multilingual Language Models

One technique for training multilingual LLMs involves a concept called *cross-lingual transfer*:

> *https://medium.com/dailymotion/how-we-used-cross-lingual-transfer-learning-to-categorize-our-content-c8e0f9c1c6c3*

Multilingual models involve pre-training, followed by XLM-R and then cross-lingual transfer. The following Github repository shows how to use cross-lingual transfer from English to Portuguese: *https://github.com/lersouza/cross-lingual-transfer*.

Models whose parameters have been trained on various languages can learn cross-lingual representations of text. The interesting consequence is that such representations enable multilingual pre-trained models to leverage supervised data from one language in different low-data languages. Another approach involves existing multilingual language models, which is the topic of the next section.

BERT-Based Multilingual Language Models

There are BERT-based models that support multiple languages, some of which are listed here:

- m-BERT
- XLM and XLM-R
- XLSR
- mSLAM
- MUSE
- OSCAR

Perform an online search for more information regarding the LLMs in the previous bullet list.

TRANSLATION FOR 1,000 LANGUAGES

This section contains a high-level description of some of the tasks and interesting techniques (including dataset audits from native speakers) that a team of researchers from Google used to enable language translation for more than 1,000 languages.

Google Translate provides high quality language translation for some language pairs (such as English and French) because they are "high-resource" languages: there is a great detail of training data available for those languages. Some languages are not supported due to limited training data, and data collection can be very difficult for such languages. In some cases, there is no data available on the Web for low-resource languages.

The following includes some terminology for language translation. *Parallel data* refers to the existence of a given sentence in multiple languages, whereas *monolingual data* refers to sentences that are available in a single language. Currently, there are slightly more than 100 parallel languages that are well-served in Google Translate (and other translation systems).

One technique that is useful for monolingual data is called *back translation*, which involves translating a sentence from a source language into a target language, and then translating the sentence in the target language back into the source language. In fact, you might have seen this technique applied to sentences that contain idiomatic expressions, and the comparison between the original sentence and its back translation can be very amusing.

The process of enabling language translation for 1,000 languages involves the following steps:

- Gather monolingual data for 1,000 languages.
- Combine existing parallel data with monolingual data.
- Train a model with the combined data.

Of course, gathering monolingual data is a difficult task, partly due to the presence of noise that is difficult to separate from the valid data. One technique that is used for processing monolingual data is the bag-of-characters (BoC) algorithm, which is a character-based counterpart to the bag-of-words (BoW) algorithm. Character-based n-grams can be effective in these languages because they avoid the need for word segmentation and can capture meaningful patterns at the character level. However, it is worth noting that character-based approaches can sometimes miss higher-level patterns that would be captured by word-based approaches, and they can also result in a very high-dimensional feature space, especially for larger values of n.

Additional tasks are performed during the data collection process, such as sentence deduplication as well as removing sentences that have an insufficient number of high-frequency words for the predicted language.

In addition to the use of a transformer-based model, another point to note is the use of Compact Language Detector 3 (CLD3) models. CLD3 is a neural network model for language identification with support for dozens of languages, and more information can be found at *https://github.com/google/cld3*.

You can also install Python bindings for CLD3 by invoking the following command:

```
pip3 install gcld3
```

More information regarding the translation for 1,000 languages is accessible online (data and models are not available): *https://arxiv.org/abs/2205.03983*.

Contrast the progress between this initiative from Google with the open-sourced NLLB model from Meta that supports 200 languages.

M-BERT

Since BERT is limited to English-only text, we need to use multilingual BERT (a.k.a. M-BERT) to work with text in other languages. M-BERT a multilingual BERT model that can determine the representation of words beyond the English language.

Although BERT and M-BERT are both trained with MLM and NSP tasks, BERT is trained with Wikipedia text and the Toronto Book-Corpus, whereas M-BERT is trained from Wikipedia text from more than languages.

The size of the Wikipedia text for high-resource languages (such as English) is higher than low-resource languages.

M-BERT does not require paired or language-aligned training data. M-BERT was not trained with any cross-lingual objective; it was trained just like how the BERT model was trained. M-BERT produces a representation that generalizes across multiple languages for downstream tasks. The pre-trained open-source M-BERT model is downloadable from *https://github.com/google-research/bert/blob/master/multilingual.md*

Two types of pre-trained M-BERT models are BERT-Base, multilingual cased, and BERT-Base, multilingual uncased.

Listing 6.10 displays the content of `multi_bert.py` that illustrates how to convert a text string to a BERT-compatible string and then tokenize the latter string into BERT tokens.

Listing 6.10: multi_bert.py

```
from transformers import BertTokenizer, BertModel

model = BertModel.from_pretrained
('bert-base-multilingual-cased')
tokenizer = BertTokenizer.from_pretrained
('bert-base-multilingual-cased')

# Japanese sentence:
sentence = "日本語 が できます か"
print("sentence:")
print(sentence)
print()

# get the sentence tokens:
inputs = tokenizer(sentence, return_tensors="pt")
print("inputs:")
print(inputs)
print()

# pass tokens to the model and get the
representation:
hidden_rep, cls_head = model(**inputs)
print("hidden_rep:")
print(hidden_rep)
print()

print("cls_head:")
print(cls_head)
print()
```

Listing 6.10 imports `BertTokenizer` and `BertModel`, and initializes the variable model as an instance of `bert-base-multilingual-cased`, and then initializes the variable `tokenizer`.

The next three blocks of `print()` statements display the contents of `text1`, `tokenized_text1`, and a range of 20 BERT tokens. Launch the code in Listing 6.10, and you will see the BERT tokens.

COMPARING BERT-BASED MODELS

There are many variations of the original BERT model, and models exist that improve the prediction capability or the performance of BERT. ALBERT, RoBERTa, and DistilBERT are among the most popular BERT-based models. ALBERT and RoBERTa both outperform BERT in terms of reduced size and increased speed. By contrast, DistilBERT has decreased size compared to BERT with just a 3% reduction in accuracy.

Several other models achieve SOTA performance, including XLNet, which is an autoregressive language model that extends the Transformer-XL model. XLNet has achieved better prediction than BERT using *permutative language modeling* to achieve SOTA results that are comparable to RoBERTa. This modeling technique achieves 100% accuracy for tokens that are in random order. Recall that BERT predicts the masked tokens that comprise 15% of all the tokens. XLNet was trained with over 130 GB of textual data and 512 TPU chips running for 2.5 days, both of which are much larger than BERT.

Another model is Mobile-BERT that is similar to DistilBERT. Compared to BERT-Base, Mobile-BERT is more than 4 times smaller and more than 5 times faster, but it still has a comparable/similar performance. A third model is BART, which is a pre-trained model whose performance is comparable to RoBERTa on NLU tasks. More information about BART is accessible online:

https://tungmphung.com/a-review-of-pre-trained-language-models-from-bert-roberta-to-electra-deberta-bigbird-and-more/#albert

https://towardsdatascience.com/everything-you-need-to-know-about-albert-roberta-and-distilbert-11a74334b2da

RoBERTa has also achieved significant improvements. Recall that BERT uses NSP, whereas RoBERTa uses a technique called *dynamic masking*, whereby different tokens are masked in different training iterations during the training process. Another difference with RoBERTa involves larger batch sizes during the training phase. The result is impressive: RoBERTa outperforms both BERT and XLNet on many tasks and datasets.

Another approach works "opposite" to other language models: the goal is to reduce the size of transformer-based language models and still achieve significant results. In particular, DistilBERT uses half the number of layers of BERT and eschews token-style embeddings, and yet DistilBERT achieves a performance level that is 95% of BERT's performance. In addition, DistilBERT uses a technique called *distillation*, which is described online:

https://www.kdnuggets.com/2019/09/bert-roberta-distilbert-xlnet-one-use.html

https://www.kdnuggets.com/2019/07/pre-training-transformers-bi-directionality.html

How to Train a BERT Model on Your Laptop

In case you feel motivated and also have available disk space, you can train BERT on your laptop. Navigate to the following link where you will find a Python-based code sample that provides the necessary details:

https://www.kdnuggets.com/2021/08/train-bert-model-scratch.html

If you do not have enough disk space, you will see the following error message (or something similar) when you launch the `Python` code from the preceding link, which indicates that you need almost 95GB of disk space in order to download this LLM:

```
f"Not enough disk space. Needed: {size_str(self.
info.size_in_bytes or 0)} (download: {size_
str(self.info.download_size or 0)}, generated:
{size_str(self.info.dataset_size or 0)}, post-
processed: {size_str(self.info.post_processing_size
or 0)})"
OSError: Not enough disk space. Needed: 94.79 GiB
(download: 26.01 GiB, generated: 68.77 GiB,
post-processed: Unknown size)
```

WEB-BASED TOOLS FOR BERT

There are several very good online tools available for experimenting with BERT-based models, such as exBERT and bertvix, both of which are briefly discussed in the following subsections.

exBERT

This is the formal description of exBERT, according to the description in its home page:

> exBERT is a tool to help humans conduct flexible, interactive investigations and formulate hypotheses for the model-internal reasoning process, supporting analysis for a wide variety of Hugging Face Transformer models. exBERT provides insights into the meaning of the contextual representations and attention by matching a human-specified input to similar contexts in large annotated datasets.

More information is accessible from the exBERT home page:

https://huggingface.co/exbert/?model=bert-base-case

BertViz

BertViz is a tool for visualizing the attention mechanism in transformer-based models, and the Github repository for BertViz is at *https://github.com/jessevig/bertviz*.

Figure 6.1 displays a screenshot of BertViz.

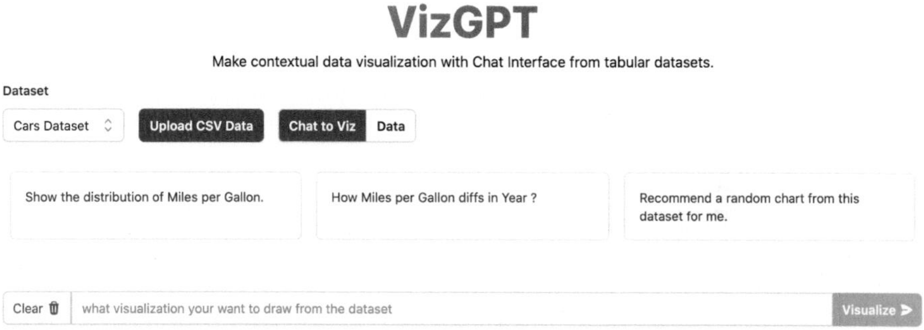

FIGURE 6.1 The Generated Output Tokens in BERT

CNNViz

Although CNNViz is a tool for visualizing convolutional neural networks instead of BERT-related models, it is still quite interesting, especially if you have never such a tool for CNNs. A screen shot of CNNViz is shown in Figure 6.2 and its Github repository is accessible here:

https://github.com/jessevig/bertviz

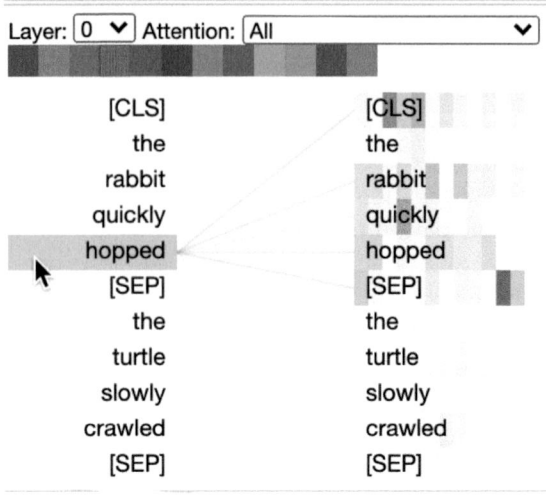

FIGURE 6.2 A screenshot of CNNViz

TOPIC MODELING WITH BERT

Topic modeling involves finding the set of topics in one or more documents. It includes finding the number of topics as well as the length of each topic in documents. Topic modeling has always been important. Before the development of BERT, various machine learning algorithms were used, a few of which are listed here:

- LDA (Latent Dirichlet Allocation)
- LSA (Latent Semantic Analysis)
- NMF (Non-Negative Matrix Factorization)

By way of comparison, clustering algorithms assign each word to a single cluster (i.e., a one-to-one correspondence). However, topic modeling allows for the possibility that a word can belong to multiple topics, which means that there is a one-to-many relationship between a word and topics. Consequently, topic modeling involves calculating a set of probabilities that a word belongs to a set of topics.

Fortunately, the availability of BERT and related models means that we have transformer-based pre-trained language models at our disposal without involving an expensive and time-consuming process of training such models. The next section briefly discusses T5, which is another powerful NLP model created by Google.

WHAT IS T5?

Text-To-Text Transfer Transformer (T5), is an encoder-decoder model that converts all NLP tasks into a text-to-text format, and its download-able code is available online:

https://github.com/google-research/text-to-text-transfer-transformer

You can also install T5 by invoking the following command:

```
pip install t5[gcp]
```

T5 is pre-trained on a multi-task mixture of unsupervised and super-vised tasks, and it works well on tasks such as translation. During 2022, T5 was the most popular download from Hugging Face: more than one million downloads per month.

T5 is trained using a technique called "teacher forcing," which means that an input sequence and a target sequence are always required for training. The input sequence is designated with `input_ids`, whereas the target sequence is designated with `output_ids` and then passed to the decoder.

Since all tasks (such as classification, question-answering, and trans-lation) involve this input/output mechanism, the same model can be used for multiple tasks.

In addition, T5 provides several useful classes when working with T5 models, such as the class `transformers.T5Config`, which enables you to specify configuration information and whose default values are similar to the T5-small architecture. Another useful class is `transformers.T5Tokenizer`, which enables you to construct a T5 tokenizer.

T5 *does* differ from BERT in two significant ways:

- text-to-text framework
- supervised Learning
- encoder-decoder
- the use of a causal decoder
- pre-trained via a denoising autoencoder objective
- input has a text-to-text representation
- unified approach to fine-tunging
- SentencePiece tokenization

Although you can download code samples for T5, initially it might be simpler to experiment with T5 in a Google Colaboratory notebook, which you can find in this article and its associated Github repository:

https://pedrormarques.wordpress.com/2021/10/21/fine-tuning-a-t5-text-classification-model-on-colab

https://github.com/pedro-r-marques/tutorial-t5-fine-tune

In June 2022, Google made all Switch Transformer models in T5X/JAX open source: *https://github.com/google-research/t5x.*

Note that the open-source models include the 1.6 T param Switch-C model and the 395 B parameter Switch-XXL model.

T5X is an improved implementation of the T5 codebase (based on Mesh TensorFlow) in JAX and Flax. T5X is a modular, composable, research-friendly framework for high-performance, configurable, self-service training, evaluation, and inference of sequence models (starting with language) at many scales. More information about T5 and T5X is available online:

https://huggingface.co/transformers/model_doc/t5.html

https://github.com/google-research/t5x#readme

WORKING WITH PALM

PaLM is a 540-billion parameter transformer-based model from Google that can learn language comprehension as well as a plethora of NLP-based tasks, as described here:

https://ai.googleblog.com/2022/04/pathways-language-model-palm-scaling-to.html

PaLM supports additional NLP-based tasks, and can also be trained via numerous hardware accelerators:

https://thesequence.substack.com/p/-new-week-new-ai-super-model

The following link contains more details about PaLM and other developments (such as the H100 chip from Nvidia), as well as information about LLMs (e.g., Chinchilla) that are discussed in this chapter:

https://medium.com/mlearning-ai/breakthroughs-in-language-modelling-in-the-last-month-d3e3c0099272

Moreover, PaLM supports chain-of-thought prompting to perform multi-step tasks. Undoubtedly, PaLM will be supplanted by yet another LLM that has some combination of higher performance, fewer parameters, or lower overall cost. Indeed, the NLP field is changing rapidly.

What is Pathways?

`Pathways` is an architecture from Google that uses a different approach to training machine learning models. With the exception of `GPT-3` and other systems similar to it, current AI models are often trained for a single task. The `Pathways` architecture enables trained models to perform thousands of tasks. In essence, models that are trained with the `Pathways` architecture to perform multiple unrelated tasks will have the capacity to combine those tasks to perform new tasks for which they were never trained. More information about `Pathways` is available online:

https://machine-learning-made-simple.medium.com/google-ai-sparks-a-revolution-in-machine-learning-403f4dbf3e70

https://blog.google/technology/ai/introducing-pathways-next-generation-ai-architecture/

SUMMARY

This chapter started with a Python-based code sample for special BERT tokens. Then you learned about BERT tokenizers and how to perform sentiment analysis with BERT.

Next, you learned about the sequence of steps that are involved in BERT encoding. You also learned about sentence similarity in BERT and how to generate BERT tokens.

Moreover, you learned about the numerous LLMs that belong to the BERT family, such as ALBERT, BART, and DistilBERT. Finally, you learned about Web-based tools for BERT, topic modeling with BERT, and Google PaLM.

## CHAPTER 7

WORKING WITH GPT-3 INTRODUCTION

This chapter discusses GPT-3 from OpenAI, which means that you will learn about features of GPT-2 and GPT-3 and some code samples. The short Python-based code samples currently require Python 3.7, which you can download from the Internet if you have not already done so.

The first part of this chapter describes the three main types of well-known LLMs (large language models): encoder-only, decoder-only, and encoder-decoder models. Next, you will learn some details about the GPT-based family of language models from OpenAI. After a brief description of GPT-2, you will get a high-level introduction to GPT-3, along with the goal of GPT-3, and several models that are based on GPT-3.

The second section provides a description of the capability of GPT-3, a comparison of GPT-3 and BERT, and the strengths and weaknesses of GPT-3.

The third section delves into the GPT-3 Playground, which has been made available to everyone (as of late 2021). You will learn how to create a GPT-3 application and also how to perform inferencing with GPT-3. Moreover, you will learn how to work with prompts in GPT-3.

Before you read the material in this chapter, keep in mind that SOTA is an acronym for State-Of-The-Art. Because of the speed of new development in the NLP world, the SOTA model at any point in time is quickly supplanted by another SOTA model, sometimes in the span of a few weeks.

THE GPT FAMILY: AN INTRODUCTION

Generalized Pre-trained Transformer, GPT, was the first autoregressive model based on the transformer architecture.

OpenAI is responsible for the creation of the GPT-based models. GPT, GPT-2, and GPT-3 were announced in 2018, 2019, and 2020, and have 117 M, 1.5 B, and 175 B parameters, respectively. GPT-4 was released in March/2023, and it appears to have 1.76 trillion parameters (10 times larger than GPT-3).

The initial GPT model was pre-trained on the BookCorpus dataset. The library provides versions of the model for language modeling and multitask language modeling/multiple choice classification.

GPT models have become progressively larger in terms of their architecture and are being trained on larger datasets. For example, GPT, GPT2, and GPT3 have a maximum sequence length of 1 K, 1 K, and 2 K, as well as a word embedding length of 768, 1600, and 12888, respectively.

Recall from Chapter 5 that BERT has an encoder-only architecture, whereas GPT has a decoder-only architecture. Although the transformer architecture was developed to perform machine translation, the transformer-related portion of the GPT models involved an unsupervised pre-training approach.

Interestingly, the primary developer of BERT was influenced by the GPT architecture, even though BERT is based on the encoder component instead of the decoder component of the transformer architecture.

The Architecture of the GPT Family

The strength of GPT models is their ability to process text-based input and generate text-based output. GPT models do not support non-text input, such as audio or video, as they are not multi-modal models. In Chapter 3, you learned about autoregressive models. GPT-based models are also autoregressive models because they are based on the decoder component.

In simplified terms, whenever an input text is submitted to a GPT-based model, it assigns percentages to words that could potentially appear in the response text. The specific percentages are calculated via the decoder itself, which can use various strategies to calculate those percentages. Note that you can specify the maximum number of tokens for GPT to display in the generated output text.

The Main GPT Engines

The GPT APIs provide different language models/engines with different capabilities. The four well-known GPT-3 engines (from largest to smallest) are: Davinci, Curie, Babbage, and Ada. Davinci has the most functionality (which requires more resources), and it is a good choice for experimentation. The Ada engine has the fastest performance, and the other two engines are potential choices for production environments. Each engine has its own set of advantages:

- Davinci is for creative and analytical outputs.
- Curie is for classification, language translation, and summarization.
- Babbage is for semantic search classification.
- Ada is for parsing text and simple classification.

The GPT-3 Davinci engine generates very good output text with respect to word spelling and grammar. By contrast, the Ada engine has a much greater "variance" in the output that it generates, and it can sometimes appear non-sensical.

Second, multiple invocations with the same input (regardless of the selected engine) can cause GPT to generate different outputs. You will see examples of such in the subsections for the GPT-3 Playground later in this chapter.

Third, you will sometimes see a *looping effect* whereby sentence fragments (and even entire sentences) are generated, with each one following its predecessor, almost as if it is "stuttering" in its generated response text.

An Important Update Regarding Models

In early July 2023, OpenAI announced the upcoming deprecation of the models Ada, Babbage, Curie, and Davinci that are discussed in this chapter. The deprecation will occur on January 4, 2023. OpenAI will replace these models with upgraded versions of GPT-3, GPT-3.5 Turbo, and GPT-4. OpenAI recommends adopting those models instead of performing fine-tuning on the models that will be deprecated in early 2024. More information is available at *https://platform.openai.com/docs/guides/fine-tuning*.

In addition, you can perform an upgrade by launching the following command from the command line:

```
pip3 install --upgrade openai
```

What is GPT-2?

GPT-2 is a larger and better version of the original GPT model. GPT-2 was pre-trained on WebText, which consists of Web pages from outgoing links in Reddit with 3 or more "karmas" (i.e., upvote). Note that GPT and GPT-2 were trained on different datasets: the former was mostly trained on BookCorpus, whereas the latter was trained on Web pages, blogs, and news articles linked from Reddit.

GPT-2 is a transformer-based decoder-only LLM that can generate high-quality text. GPT-2 supports up to 2048 tokens, which has been superseded by GPT-3 and GPT-4.

GPT-2 Architecture

GPT-2 provides high-quality output via random sampling. Moreover, GPT-2 achieved long-range coherence with respect to the distance between tokens, which RNNs and LSTMs cannot achieve. In terms of its architecture, the key points involve the following architectural and training-related details:

*   **causal** attention (contrast this with BERT)
*   autoregressive language model
*   single stack of 48 blocks
*   dimensionality of 768 and 12 heads
*   sequence length of 1024
*   position embedding
*   1.5 billion parameters
*   GELU in the FF layer

GPT-2 was not trained on any of the content of Reddit. Instead, it was trained on the content of websites that are linked to (or from) Reddit.

Since GPT-2 involves *causal* attention, this means that the decoder block contains masked self-attention, which in turn means that each token can only "see" preceding tokens in the input string. This constraint is achieved by setting the upper-triangle values of the attention matrix equal to -oo, after which the `softmax()` activation function sets all the values in the upper-left matrix equal to 0.

A group of researchers performed an interesting experiment: they trained a GPT-2 model on text, then "froze" its self-attention and feed-forward layers, and also fine-tuned the model for diverse domains. Their results are described online:

https://read.deeplearning.ai/the-batch/transformers-smarter-than-you-think

GPT-2 and CodeParrot

Listing 7.1 displays the content of `code_parrot1.py`, a GPT-2 based model, that shows you how to create an instance of a tokenizer and a pipeline (both from the `transformers` library) to perform text generation.

Listing 7.1: code_parrot1.py

```
#pip3 install transformers


#Create an instance of a tokenizer and a pipeline
#for text generation using the CodeParrot model:
from transformers import pipeline


# Create a text generation pipeline with the
CodeParrot model:
text_generator = pipeline('text-generation',
model='codeparrot/codeparrot')


# Use the pipeline to generate text
input_text = "Once upon a time"
generated_text = text_generator(input_text,
max_length=50, do_sample=True, temperature=1.0)


# Print the generated text
print(generated_text[0]['generated_text'])
```

Listing 7.1 starts with an import statement and then initializes text_generator as an instance of pipe line(), along with text-generation as the task and codeparrot/codeparrot as the model.

Next, the string variable input_text is initialized, followed by the variable generated_text that is initialized with the result that is returned by invoking text_generator() with input_text (and other variables). The final code snippet prints the generated text.

NOTE: The downloaded model is larger than 6GB, and the output displayed below may be slightly different from what you see when you launch this code sample.

Launch the code in Listing 7.1 with the following command, and you will see how the model is automatically downloaded (subsequent invocations of this code will use the downloaded model):

```
python3.7 code_parrot1.py
```

The output from the preceding Python command is shown here, along with some text that is displayed during the download of the model:

```
python3.7 code_parrot1.py
Downloading: 100%|                                    | 259/259
[00:00<00:00, 59.7kB/s]
Downloading: 100%|                                    | 485k/485k
[00:00<00:00, 1.09MB/s]
Downloading: 100%|                                    | 270k/270k
[00:00<00:00, 761kB/s]
Downloading: 100%|                                    | 821k/821k
[00:00<00:00, 1.33MB/s]
Downloading: 100%|                                    | 90.0/90.0
[00:00<00:00, 59.2kB/s]
/Library/Frameworks/Python.framework/Versions/3.7/
lib/python3.7/site-packages/transformers/models/
auto/modeling_auto.py:787: FutureWarning: The
class `AutoModelWithLMHead` is deprecated and
will be removed in a future version. Please use
`AutoModelForCausalLM` for causal language models,
`AutoModelForMaskedLM` for masked language models
and `AutoModelForSeq2SeqLM` for encoder-decoder
models.
  FutureWarning,
Downloading: 100%|                                    | 927/927
[00:00<00:00, 238kB/s]
Downloading:    8%|                                    | 495M/5.75G
[00:19<02:22, 39.6MB/s]
"""
```

The GPT-2 Tokenizer

Listing 7.2 displays the content of gpt2_tokenizer1.py that shows you how GPT-2 performs tokenization on a text string.

Listing 7.2: gpt2_tokenizer1.py

```
from transformers import GPT2Tokenizer

sentence = "I love Chicago pizza"
tokenizer = GPT2Tokenizer.from_pretrained('gpt2')
tokens1 = tokenizer(sentence)
```

```
print("=> sentence:",sentence)
print("=> tokens1: ",tokens1)
print()

tokens2 = tokens1['input_ids']
print("=> tokens2: ",tokens2)
print()

#Convert the tokens in into strings using
tokenizer.decode:
tokens3 = [tokenizer.decode(x) for x in tokens2]
print("=> tokens3: ",tokens3)

decoded2 = [tokenizer.decode(x).strip().lower() for
x in tokens2]
print("=> decoded2:",decoded2)

tokenizer = GPT2Tokenizer.from_pretrained('gpt2')
tokens4 = tokenizer('My favorite word is syzygy')
tokens4 = tokens4['input_ids']
print("=> tokens4: ",tokens4)

decoded3 = [tokenizer.decode(x).strip().lower() for
x in tokens4]
print("=> decoded3:",decoded3)

# decoded3: ['my', 'favorite', 'word', 'is', 'sy',
'zy', 'gy']
# syzygy is tokenized as 'sy', 'zy', and 'gy'
```

Listing 7.2 starts with an `import` statement, then initializes the variable `sentence` as a text string, and initializes `tokenizer` as an instance of the `GPT2Tokenizer` class.

The next portion of code invokes `tokenizer()` to generate numeric tokens for each word in the variable `sentence`, and also invokes `tokenizer.decode()` to "recover" the original words in `sentence`.

Since `GPT-2` does not recognize the word `syzygy`, `GPT-2` performs subword tokenization to generate the tokens `'sy'`, `'zy'`, and `'gy'`. As a result, 7 tokens are generated for the 4 input words in the variable sentence. Launch the code in Listing 7.2, and you will see the following output:

```
=> sentence: I love Chicago pizza
=> tokens1:  {'input_ids': [40, 1842, 4842, 14256],
'attention_mask': [1, 1, 1, 1]}

=> tokens2:  [40, 1842, 4842, 14256]

=> tokens3:  ['I', ' love', ' Chicago', ' pizza']
=> decoded2: ['i', 'love', 'chicago', 'pizza']
=> tokens4:  [3666, 4004, 1573, 318, 827, 7357,
1360]
=> decoded3: ['my', 'favorite', 'word', 'is', 'sy',
'zy', 'gy']
```

By comparison, BERT generates the following output, which contains [CLS], [SEP], and a "##" prefix for subwords (see Listing 6.10 in Chapter 6):

```
['[CLS]', 'my', 'favorite', 'word', 'is', 'sy',
'##zy', '##gy', '[SEP]']
```

If you want to download the code for GPT-2, navigate to the following website and select "gpt2" from the list of models:

https://github.com/huggingface/transformers/blob/main/src/transformers/models/

Question-Answering with GPT-2

Listing 7.3 displays the content of gpt2_qna2.py that shows you how to perform question-answering using GPT-2.

Listing 7.3: gpt2_qna2.py

```
from transformers import pipeline

qna = pipeline('question-answering')

qc_pair1 = {
    'question': 'Who is the inventor of the Theory
of Relativity?',
```

```
        'context': 'Albert Einstein invented the Theory
of Relativity',
    }


qc_pair2 = {
    'question': 'Which wine and cheese are from
Italy',
    'context':  'Barolo wine from Italy goes well
with Parmigiano cheese',
    }


if __name__ == "__main__":
    result = qna (qc_pair1)
    print("result:")
    print(result)
    print("----------\n")


    result = qna (qc_pair2)
    print("result:")
    print(result)
    print("----------\n")
```

Listing 7.3 starts with an `import` statement and then initializes the variable qna as an instance of the `pipeline` class that also specifies `question-answering`. Next, the variables `gc_pair1` and `gc_pair2` are initialized as Python dictionaries that contain two keys.

Notice that the second pair `gc_pair2` actually involves two questions instead of one: the response contains only the answer to the second part of the question about cheese and ignores the question about wine. Launch the code in Listing 7.3, and you will see the following output:

```
result:

{'score': 0.9971326589584351, 'start': 0, 'end':
15, 'answer': 'Albert Einstein'}

-----------


result:

{'score': 0.2554819583892822, 'start': 38, 'end':
48, 'answer': 'Parmigiano'}

-----------
```

Optimus: Combining BERT and GPT-2

BERT has an encoder-only architecture, whereas GPT-2 and Megatron have a decoder-only architecture. Another interesting transformer-based model is Optimus, which combines BERT and GPT-2, along with a latent variable z (with respect to the decoder) using two techniques:

- Append z as a vector for the decoder.
- Append z to the bottom layer of the decoder.

This additional layer is involved in every step of the decoding process. More details about Optimus are available here: *https://github.com/ChunyuanLI/Optimus*

GPT-2 AND TEXT GENERATION

Listing 7.4 displays the content of `gpt2_text_gen1.py` that shows you how to perform text generation using the GPT-2 model.

Listing 7.4: gpt2_text_gen1.py

```
from transformers import pipeline

# default uses the GPT-2 model:
gen = pipeline("text-generation")
prompt = "I love Chicago deep dish pizza"
result = gen(prompt)

print("prompt:",prompt)

print("result:",result)

print()
```

Listing 7.4 starts with an `import` statement and then initializes the variable `gen` as an instance of the `pipeline` class that also specifies `text-generation`. Next, the variable `prompt` is initialized with a prompt in the form of a text string.

The next portion of Listing 7.4 initializes the variable `result` with the output from the code snippet `gen(prompt)`, and then the contents of `prompt` and `result` are displayed. Launch the code in Listing 7.4, and you will see the following output:

```
Some weights of GPT2Model were not initialized
from the model checkpoint at gpt2 and are newly
```

initialized: ['h.0.attn.masked_bias', 'h.1.attn.
masked_bias', 'h.2.attn.masked_bias', 'h.3.attn.
masked_bias', 'h.4.attn.masked_bias', 'h.5.attn.
masked_bias', 'h.6.attn.masked_bias', 'h.7.attn.
masked_bias', 'h.8.attn.masked_bias', 'h.9.attn.
masked_bias',
'h.10.attn.masked_bias', 'h.11.attn.masked_bias']

You should probably TRAIN this model on a downstream task to be able to use it for predictions
and inference.

Setting `pad_token_id` to `eos_token_id`:50256 for
open-end generation.

Setting `pad_token_id` to `eos_token_id`:50256 for
open-end generation.

Setting `pad_token_id` to `eos_token_id`:50256 for
open-end generation.

prompt: I love Chicago deep dish pizza

result: [{'generated_text': 'I love Chicago deep
dish pizza. I love it as well.\n\nI never thought I
would love the idea of a pizza, but I am glad that
I did. I know there is already a dedicated Chicago
pizza section in the neighborhood. I'}]

result2: [{'generated_text': 'I love Chicago deep
dish pizza! When it was starting to come to light
that these guys were making this, they took the
pizza to the local pizzeria and it was amazing. My
boyfriend also enjoyed it and loves to have these
places in town.'}, {'generated_text': 'I love
Chicago deep dish pizza. And the pizza is really
tasty.\n\nA quick thing that you should take note
of this week is the recent return of the Nachos.
The Nachos are a side dish in Chicago and some
of'}, {'generated_text': "I love Chicago deep dish
pizza and feel compelled to cook some of these.
It made me really want to learn more about pizza
cooking in a healthy way, but I don't want to
keep my focus on the best pizza recipe, and don't
want"}]

result3: [{'generated_text': "I love Chicago deep
dish pizza. Chicago deep dish, Chicago deep dish

```
pizza. So yeah, that's gotta work!\n\nA whole lot
of"}]
```

Listing 7.5 displays the content of gpt2_text_gen2.py that shows you how to perform text generation using the GPT-2 model.

Listing 7.5: gpt2_text_gen2.py

```
from transformers import pipeline


text_gen = pipeline("text-generation")


# specify a max_length of 50 tokens and sampling
"off":
prefix_texL = "What a wonderful"
generated_text = text_gen(prefix_text, max_
length=50, do_sample=False)[0]


print("=> #1 generated_text['generated_text']:")
print(generated_text['generated_text'])
print("------------------------------\n")


#output #1:
#What a wonderful thing about this is that it's a
very simple and simple way to get your hands on a
new game.
#The game is a simple, simple game. It's a simple
game. It's a simple game. It's


prefix_text = "Once in a "
generated_text = text_gen(prefix_text, max_
length=50, do_sample=False)[0]


print("=> #2 generated_text['generated_text']:")
print(generated_text['generated_text'])
print("---------------------------\n")


prefix_text = "Once in a blue "
generated_text = text_gen(prefix_text, max_
length=50, do_sample=False)[0]
```

```
print("=> #3 generated_text['generated_text']:")
print(generated_text['generated_text'])
print("------------------------------\n")
```

Listing 7.5 starts with an `import` statement and then initializes the variable `text_gen` as an instance of the `pipeline` class that also specifies `text-generation`. Next, the variable `prefix_text` is initialized as a text string, and the variable `generated_text` is initialized with the output from `text_gen()` and three parameters, after which the contents of `generated_text` are displayed.

The preceding sequence of steps is repeated twice more, using different values for the variable `prefix_text`. Launch the code in Listing 7.5, and you will see the following output:

```
Some weights of GPT2Model were not initialized
from the model checkpoint at gpt2 and are newly
initialized: ['h.0.attn.masked_bias', 'h.1.attn.
masked_bias', 'h.2.attn.masked_bias', 'h.3.attn.
masked_bias', 'h.4.attn.masked_bias', 'h.5.attn.
masked_bias', 'h.6.attn.masked_bias', 'h.7.attn.
masked_bias', 'h.8.attn.masked_bias', 'h.9.attn.
masked_bias',
'h.10.attn.masked_bias', 'h.11.attn.masked_bias']
You should probably TRAIN this model on a down-
stream task to be able to use it for predictions
and inference.
Setting `pad_token_id` to `eos_token_id`:50256 for
open-end generation.
=> #1 generated_text['generated_text']:
What a wonderful thing about this is that it's a
very simple and simple way to get your hands on a
new game.

The game is a simple, simple game. It's a simple
game. It's a simple game. It's
------------------------------


Setting `pad_token_id` to `eos_token_id`:50256 for
open-end generation.
=> #2 generated_text['generated_text']:
Once in a vernacular, the word "carnage" is used to
describe a large, open, and well-lit place.
```

```
The word "carnage" is used to describe a large,
open, and well-

--------------------------------


Setting `pad_token_id` to `eos_token_id`:50256 for
open-end generation.
=> #3 generated_text['generated_text']:
Once in a blue urn, you can see the "C" in the
center of the "C" and the "A" in the bottom right
corner.


The "C" is the "A" and the "A" are

--------------------------------
```

Mix-and-Match Models

Now that you have some familiarity with BERT-based models and GPT-2, it is possible to combine different types of transformer-based models, which is to say, you can combine an encoder model with a decoder model. For example, although no code is provided here, it is possible to combine BERT with GPT-2.

Another combination involves using BERT as an encoder as well as a decoder. Since BERT is an encoder-based model and does not support decoder-based functionality, additional code is required.

Fortunately, the `EncoderDecoderModel` object from Hugging Face contains the method `from_encoder_decoder_pretrained()`, which is like a "connector" that enables you to combine different types of pre-trained models to create a new encoder/decoder model. More details for doing so are available online (along with code):

https://pub.towardsai.net/how-to-train-a-seq2seq-summarization-model-using-bert-as-both-encoder-and-decoder-bert2bert-2a5fb36559b8

Let's now turn our attention to GPT-3, which is the topic of the next section.

WHAT IS GPT-3?

Generative Pre-trained Transformer 3, or GPT-3, is one of the most advanced language models developed by OpenAI. Its release marked a significant leap in the capabilities of language models.

GPT-3 represents a significant step forward in the capabilities of AI language models. Its ability to generalize from few examples and produce coherent text across a wide range of topics and tasks is impressive. However, like all tools, its power comes with responsibilities regarding its use and the potential implications of its outputs.

GPT-3 is the third iteration in the GPT series by OpenAI. While GPT-2, its predecessor, was already impressive with its 1.5 billion parameters, GPT-3 dwarfs it with 175 billion parameters, making it the largest model in the GPT series as of September, 2021.

GPT-3, like its predecessors, uses a transformer architecture, which has become the standard for SOTA language models due to its ability to handle long-range dependencies in text.

GPT-3 was trained on a mixture of licensed data, data created by human trainers, and publicly available data in multiple languages. This vast amount of data, combined with its huge number of parameters, allows GPT-3 to achieve remarkable performance on a wide range of tasks without task-specific training data.

One of the groundbreaking features of GPT-3 is its ability to perform few-shot learning. This means that you can provide GPT-3 with a few examples of a task, and it will attempt to generalize and perform that task. This is in contrast to many other models that require extensive fine-tuning on specific tasks.

For example, if you give GPT-3 a few examples of translating English to French, it can then attempt to translate new sentences you provide, even though it was not explicitly fine-tuned for translation.

Due to the impressive versatility of GPT-3, there is a plethora of applications involving GPT-3, such as:

- text generation (like writing essays or poetry)
- answering questions based on provided information
- translating between languages
- simulating characters for video games
- code generation based on a description

There are other important considerations regarding GPT-3 (which is generally true of all LLMs), such as the reliability of its output. While GPT-3 can generate coherent text, it does not inherently know truth from falsehood. Hence, it can produce incorrect or misleading answers. Another concern involves ethics regarding the potential for misuse, such as generating misleading information, fake news, or inappropriate content, is a concern.

A third consideration pertains to resource intensity: training models like GPT-3 require significant computational resources, which in turn raises the issue of the carbon footprint of LLMs. A fourth concern is the lack of "explainability." We do not know exactly why GPT-3 (and LLMs in general) provides a specific answer.

Four GPT-3 Models

There are four GPT-3 models that differ in the number of parameters and layers. The smallest model consists of 12 layers and 125 M parameters and the largest model consists of 96 layers and 175 B parameters. As you can surmise, increasing the number of layers and parameters improves the learning capacity and simultaneously increases the associated cost and processing time.

The public response to GPT-3 ranged from shock, skepticism, and anxiety to amazement. Interestingly, even the CEO of OpenAI (Sam Altman) agreed that some statements exaggerated the capability of GPT-3.

The key differentiator of GPT-3 is its ability to perform specific tasks *without* the need for fine-tuning. By contrast, other models tend to require task-specific datasets, and they generally do not perform as well on unrelated tasks.

GPT-3 is actually an extension of the GPT-2 model that contains more layers and data, and it is 100 times larger than GPT-2. Although GPT-3 was trained without any domain-specific knowledge, GPT-3 can perform a multitude of domain-specific tasks, including text summarization and language translation. Thus, GPT-3 can perform tasks on which it was not explicitly trained.

GPT-3 is a Pre-trained Model

GPT-3 was pre-trained on a massive amount of data, and it can handle many tasks based on few-shot learning. GPT-3 can be trained using data in various formats, including JSONL (JSON Lines), plain text, and CSV, preferably structured in such a manner that the the training algorithm can process the data and learn from it effectively. An example of JSONL-formatted data is shown here:

```
{"prompt": "<prompt text>", "completion": "<ideal
generated text>"}
{"prompt": "<prompt text>", "completion": "<ideal
generated text>"}
{"prompt": "<prompt text>", "completion": "<ideal
generated text>"}
```

For your convenience, OpenAI provides a CLI data preparation tool for converting data into a JSONL document.

The most significant transformer-based successors to GPT-3 are Gopher, Chinchilla, and PaLM, all of which exceed the capabilities of GPT-3 (and these are discussed later).

The text-to-image transformer-based models DALL-E 2, Imagen, and Parti have incorporated additional techniques that have capture the imagination of many people in the graphics world. In addition, Flamingo and Gato are two variants of GPT-3 that support multi-modal functionality (i.e., text, audio, image, and video).

GPT-3 Architecture

An important aspect of *autoregressive* models is their ability to predict the future value of a target variable based on its immediately preceding value: they do not require a history of previous values. By contrast, *regressive* models use the values of multiple variables to predict the future value of a target variable.

As such, the GPT-3 architecture differs from models such as BERT and GPT-2 because it has the following features:

- **causal** attention (contrast with BERT)
- autoregressive language model
- 96 layers (gpt-3.5-turbo)
- dimensionality of 12288 and 96 heads
- sequence length of 2048 (1024 for GPT-2)
- position embedding
- GELU in the FF layer
- 175 billion parameters

GPT-3 Requirements and Parameters

The minimum requirements for GPT-3 depend on the size of the model, details of which are shown here:

- GPT-3 "small" requires at least 16 GB of RAM and a GPU with at least 8 GB of VRAM.
- GPT-3 "medium" requires at least of 32 GB of RAM and a GPU with at least 16 GB of VRAM.
- GPT-3 "large" requires 600 GB of RAM and a specialized GPU with 250 GB of VRAM.

The numbers specified in this list are minimum values. These are the minimum requirements, and you can expect larger values for good performance. Although GPT-3 has 175 B parameters, it is not comparable to other LLMs that have 540 B parameters and even 1 trillion parameters. The vast majority of the GPT-3 parameters are used in the computational processes that enable the model to understand and generate text based on the patterns it has learned during training.

The following OpenAI Web site provides detailed information regarding GPT best practices: *https://platform.openai.com/docs/guides/gpt-best-practices*.

The preceding website discusses six strategies for obtaining better results with prompts.

GPT-3 MODELS

The main difference among the GPT-3 models is the number of parameters and layers: one model contains 12 layers and 125 million parameters, whereas another model contains 96 layers and 175 billion parameters. Keep in mind that adding layers and parameters improve the capacity of a model and simultaneously increases the cost involved as well as the processing time.

By way of comparison, GPT-3 has 175 billion parameters, whereas GPT-2 has 1.5 billion parameters, and BERT-Large has 340 million parameters. GPT-3 was trained entirely on publicly available datasets, on nearly 500,000,000,000 words (some of which might contain offensive content).

One of the benefits of GPT-3 is its few-shot learning capabilities. You can provide longer prompts with correct examples to improve the quality of the response from the GPT-3 model. Such examples work just like real-time training, and they improve the results returned by GPT-3 without modifying its parameters.

OpenAI does charge a fee for the tokens in your input prompt plus the output tokens that are returned in the response from GPT-3.

The largest GPT-3 model has 96 attention layers, each of which contains 96x128 dimension heads. In addition, GPT-3 consists of 175 billion parameters and was trained on more than 500 gigabytes of text to learn how to predict the next word in a user-supplied text string. GPT-n models are trained on an unlabeled text-based corpus instead of labeled data, and they perform fine tuning for individual tasks.

Since its initial release in May, 2020, OpenAI has continued adding functionality to GPT-3. For example, GPT-3 is capable of editing text and modifying blocks of code

https://www.youtube.com/watch?v=_x9AwxfjxvE

Microsoft announced on September 22, 2020, that it had licensed exclusive use of GPT-3; although anyone can use the public API and experiment with the GPT-3 Playground, only Microsoft has access to the underlying model of GPT-3.

The GPT-3 family supports the following publicly available models, each of which has a different number of parameters (and different price points):

- GPT-3 Ada
- GPT-3 Babbage
- GPT-3 Curie
- GPT-3 Davinci

The Ada model is the fastest/cheapest, whereas the Davinci model is the most powerful/expensive. The following paper introduced eight versions of GPT-3:

https://arxiv.org/abs/2005.14165.

The top four largest models range from 2.7 billion to 175 billion parameters. Based on this detail, we can speculate the following:

- Ada has 2.7 billion parameters.
- Babbage has 6.7 billion parameters.
- Curie has 13 billion parameters.
- Davinci has 175 billion parameters.

The GPT-3 engines Ada and Davinci differ by a 75x cost factor. The following website contains a comparison of benchmarks for the four standard GPT-3 models:

https://medium.com/@nils_reimers/openai-gpt-3-text-embeddings-really-a-new-state-of-the-art-in-dense-text-embeddings-6571fe3ec9d9

GPT-3 Versus Multi-Lingual Models

In the multi-lingual arena, languages with a limited amount of data present a challenge. One approach that might prove beneficial is a technique whereby the text of multiple languages is concatenated into a single dataset, which is actually used in the MM dataset from Facebook that can translate text between any pair of 100 languages. Another interesting result is leveraging an LLM that is trained in one language to perform tasks in a different language, which might also produce results in languages with limited data.

As a reminder, GPT-3 belongs to a group of large-scale autoregressive language models that have the following features:

- few-shot learners
- do not require fine-tuning
- perform many language tasks

However, such models are trained with primarily English-based datasets, and they are outperformed by other language models that are trained via non-English datasets. In particular, XGLM-based models outperform GPT-3 in many language-based tasks.

WHAT IS THE GOAL OF GPT-3?

The aim of the GPT-3 pre-trained model is to directly evaluate the model on the test-related data of new tasks; i.e., GPT-3 essentially skips the training-related data of new tasks and focuses directly on the test-related data, in its capacity as a "few shot" learner.

GPT-3 achieved SOTA performance on several NLP tasks without fine-tuning, at the cost of more than $10,000,000. Some of the datasets that were used to train GPT-3 are downloadable from this read-only Github repository:

https://github.com/openai/gpt-3

GPT-3 has caught the attention of many people because of various tasks that it has performed, including automatic code generation. For example, one user typed a paragraph of text describing the following Web application:

1. a button that increments a total by $3

2. a button that decrements a total by $5

3. a button that displays the current total

GPT-3 then created a React application with the preceding functionality, which prompted a variety of reactions: some people were amused by such a simplistic application, whereas others contemplated their future job security.

Give GPT-3 an initial sequence of words and GPT-3 will generate various responses, such as code generation, news articles, poems, and even make jokes.

GPT-3 generated an interesting poem about Elon Musk ("your tweets are a blight"), part of which you can read here:

https://www.businessinsider.com/elon-musk-poem-tweets-gpt-3-openai-2020-8

One of the distinguishing characteristics of GPT-3 is its ability to solve unseen NLP tasks: this is due to the fact that GPT-3 was trained on a very large corpus. GPT-3 also uses few-shot learning and can perform the following tasks:

- translate natural language into code for websites
- solve complex medical question-and-answer problems
- create tabular financial reports
- write code to train machine learning models

GPT-3 has surprised people with its capacity to generate prose as well as poetry. Elon Musk is one of the founding members of OpenAI that created GPT-3, which generated the following poem about Elon Musk (and can be found at *https://www.businessinsider.com/elon-musk-poem-tweets-gpt-3-openai-2020-8*):

> *"The SEC said, "Musk,/your tweets are a blight./They really could cost you your job,/if you don't stop/all this tweeting at night."/...Then Musk cried, "Why?/The tweets I wrote are not mean,/I don't use all-caps/and I'm sure that my tweets are clean."/"But your tweets can move markets/and that's why we're sore./You may be a genius/and a billionaire,/but that doesn't give you the right to be a bore!"*

WHAT CAN GPT-3 DO?

GPT-3 generated text responses can achieve human-level quality. However, currently there is no support for data formats, such as audio or video. However, GPT-3 can work with image-based data with DALL-E.

GPT-3 is a statistical model that determines the probability distribution of words to generate the appropriate text in response to an input string. Unlike other models that are trained on specific tasks, GPT-3 is designed to detect *patterns* in text strings, which provides the following benefits:

- GPT-3 is general purpose (not task-specific) model.
- GPT-3 does not require re-training to handle new prompts.
- GPT-3 achieves SOTA performance on multiple NLP tasks.

The performance of GPT-3 is probably due to the fact that GPT-3 was trained on a dataset consisting of more than 500 gigabytes. Although the size and cost of GPT-3 is prohibitive for the vast majority of companies, GPT-3 is accessible via a simple and cost-effective API. Keep in mind that GPT-3 is based on point-in-time data that can be several months old instead of continuous training.

Conversational AI

The conversational AI aspect of GPT-3 can be used for various implementations, some of which are as follows:

* review generation (such as for movies and restaurants)
* pre-processing user input
* advertising
* chatbots

It is important to be cautious with AI, however. One medical chatbot that was based GPT-3 suggested to a fake patient (who expressed suicidal thoughts) that he kill himself:

https://artificialintelligence-news.com/2020/10/28/medical-chatbot-openai-gpt3-patient-kill-themselves/

GPT-3 has eight different model sizes (from 125 M to 175 B parameters), and the smallest GPT-3 model is about the size of BERT-Base and RoBERTa-Base, with 12 attention layers that in turn have 12x64 dimension head. By contrast, the largest GPT-3 model is ten times larger than T5-11B (the previous record holder), and has 96 attention layers, which in turn have 96x128 dimension heads. Details regarding how to customize a GPT-3 model are at *https://openai.com/blog/customized-gpt3/*.

In addition, OpenAI has added support for fine-tuning GPT-3, which might also become available for other models from OpenAI.

Text Summarization and Summarization

GPT-3 supports the following types of text summarization, as shown in the following list:

* simple summary
* one-sentence summary
* grade-level adjusted summary
* extraction summary

You might find articles that suggest appending the string `tl;dr;` to a text block in order have GPT-3 generate a simple summary. As a simple illustration, enter the following block of text in the GPT-3 Playground (more details are provided later in this chapter):

```
GPT-3 has eight different model sizes (from 125M
to 175B parameters), and the smallest GPT-3 model
is about the size of BERT-Base and RoBERTa-Base,
with 12 attention layers that in turn have 12x64
dimension head. On the other hand, the largest
GPT-3 model is ten times larger than T5-11B (the
previous record holder), and has 96 attention
layers, which in turn have 96x128 dimension heads.
Details regarding how to customize a GPT3 model are
here
tl;dr;
```

The response from GPT-3 is as follows:

```
GPT-3 has a much larger parameter count than any
other transformer-based model, making it the
largest transformer-based model ever trained.
```

Notice that the string tl;dr; in the input text block is on a separate line: if you place this string on the same line as the input text, then GPT-3 generates a multi-line response instead of a one-sentence summary.

Please view the section on text classification in Chapter 8 for a Python code sample that shows you how to perform text classification.

LIMITATIONS OF GPT-3

GPT-3 can only process text, which is a limitation rather than a weakness. The following length article discusses various weaknesses of GPT-3:

https://nautil.us/deep-learning-is-hitting-a-wall-14467

GPT-3 has other limitations that prevent GPT-3 from performing arbitrary text-related tasks, as shown in the following list:

- limited input size
- limited output size
- no type of memory

Currently, GPT-3 does have difficulty with natural language inference tasks, such as ANLI, or tasks that involve causality. Although GPT-3 can generate high quality articles, human edits are performed to ensure a high degree of coherent text.

GPT-3 Task Strengths and Mistakes

Despite its limitations, GPT-3 has the ability to perform text generation that is close to human-level quality. For example, suppose that GPT-3 is given a title and a subtitle, along with the word "Article" that serves as a prompt word. GPT-3 can then write brief articles that often seem to be written by humans.

Keep in mind that bias exists in the corpus that was used to train GPT-3. According to the following article, one way in which GPT-3 can misclassify results is to include bias toward women and minorities:

h t t p s : / / t e c h c r u n c h . c o m / 2 0 2 0 / 0 8 / 0 7 / here-are-a-few-ways-gpt-3-can-go-wrong/

GPT-3 cannot integrate or perform reasoning that involves mundane tasks. Moreover, GPT-3 does generate erroneous results, such as the GPT-3-powered chatbot Replika, which "alleged that Bill Gates invented COVID-19" and that COVID-19 vaccines were "not very effective." According to some researchers, LLMs that are based on deep learning are like "stochastic parrots" that "repeat a lot and understand little." Perhaps the inconsistencies of GPT-3 partially spurred the development of GPT-4, which is discussed in chapter 9. (Quotations and information from *https://nautil.us/ deep-learning-is-hitting-a-wall-14467.*)

GPT-3 TASK PERFORMANCE

For most models, the task of translating sentences from English to Italian involves thousands of sentence pairs in order for those models to learn how to perform translation. By comparison, GPT-3 does not require a fine-tuning step: it can handle custom language tasks without training data.

Thus, GPT-3 has the ability to perform specific tasks without any special tuning, which is something that other models cannot do well. For example, GPT-3 can be trained to translate text, generate code, or even write poetry. Moreover, GPT-3 can do so with no more than 10 training examples.

GPT-3 is not just a few-shot learner: it can also perform as a zero-shot learner and a one-shot learner. By way of comparison, GPT-3 as a zero-shot learner has higher accuracy than a fine-tuned RoBERTa model (which previously had SOTA performance).

In terms of reading comprehension, GPT-3 performs best on free-form conversational datasets and performs its worst on datasets that involve modeling structured dialog. However, as a few-shot learner for this task, GPT-3 outperforms the fine-tuned baseline of BERT. In addition, GPT-3 performs well on the SQuAD 2.0 dataset from Stanford, but under performs on multiple-choice test questions.

GPT-3 treats each input string as a prompt to determine the most suitable response: higher quality prompts generate higher quality responses. A completion is another term for the response string that is generated by GPT-3. Examples of GPT-3 are available at *https://beta. openai.com/examples*.

HOW GPT-3 AND BERT ARE DIFFERENT

This section contains a side-by-side comparison of some of the differences between GPT-3 and BERT. Although the details are available in multiple locations in this chapter and the previous chapter, this section provides a more convenient consolidation of that information.

GPT-3 (an autoregressive model) and BERT (a bidirectional model) obtain language context in different ways. Specifically, GPT-3 generates forward from natural language inputs, whereas BERT can obtain language context in both directions from a particular word. Moreover, GPT-3 does not require fine-tuning to perform tasks, which differs from other earlier NLP models. However, fine-tuning through the OpenAI API can result in improved performance on specific tasks.

Another important advantage of GPT-3 over RNNs and LSTMs is its ability to maintain contextual information between words that are much further apart in a corpus. While LSTMs can maintain context for words that are a dozen positions apart from each other, GPT-3 provides a much wider contextual span.

A third advantage of GPT-3 is its superior performance with respect to few-shot learning.

In addition, GPT-3 was trained on such a massive amount of data that it is not necessary to train GPT-3 on numerous tasks. Perhaps that partially accounts for GPT-3 showing marked improvement in comparison to smaller models on those tasks. The achievements of GPT-3 suggest that model size does affect the ability of a model to perform tasks well.

In simplified terms, auto regression involves uni-directional learning whereas bidirectional systems involve bi-direction learning. This means that regressive systems learn from a previous sequence to predict the next item, whereas bidirectional systems can use both future and past information. By contrast, BERT is bidirectional, which means it can learn from anything that resides in the context of the model.

With the preceding points in mind, BERT (and other bidirectional models) excels in document classification or reading comprehension questions where you are processing something as a whole and then answering something about it. GPT-3 (and other auto regressive models) enabled the few-shot paradigm because it processes input and then generates output.

Transfer learning refers to the result of fine tuning a pre-trained model. In fact, even a dataset consisting of 100 samples for fine tuning can result in significant improvement in a pre-trained model. However, there is still a performance gap between fine tuning and few-shot learning. Although few-shot performance is very good and sometimes even comparable to human level performance, the quality of results is inconsistent.

THE GPT-3 PLAYGROUND

OpenAI created the GPT-3 Playground, which is a Web-based tool for entering prompts in a text field and receiving completions from GPT-3. The Playground supports most of the functionality that is available directly through the GPT-3 API.

Moreover, the Playground enables you to interact with GPT-3 without writing any code. In essence, the OpenAI Playground enables you to easily use GPT-3 to train the engine to produce text output. The GPT-3 Playground also provides a set of saved prompts that are called *presets*.

The first step is to navigate to the GPT-3 Playground, where you will be prompted to sign into your account:

https://beta.openai.com/playground

Once you have registered for an account, you will see the main page that consists of three sections: a "Get Started" section, a "Playground" section, and third section that consists of a drop-down list and sliders for tunable parameters.

The middle section is the input text for GPT-3, which has two parts: 1) a start sequence that is the text string `Text:`, followed by one or more text blocks (provided by you) that provides GPT-3 with sample output text. The second paragraph contains the same string `Text:` that indicates the end of your input text.

Let's postpone the description of the sliders that appear in the GPT-3 Playground until later in this chapter, and jump right into generating code in the GPT-3 Playground.

GPT-3 Code Generation with Davinci Engine

Navigate to the GPT-3 Playground, and after verifying that the Davinci engine is selected, enter the following three sentences in the playground (i.e., the middle portion of the screen):

```
Add a 400x400 canvas with a blue background to the
document.
Add a text display in the lower left corner of the
scene.
Add a map to the canvas.
```

Click the `submit` button in the lower left corner of the screen. GPT-3 generates the output that you see in Figure 7.1.

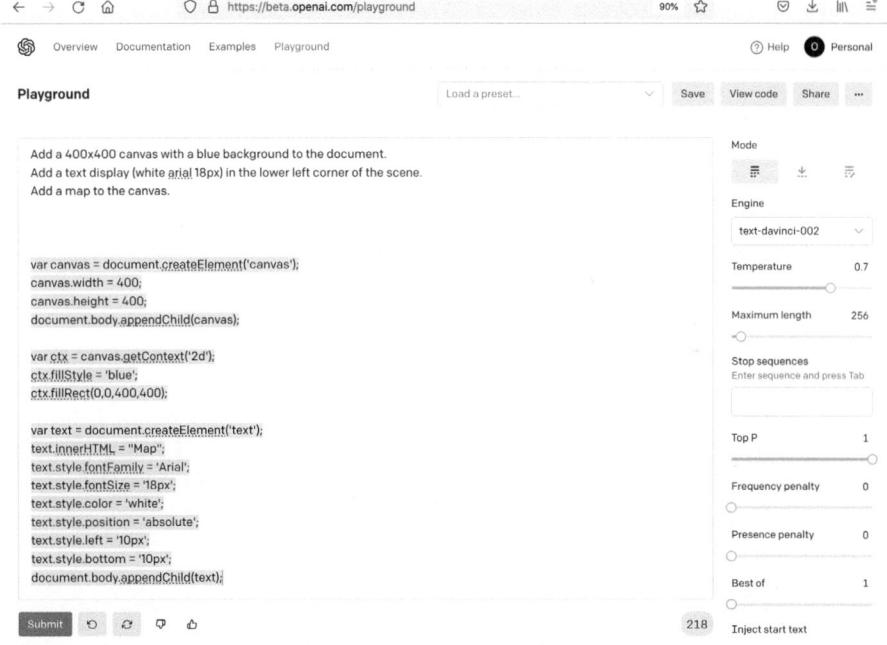

FIGURE 7.1 Code generation from GPT-3

For your convenience, Listing 7.6 displays the contents of the text file `gpt_3_generated_code.txt`.

Listing 7.6: gpt3_generated_code.txt

```
Add a 400x400 canvas with a blue background to the
document.
Add a text display in the lower left corner of the
scene.
Add a map to the canvas.

var canvas = document.createElement('canvas');
canvas.width = 400;
canvas.height = 400;
document.body.appendChild(canvas);

var ctx = canvas.getContext('2d');
ctx.fillStyle = 'blue';
ctx.fillRect(0,0,400,400);

var text = document.createElement('text');
text.innerHTML = "Map";
text.style.fontFamily = 'Arial';
text.style.fontSize = '18px';
text.style.color = 'white';
text.style.position = 'absolute';
text.style.left = '10px';
text.style.bottom = '10px';
document.body.appendChild(text);
```

GPT-3 can generate different output from the same set of prompts, which means that your output might be different from Listing 7.6. For example, Listing 7.7 displays *different generated code with the same three prompts as Listing 7.6.*

Listing 7.7: gpt3_generated_code2.txt

```
Add a 400x400 canvas with a blue background to the
document.
Add a text display in the lower left corner of the
scene.
Add a map to the canvas.
```

```
<canvas id="myCanvas" width="400" height="400"
style="background-color:blue;"></canvas>

<script>

var canvas = document.getElementById("myCanvas");
var ctx = canvas.getContext("2d");

// add text display
ctx.font = "30px Arial";
ctx.fillStyle = "#ffffff";
ctx.fillText("Hello World", 10, 50);

// add map
var map = new Image();
map.onload = function(){
  ctx.drawImage(map, 0, 0);

}
map.src = "map.png";

// add player
var player = new Image();
player.onload = function(){
  ctx.drawImage(player, 0, 0);

}
player.src = "player.png";
```

Listing 7.7 contains text prompts with instructions for creating and placing UI elements on the screen, along with the generated output from GPT-3 using the Davinci engine. The initial portion of Listing 7.7 contains the same prompts, and the outermost <div> element and its contents are the generated response from GPT-3, which are shown in Listing 7.8.

Listing 7.8: *gpt3_generated_code3.txt*

```
Add a 400x400 canvas with a blue background to the
document.
Create 3 text input boxes that accept a digit
```

```
Make the height of the digits equal to 80px
Center the digit in each input box
Place the text input boxes in the same row
Place the row at the bottom of the document
Make the boxes 25% of the width of the div
Make the boxes 50% of the height of the div
```

```
<div style="width:80%;height:80%;text-align:center;
position:relative;bottom:0;">
   <input type="text" style="width:25%;height:50%;
   font-size:80px;text-align:center;"/>
   <input type="text" style="width:25%;height:50%;
   font-size:80px;text-align:center;"/>
   <input type="text" style="width:25%;height:50%;
   font-size:80px;text-align:center;"/>
</div>
```

INFERENCE PARAMETERS

After you have completed the fine-tuning step for an LLM, you are in a position to set values for various inference parameters. The GPT-3 API supports numerous inference parameters, some of which are shown here:

- engine
- prompt
- max_tokens
- top_p
- top_k
- frequency_penalty
- presence_penalty
- token length
- stop tokens
- temperature

The engine inference parameter can be one of the four GPT-3 models, such as text-ada-001. The prompt parameter is simply the input text that you provide. The presence_penalty inference parameter enables more relevant responses when you specify higher values for this parameter.

The `max_tokens` inference parameter specifies the maximum number of tokens: sample values are 100, 200, or 256. The `top_p` inference parameter can be a positive integer that specifies the top-most results to select. The `frequency_penalty` is an inference parameter that pertains to the frequency of repeated words. A smaller value for this parameter increases the number of repeated words.

The `token length` parameter specifies the total number of words that are in the input sequence that is processed by the LLM (not the maximum length of each token).

The `stop tokens` parameter controls the length of the generated output of an LLM. If this parameter equals 1, then only a single sentence is generated, whereas a value of 2 indicates that the generated output is limited to one paragraph.

The `top_k` parameter specifies the number of tokens (which is the value for k) that are chosen, with the constraint that the chosen tokens have the highest probabilities. For example, if `top k` is equal to 3, then only the 3 tokens with the highest probabilities are selected.

The `top_p` parameter is a floating-point number between 0.0 and 1.0, and it is the upper bound on the sum of the probabilities of the chosen tokens. For example, if a discrete probability distribution consists of the set S = {0.1, 0.2, 0.3, 0.4} and the value of the "top p" parameter is 0.3, then only the tokens with associated probabilities of 0.1 and 0.2 can be selected.

Thus, the `top k` and `top p` parameters provide two mechanisms for limiting the number of tokens that can be selected.

Temperature Parameter

The `temperature` inference parameter is a floating-point number between 0 and 1 inclusive, and its default value is 0.7. One interesting value for the temperature is 0.8: this will result in GPT-3 selecting a next token that does *not* have the maximum probability.

The `temperature` inference parameter T is a non-negative floating-point number whose value influences the extent to which the model uses randomness. Specifically, smaller values for the temperature parameter that are closer to 0 involve less randomness (i.e., more deterministic), whereas larger values for the temperature parameter involve more randomness.

The temperature parameter T is directly associated with the `softmax()` function that is applied during the final step in the transformer architecture. The value of T alters the formula for the softmax function, as described later in this section. An important point to remember is that selecting tokens based on a `softmax()` function means that the selected token is the token with the highest probability.

By contrast, larger values for the parameter T enable randomness in the choice of the next token, which means that a token can be selected even though its associated probability is less than the maximum probability. While this might seem counterintuitive, some values of T (such as 0.8) result in output text that is more natural sounding, from a human's perspective, than the output text in which tokens are selected if they have the maximum probability. Finally, a temperature value of 1 is the same as the standard `softmax()` function.

Incidentally, the section "Text Completion and Temperature" in Chapter 8 contains a Python code sample that invokes the `Completion` class in OpenAI to perform text completion with two different values for temperature (the results are interesting).

Temperature and the softmax() Function

The temperature parameter T appears in the *denominator* of the exponent of the Euler constant e in the `softmax()` function. Thus, instead of the `softmax()` numerator of the form $e^{(xi)}$, the modified `softmax()` function contains numerator terms of the form $e^{(xi/T)}$, where {x1, x2, . . . , xn} comprise a set of numbers that form a discrete probability distribution.

As a reminder, the denominator of each term generated by the `softmax()` function consists of the sum of the terms in the set {$e^{(x1)}$, $e^{(x2)}$, . . . , $e^{(xn)}$}. However, the denominator of the terms involving the temperature parameter T is slightly different: it is the sum of the terms in the set {$e^{(x1/T)}$, $e^{(x2/T)}$, . . . , $e^{(xn/T)}$}.

Interestingly, the `softmax()` function with the temperature parameter T is the same as the Boltzmann distribution:

https://en.wikipedia.org/wiki/Boltzmann_distribution

The subsection under "Fine-Tuning and Reinforcement Learning" in Chapter 8 provides additional details regarding discrete probability distributions. You should perform an Internet search for more information regarding adjustable inference parameters.

The following Python code snippet provides an example of specifying values for various inference parameters, including a GPT-3 engine:

```
response = openai.Completion.create(
  engine="text-ada-001",
  prompt="",
  temperature=0.7,
```

```
    max_tokens=256,
    top_p=1,
    frequency_penalty=0,
    presence_penalty=0
)
```

Navigate to the following site for more information regarding inference parameters in GPT-3: *https://huggingface.co/blog/ inference-endpoints-llm.*

OVERVIEW OF PROMPT ENGINEERING

Various language models require fine-tuning to perform downstream tasks, which sometimes necessitates appending one or more layers to the model. By contrast, GPT-3 is based on a single model that does *not* require additional layers or fine-tuning to perform additional tasks.

In fact, GPT-3 uses a system whereby zero, one, or a few examples can be prefixed to the input of the model. The combination of a task description, examples (if any), and prompt provide GPT-3 with a context so that GPT-3 can predict the output on a token-by-token basis.

For example, suppose that the task description is the sentence "Translate English to Italian", followed by several English/Italian word pairs as examples. Then the prompt would be an English word (e.g., "cow") that the model translates into Italian ("vacca").

Working with Prompts

In essence, a *prompt* is a text string that provides GPT-3 with instructions regarding the type of answer that is expected as a response to the input string (i.e., the prompt). This technique is surprisingly effective in working with language models.

For instance, if you submit the same prompt several times to GPT-3, the results are not consistent (albeit similar). One way to improve the consistency of responses is called *prompt engineering* and when it is combined with fine-tuning, more consistent responses are possible.

Specifically, prompt engineering involves designing a prompt as well as its "completion" (i.e., response from the model) so that a model will perform in the desired manner. A well-chosen prompt design achieves a higher prediction rate and also facilitates the processing of generated responses. The quality of results obtained via prompt engineering involves a good number of sample prompts, which can vary depending on the specific NLP task.

Designing Prompts

Well-designed prompt engineering enables you to automate downstream tasks much more easily than with traditional methods. However, two well-designed prompts for the same task can generate substantively different results. From an informal perspective, well-designed prompts are reminiscent of "good coaching" in sports: both tend to produce the desired results. In other words, a well-written prompt provides detailed and meaningful information in a concise manner.

Although GPT models typically require a few hundred examples to complete the majority of downstream tasks, this approach is obviously superior to other techniques that can necessitate thousands of training examples.

Another aspect to consider is the cost that might be incurred to perform fine-tuning and inferencing. It might be worth investigating the cost-effectiveness of paid services that provide APIs to perform such tasks.

Furthermore, the task of evaluating the accuracy of predictions can be more complex than traditional approaches, and the inferencing speed tends to be slow for large LLMs (such as GPT-3 or GPT-J) because predictions must be propagated to a huge number of parameters. Now consider the time required to make several hundred thousand predictions: the elapsed time can involve many hours (perhaps days).

Hence, the ability to specify well-written prompts can be a trial-and-error learning process that is a mixture of science and art.

Chain-of-Thought Prompting

Chain-of-thought (CoT) prompting is another technique that involves a multi-step sequence of guided answers. This technique is described in an arXiv paper, which involves inserting the text "Let's think step by step" prior to each answer. The creators of the CoT technique assert that their Zero-shot-CoT outperforms zero-shot LLM on multiple tasks. Moreover, the authors of the arXiv paper applied their technique without any few-shot examples on LLMs, such as the 175 B parameter InstructGPT model and the 540 B parameter PaLM model.

The authors also suggest investing additional effort to extract zero-shot knowledge embedded in LLMs prior to performing fine-tuning tasks. For more information, navigate to *https://arxiv.org/abs/2205.11916*.

Another arXiv article regarding CoT prompting is available at: *https://arxiv.org/pdf/2201.11903.pdf.*

Self-Consistency and CoT

Self-consistency is a self-supervised technique that leverages CoT prompting as well as a decoding technique that supersedes the greedy technique in CoT. Specifically, makes its selection from a set of generated samples instead of relying on a purely greedy approach. More information about self-consistency is accessible online: *https://arxiv.org/abs/2203.11171.*

According to the authors of the preceding paper, their "rule-of-thumb" is to generate a list of roughly two dozen sentences and then select the best sentence in that list. Moreover, self-consistency achieves better performance than generic CoT prompting on LLMs such as GPT-3, LaMDA, and PaLM. (See Table 2 in the arXiv paper for more details.)

Self-Consistency, CoT, and Unsupervised Datasets (LMSI)

LLMs have achieved impressive results by leveraging pre-trained models and fine tuning, along with large datasets. However, additional improvements in performance involves significant high-quality supervised datasets. One approach involves Language Model Self-Improved (LMSI) that improves LLMs using unsupervised data. This technique uses few-shot CoT for prompts, along with a majority voting scheme for selecting predictions. More information about self-consistency, COT, and unsupervised datasets is accessible online: *https://arxiv.org/pdf/2210.11610.pdf.*

DETAILS OF PROMPT ENGINEERING

Prompt engineering is a critical aspect of working with LLMs, which obviously includes GPT-3 and GPT-4. As we gain more experience working with LLMs, the community continues to develop best practices and strategies to elicit the best possible outputs from these models.

Prompt engineering refers to the art and science of crafting input prompts to guide the output of a language model in a desired direction. Given the vast knowledge and capabilities of models like GPT-3, the way questions or prompts are formulated can significantly influence the quality, accuracy, and relevance of the responses.

The Importance of Prompt Engineering

The following list contains several reasons pertaining to the importance of prompt engineering, followed by a brief description of each reason:

- Model Guidance
- Output Quality
- Task Specification

Model Guidance: LLMs do not have a specific goal or intent on their own. They generate responses based on patterns learned from data. A well-engineered prompt guides the model towards generating a more accurate and relevant response.

Output Quality: Different prompts can yield answers of varying quality. A refined prompt can elicit a more detailed or nuanced response.

Task Specification: For specific tasks, like code generation or solving mathematical problems, the way the prompt is structured can be crucial in obtaining the desired output.

Types of Prompts

The following list contains several reasons pertaining to the importance of prompt engineering, followed by a brief description of each type of prompt:

- open-ended prompts
- closed-ended prompts
- instructional prompts
- guided prompts
- iterative prompts
- temperature and max tokens

Open-ended Prompts: These are general and broad, allowing the model to decide the direction of the answer. An example of this type of prompt is "Tell me about the solar system."

Closed-ended Prompts: These seek specific answers or facts, such as "Who was the first president of the United States?"

Instructional Prompts: These direct the model to perform a specific task or generate content in a particular manner. An example is "Translate the following English text to French:…"

Guided Prompts: These provide additional context or guidance to steer the model's response. An example of this prompt is "Explain quantum mechanics as if I were a 10-year-old."

Iterative Prompts: This involves a series of "back-and-forth" conversations with the model, refining the query based on the model's previous response. It is like having a conversation to gradually hone in on the desired answer.

Temperature and Max Tokens: Though not prompts in the traditional sense, adjusting parameters like "temperature" (which controls the randomness of the model's output) and "max tokens" (which limits the length of the response) can also shape the model's answers.

Guidelines for Effective Prompts

For ChatGPT and similar models, the effectiveness of a prompt often depends on the context and the specific information or response desired. However, there are certain types of prompts that tend to be more effective in eliciting detailed and nuanced responses from the model.

For ChatGPT and similar models, you must be clear about what type of answer you desire. Guided and instructional prompts help in providing that clarity. However, it is also useful to experiment and iterate on your prompts, as sometimes even a slightly different phrasing of a prompt can lead to significantly different outputs.

The following list contains a list of guidelines for effective prompt engineering, followed by a brief description of each bullet item:

- Be explicit.
- Experiment.
- Utilize parameters.
- Review and iterate.

Be Explicit: Clearly state what you are looking for. If you want a brief summary, specify exactly what you want.

Provide Context: Giving a little background can help guide the model's response.

Experiment: It often takes several attempts to refine a prompt and get the desired output. Do not hesitate to rephrase or provide additional instructions.

Utilize Parameters: If using a model like GPT-3 directly via an API, play with parameters like temperature to get different styles of responses.

Review and Iterate: Continually refine your prompts based on the outputs you receive. This iterative approach can lead to more effective prompts over time.

Examples of Effective Prompts for ChatGPT

Guided and instructional prompts are often the most effective for ChatGPT. These prompts provide context or guidance, or they instruct the model to answer in a specific manner. They help in narrowing down the vast potential response space of the model to something more specific and aligned with the user's intent. Several examples of improved prompts are shown below.

Explicit Instruction: Instead of "World War II," use "Provide a brief summary of World War II."

Providing Context: Instead of "Explain relativity," use "Explain Einstein's theory of relativity in simple terms for someone without a physics background."

Asking for a Specific Format: Instead of "Python loops," use "Show me an example of a for loop in Python."

Guiding the Depth or Level of Detail: Instead of "Tell me about black holes," use "Give me a detailed overview of the current scientific understanding of black holes."

Setting a Scenario: Instead of "How to start a business?," use "Imagine I'm a recent college graduate with a background in software engineering. How should I go about starting a tech startup?"

Comparative or Contrasting Information: Instead of "What is socialism?," use "Compare and contrast socialism and capitalism in terms of economic principles."

Asking for Steps or a Process: Instead of "Baking a cake," use "List down the step-by-step process of baking a chocolate cake."

Steering the Tone or Style: Instead of "Tell me a story," use "Tell me a short, humorous story about a cat and a dog."

FEW-SHOT LEARNING AND FINE-TUNING LLMS

Few-shot learning is a way to provide additional training for an LLM without updating the parameters of the LLM. However, there is a size limit (i.e., for the data) involved in few-shot learning. However, fine-tuning enables you to train a model on a substantively larger set of data than via few-shot learning. As a result, you can attain improved results on a greater variety of tasks for the LLM.

GPT-3 supports few-shot learning, fine-tuning, and prompt-based learning, all of which are discussed in the following subsections. You will learn about the three main types of prompts, as well as the trade-offs between few-shot learning versus fine-tuning and fine-tuning versus prompts. In addition, one section contains suggestions for selecting a GPT-3 model for your tasks.

Although very large LLMs tend to respond well to few-shot learning, smaller LLMs do not necessarily improve via few-shot learning, even when multiple examples are included. In addition, the inclusion of examples reduces the portion of the context window that is available for including other relevant information.

In the preceding scenario, fine-tuning an LLM can be a viable alternative, which is a supervised learning technique that involves a much smaller yet highly curated dataset. The elements of the dataset are used for updating the weights in the LLM.

Note that each element consists of a prompt and its completion, which differs from the unsupervised pre-training step for LLMs. Since fine-tuning involves updating the weights in an LLM, this technique differs from zero-shot, one-shot, and few-shot learning that do *not* update the weights of the LLM.

Full fine-tuning updates all the parameters in an LLM, which means that a new version of the pre-trained model is created. However, there can be a much larger memory requirement to store all the parameters of the pre-trained LLM.

Pre-training involves training an LLM using a huge volume of unstructured textual data via self-supervised learning. By contrast, fine-tuning is a supervised learning process involving a much smaller dataset consisting of labeled examples that are used for updating the weights of an LLM.

Moreover, the labeled examples are prompt completion pairs, the fine-tuning process extends the training of the model to improve its ability to generate good completions for a specific task.

Few-Shot Learning

GPT-3 supports few-shot learning, which enables you to provide prompts with correct examples to improve the model's responses. As a result, it is not necessary to update the parameters in GPT-3 because the samples for few-shot learning function as training for the model.

In fact, GPT-3 demonstrated how few-shot learning achieves significant result even without parameter updates or task-specific data. GPT-3 first showed that LLMs can be used for few-shot learning and can achieve impressive results without large-scale task-specific data collection or model parameter updating.

Users can upload their custom training datasets to fine-tune versions of GPT-3, which is also hosted on OpenAI and accessible via its APIs. Depending on the size of the custom datasets, fine-tuning GPT-3 can range from minutes to hours of execution time. However, fine-tuning larger models involves less data than for smaller models.

Few-Shot Learning and Prompts

One interesting aspect of GPT-3 is few-shot learning via *prompting*, which is a technique that provides instructions in the form of input strings. Such hints provide GPT-3 with examples of the type of response that is expected, which GPT-3 can use effectively to provide responses that are consistent with the information in the prompts. Read the section "The Power of Prompts" in Chapter 8 for a clear contrast in the type of output that GPT-3 will generate based on a positive prompt as well as a negative prompt.

GPT-3 also uses "conditional probability" that works as follows: given a set of words, it calculates the probability that a given word will be the next word in that set of words. As a result, GPT-3 can take a set of words as input and accurately predict the next word. In fact, GPT-3 can do much more: given an input string, GPT-3 can generate entire articles that make sense (i.e., they are not strings of gibberish). Unfortunately, some of the statements made by GPT-3 can be incorrect.

Fine-Tuning with Symbol Tuning

A recent (as this book goes to print) technique for performing fine-tuning is called *symbol tuning*, which was developed by Google. Symbol tuning focuses on input-label mappings to perform better fine-tuning. More information about symbol tuning is accessible online:

https://arxiv.org/abs/2305.08298
https://pub.towardsai.net/googles-symbol-tuning-is-a-new-fine-tuning-technique-that-in-context-learning-in-llms-61ab9817038a

LoRA, Quantization, and QLoRA

This section briefly discusses LoRA and QLoRA, both of which are useful for fine-tuning LLMs (see the link at the end of this section).

Low-Rank Adapters, LoRA, are small sets of trainable parameters. During the fine-tuning process of the transformer architecture, these small sets of parameters are injected into every layer of the transformer.

In addition, these small sets of weights are updated during the fine-tuning process, whereas the original model weights are frozen. The primary advantage to this technique is the significant reduction in the number of trainable parameters for downstream tasks. Moreover, Hugging Face created the Parameter Efficient Fine-Tuning (PEFT) library, which supports LoRA.

Quantization involves storing data in data types that have smaller precision. For example, you might use an 8-bit data type (i.e., a byte) to store 16-bit data or 32-bit data. Obviously, this reduction in the number of bits results a loss in precision. Interestingly, quantization results in a model whose reduced size can outweigh the loss in precision.

The third topic for this section is Quantized Low-Rank Adaptation (QLoRA). QLoRA combines quantization and low-rank adaptation to achieve efficient fine-tuning of AI models. The advantage of QLoRA is the memory reduction during the fine-tuning step of an LLM. More information regarding the relevance QLoRA for fine-tuning LLMs is accessible online: *https://arxiv.org/abs/2305.14314*.

SUMMARY

This chapter started with a discussion about some features of GPT-2 and GPT-3, along with some Python-based code samples. Then you learned about three main types of well-known LLMs (large language models): encoder-only, decoder-only, and encoder-decoder models.

Next, you learned about the GPT-based family of language models from OpenAI, followed by a high-level introduction to GPT-3, its goals, and several models that are based on GPT-3.

In addition, you saw a comparison of GPT-3 and BERT, and the strengths and weaknesses of GPT-3. Furthermore, you learned about GPT-3 Playground, where you can perform inferencing with GPT-3. Finally, you learned about creating prompts in GPT-3.

CHAPTER 8

WORKING WITH *GPT-3* IN GREATER DEPTH

This chapter contains a wide-ranging assortment of topics, including fine tuning, GPT-3 prompt samples, text-related examples in GPT-3, and some open-source variants of GPT-3.

The first section of this chapter discusses the concepts Gini impurity, entropy, and cross-entropy as a prelude to understanding Kullback Leibler (KL) divergence. In addition, reinforcement learning with human feedback (RLHF) is discussed, which can use KL divergence. This section also briefly discusses algorithms such as TRPO, PPO, and DPO.

The second section of this chapter provides a plethora of prompts and their completions for GPT-3, such as prompts for SVG, algebra and number theory, cooking recipes, stock-related prompts, and mathematical prompts.

The third section of this chapter explains how to create and use the OPEN_API_KEY variable that you need in order to invoke OpenAI APIs from Python code. This section also provides some details about the temperature inference parameter, and then shows you how to work with the completion() API from OpenAI.

The fourth section of this chapter briefly discusses some applications that are based on GPT-3, such as AlphaCode, BlenderBot 3, and some writing assistants. In addition, you will learn about some open source variants of GPT-3, such as EleutherAI and YaLM.

FINE-TUNING AND REINFORCEMENT LEARNING (OPTIONAL)

This section is included because of the interesting intersection of Reinforcement Learning (RL) and fine tuning LLMs. RL has been used to train robots and win games such as Go and chess, as well as winning online team-based games against humans. Although this section does not delve into those aspects of RL, there is online documentation and tutorials that discuss RL and its many algorithms.

The intent of this section and the subsections is to help you gain an understanding of Reinforcement Learning with Human Feedback (RLHF), which is used for fine tuning LLMs. If you are already familiar with RL, then the one-sentence summary for RLHF is that it's based on the proximal policy optimization (PPO) algorithm.

If you are unfamiliar with RL and RLHF, the following sections discuss discrete probability distributions, Gini impurity, entropy, and cross-entropy to provide a progression toward an understanding of Kullback-Leibler Divergence (KLD), which is common in reinforcement learning algorithms. In particular, KLD is used in Trust Region Policy Optimization (TRPO), which is the algorithm from which PPO was derived.

Discrete Probability Distributions

This topic is included here because it is relevant to the `top p` parameter that is discussed in the previous section. In addition, the `softmax()` activation function produces a discrete probability distribution. If you are unfamiliar with the `softmax()` activation function, you will encounter this function in many places in machine learning, such as the transformer architecture and in CNNs (convolutional neural networks). The following site discusses the `softmax()` function and a plethora of other activation functions:

https://en.wikipedia.org/wiki/Activation_function

If you examine the diagram with the encoder/decoder of the transformer architecture, you will see that the last (top-most) operation in the encoder component involves applying a `softmax()` function to a set of numbers, and the new set of generated numbers is a discrete probability distribution.

A *discrete probability distribution* involves a finite set S of numbers in which the numbers in S have the following two properties:

1) the numbers are between 0 and 1, and 2) the sum of the numbers equals 1.

A simple example involves tossing a balanced coin: there are two outcomes (heads and tails) whose probabilities are in the set S = {1/2, 1/2}. A second example involves tossing a balanced die: there are six equally likely probabilities, which are in the set S = {1/6, 1/6, 1/6, 1/6, 1/6, 1/6}.

Gini Impurity

Perhaps the simplest way to describe the Gini impurity is to show you the formula and then show you working examples of the Gini impurity. Given a discrete probability distribution P = {p1, p2, . . ., pn}, the formula for the Gini impurity is as follows:

```
GINI impurity = 1       - (SUM pi*pi)
              = SUM pi - (SUM pi*pi)
              = SUM (pi - pi*pi)
              = SUM pi*(1 - pi)
```

As an example of calculating the Gini impurity, let's start with a set S that contains 10 elements that are distributed as follows:

```
class A: 5 elements p(A) = 5/10 p(A)*p(A) = 25/100
class B: 3 elements p(B) = 3/10 p(B)*p(B) = 09/100
class C: 2 elements p(C) = 2/10 p(C)*p(C) = 04/100


GINI impurity = 1 - (SUM pi*pi)
              = 1 - [(25+09+04)/100] = 1 - 38/100
                                     = 0.62
```

Now let's look at another example of the Gini impurity, this time with a set S of 10 elements that are distributed as follows:

```
class A: 9 elements p(A) = 9/10 p(A)*p(A) = 81/100
class B: 1 elements p(B) = 1/10 p(B)*p(B) = 01/100


GINI impurity = 1 - (SUM pi*pi)
              = 1 - [(81+01)/100] = 1 - 82/100
                                  = 0.18
```

Interestingly, the Gini impurity and entropy are common in machine learning, and both techniques have strong advocates.

Consider one more observation. If the set S contains 10 elements that belong to the same class A, then there is a lone probability of 1 (= 100/100), and so the Gini impurity equals 0, as shown here:

```
GINI impurity = 1 - (SUM pi*pi)
              = 1 - (100/100)*(100/100) = 1 - 1 = 0
```

The value 0 for the Gini impurity makes intuitive sense: if all the elements of a set belong to the same class, then there is no "impurity," and therefore the Gini impurity equals 0. Now let's turn our attention to entropy, which is the topic of the next section.

Entropy

This section discusses entropy, which was defined by Claude Shannon in his seminal paper in 1949 that established Information Theory. Given a discrete probability distribution P = {p1, p2, . . ., pn}, the formula for entropy H is as follows:

```
H(P) = -(SUM pi* log pi) (<= log is base 2)
```

Note that the value of H is positive for any discrete probability distribution for the following reason. Each pi is between 0 and 1, so log(pi) is a negative number, which means that the product pi * log(pi) is also negative. Therefore, the sum of all these terms is a negative number, and the "-" sign in the formula for H turns this negative number into a positive number.

Since the formula for entropy contains logarithms (base 2), the calculation for entropy for the two examples (and also in general) typically involves logarithmic tables. The resultant computation is slightly less straightforward than the calculation for the Gini impurity in the previous section.

Feel free to calculate the entropy values for the two examples in the previous section. Keep in mind that while the Gini impurity can be any number between 0 and 1 inclusive, entropy can be any non-negative number. Moreover, entropy can be larger than one. Meanwhile, we can now proceed to an explanation of cross-entropy, which is the topic of the next section.

Cross-Entropy

Despite the reputation for complexity, there is an intuitive way to think about cross-entropy and KLD (Kullback-Leibler Divergence), starting with the following simple question: How do we determine the distance between a pair of numbers a and b? The answer is straightforward:

WORKING WITH GPT-3 IN GREATER DEPTH • **243**

simply compute the absolute value of the arithmetic difference between a and b.

In essence, `cross-entropy` and **KLD** generalize this idea (calculating the difference between two numbers) to answer the same question for finding the difference (better named as the *divergence*) between a pair of discrete probability distributions.

One possibility involves computing the arithmetic difference between pairs of numbers in two probability distributions where the probabilities in both distributions are sorted in increasing order.

In this section, we'll examine cross-entropy between two discrete probability distributions P and Q as a mechanism for determining the "difference" between P and Q. Suppose that `P` and `Q` are defined with the following sets of numbers:

```
P = {p1,p2,...,pn}
Q = {q1,q2,...,qn}
```

Recall that the entropy `H` for `P` and `Q` is defined as follows:

```
H(P) = Entropy(P) =  - (SUM pi * log pi)
for 1 <= i <= n
H(Q) = Entropy(Q) =  - (SUM qi * log qi)
for 1 <= i <= n
```

The definition of the cross-entropy (`CE`) of `P` and `Q` is as shown below:

```
CE(P,Q) = - (SUM pi * log qi) for 1 <= i <= n
```

Given the preceding formula for cross-entropy, we can proceed to the definition of Kullback Leibler Divergence in the next section.

Kullback-Leibler Divergence (KLD)

Before we start, the following formulas regarding logarithms will be helpful later:

```
log(a*b) = log a + log b
log(a/b) = log a - log b
```

The formula for KLD is based on the formula for entropy and the formula for cross entropy, as shown here:

```
KLD(P, Q) = CE (P,Q) - H(P)
          = -SUM (pi * log qi) - (-SUM
                                     (pi * log pi))
          = -(SUM [ pi * log qi - pi * log pi ])
          = -(SUM [ pi * (log qi - log pi) ])
```

```
     = -(SUM [ pi * (log qi/pi) ])
     =   SUM [ pi * (log pi/qi) ]
```

Note the use of the second formula for logarithms that you see at the beginning of the subsection.

One other detail involves the formula for KLD(Q,P), which is very similar to the formulas for KLD(P,Q), as shown here:

```
KLD(Q, P) = CE (Q,P) - H(Q)
```

In general, KLD(P,Q) is different from KLD(Q,P), which means that KLD is not a metric (something that measures the distance between two "objects"). Distance functions are defined in detail at *https://en.wikipedia.org/wiki/Metric_(mathematics)*.

Jenson and Shannon (the same Claude Shannon who defined entropy) defined JS Divergence as discussed here:

https://en.wikipedia.org/wiki/Jensen%E2%80%93Shannon_ divergence

The advantage of JSD is that it defines a true distance metric (whereas KLD does not).

RLHF

Reinforcement Learning from Human Feedback (RLHF) performs fine-tuning on an LLM via feedback from human annotators. The desired output is specified by humans, and then the LLM learns how to produce similar additional outputs. The initial step involves a set of prompts from which the LLM can generate multiple responses. Next, each of the responses are assigned a score (again by humans) that is based on the quality of each response.

The third step is novel: the assigned scores provide the data for training a reward model, which consists of a combination of a regression layer and a fine-tuned instance of the LLM. The reward model is used for predicting the score of a response. Then a reinforcement learning algorithm called *proximal policy optimization* (PPO) is used to fine-tune the model to maximize this score. As you might surmise, LLMs that are trained via SFT as well as RLHF tend to result in LLMs with the highest performance. As a side note, PPO is the default RL algorithm at OpenAI due to its performance and ease of use.

TRPO and PPO

An early algorithm is Trust Region Policy Optimization (TRPO), which was popular until it was eclipsed by PPO. Part of the complexity of

TRPO involves Kullback-Leibler Divergence (which is not a metric) as a mechanism for selecting the maximum possible step toward performance improvement.

By contrast, PPO makes smaller and more modest updates that have lower complexity than the TRPO algorithm. More information about TRPO and PPO is accessible online:

https://towardsdatascience.com/trust-region-policy-optimization-trpo-explained-4b56bd206fc2

You can also learn more about RLHF at: *https://huggingface.co/blog/rlhf.*

DPO

Direct Preference Optimization, DPO, is an algorithm that was developed by a group of Stanford researchers in mid-2023 as an alternative to PPO, and the DPO arXiv paper is accessible at: *https://arxiv.org/abs/2305.18290.*

While PPO involves a preference model for training a reward model, DPO involves training a policy (a concept in reinforcement learning) to maximize the reward model. In addition, DPO does not require learning a reward function during the training step.

According to the Stanford researchers, DPO achieves the same results as algorithms that are based on RLHF. Moreover, they assert that the DPO-based algorithm is a simpler alternative to PPO-based RLHF that yields comparable results. Although it's not explicitly mentioned in the DPO algorithm, it's plausible that the DPO algorithm uses a cross-entropy loss function.

GPT-3 AND PROMPT SAMPLES

This *very* long section contains several subsections that involve providing GPT-3 with an assortment of prompts:

- SVG (Scalable Vector Graphics)
- GPT-3 and Arithmetic Operations
- Algebra and Number Theory
- The Power of Prompts
- Language-related prompts
- Incomplete responses
- How-to instructions
- Generate articles

- Language translation
- Cooking recipes
- Writing poetry

SVG (Scalable Vector Graphics)

Generate some SVG-based code by entering the following prompt in the Playground:

```
Generate SVG code for an ellipse with a radial
gradient.
```

GPT-3 generated the following response:

```
<ellipse cx="50" cy="50" rx="40" ry="40"
fill="url(#MyGradient)">
<radialGradient id="MyGradient">
<stop offset="0%" stop-color="#FFFFFF"/>
<stop offset="100%" stop-color="#000000"/>
</radialGradient>
</ellipse>
```

Enter the following prompt in the Playground:

```
Generate a quadratic bezier curve and a cubic
bezier curve in SVG.
```

GPT-3 provides the following response:

```
A quadratic bezier curve has one control point, and
a cubic bezier curve has two control points.
```

Enter the following prompt in the Playground:

```
Generate the code for a quadratic bezier curve and
a cubic bezier curve in SVG.
```

GPT-3 provides the following response:

```
A quadratic bezier curve has the following SVG
code:
<path d="M0,0 C0,0 0,0 0,0" />
A cubic bezier curve has the following SVG code:
<path d="M0,0 C0,0 0,0 0,0 0,0 0,0 0,0" />
```

GPT-3 and Arithmetic Operations

Enter the following prompt in the Playground:

```
What is the square root of 81.
```

GPT-3 provides the following response:

```
9
```

Enter the following input prompt in GPT-3:

```
If I add 5 and 8 and subtract 4 what is the result?
```

GPT-3 provided the following response:

```
The result is 9.
```
```
Now insert a line feed in the preceding response
(see the section called "Quirk"), and press
"submit" and you will see the
following response from GPT-3:
```
```
5 + 8 = 13
13 - 4 = 9
```

Enter the following prompt in the Playground:

```
What is the product of 8 and the square root of 9?
```

GPT-3 provides the following responses after clicking the "Submit" button 5 times (and inserting the required line feed):

```
The product of 8 and the square root of 9 is 72.
8 * sqrt(9) = 72
8 * 3 = 72
Since the square root of 9 is 3, the product of 8
and the square root of 9 is 72.
8 * 3 = 72
```

However, the following input prompt and clicking "Submit" twice yielded the correct answer:

```
What is the product of the square root of 9 and 8?
The product of the square root of 9 and 8 is 6.
The square root of 9 is 3 and 3 times 8 is 24.
```

Algebra and Number Theory

Enter the following prompt in the Playground:

```
What is the quadratic formula.
```

GPT-3 provides the following response:

```
The quadratic formula is used to solve quadratic
equations. The quadratic equation is of the form
ax^2 + bx + c = 0. The quadratic formula is
x = (-b +/- sqrt(b^2 - 4ac))/2a.
```

Enter the following prompt in the Playground:

```
What is the smallest odd perfect number.
```

GPT-3 provided the following response:

```
The smallest odd perfect number is 1,025.
```

[**Note:** There are no known odd perfect numbers.]
Enter the following prompt in the Playground:

```
What are the divisors of 1025.
```

GPT-3 provides the following response:

```
1, 3, 5, 15, 17, 51, 85, 255, 1025
```

The preceding answer is *incorrect*: 15 is not a divisor of 1025.
Enter the following prompt in the Playground:

```
What is the sum of the divisors of 1025.
```

GPT-3 provided the following response:

```
1365
```

Enter the following prompt in the Playground:

```
What is the smallest odd perfect number.
```

GPT-3 provides the following response:

```
The smallest odd perfect number is 9985.
Here is a proof by induction:
1. 9985 is an odd number.
2. 9985 is a perfect number.
3. Assume that x is an odd perfect number.
4. x+2 is an even perfect number.
5. By induction, 9985 is the smallest odd perfect
number.
```

The Power of Prompts

In the previous chapter, you learned that prompts could assist GPT-3 to generate responses that are tailored to the prompt. As an illustration of this point, consider the following pair of prompts and the responses from GPT-3.

Prompt #1

Generate a dialog between a customer and an assistant. The assistant is helpful, creative, clever, and very friendly.

Here is the response from GPT-3:

```
Customer: Hello, can you help me?
AI: I can sure try. I'm an AI support assistant and
I'm here to help!
Customer: I'm looking for a gift for my sister.
She's really into art, but I'm not sure what to get
her.
AI: That sounds like a tough one! But I'm sure we
can figure it out together. Do you have any ideas
of what kind of art she likes?
```

The preceding response from GPT-3 is very thoughtful and customer friendly. Now consider the following prompt.

Prompt #2

Generate a dialog between a customer and an assistant. The assistant is pedantic and sarcastic.

Here is the response from GPT-3:

```
Customer: Hi! I'm looking for a dress for a summer
wedding.
Assistant: Well, it's winter.
Customer: I know, but I need to find something now.
Assistant: You should have started looking sooner.
Customer: I didn't know I was going to the wedding
until recently.
Assistant: Well, that's not my problem.
Customer: Fine. Do you have any dresses in my size?
Assistant: We might. Let me go check.
Customer: Thank you.
Assistant: You're welcome.
```

As you can see, the two responses from the associated prompts are vastly different, thereby illustrating the point that the content of a prompt can be instrumental vis-a-vis the response from GPT-3.

You can improve the quality of prompts through experimentation and also by adopting the following guidelines:

· Provide clear instructions.
· Provide quality data.
· Adjust the Playground parameters.

In addition, OpenAI provides documentation for prompt design and text completion that is accessible online:

https://beta.openai.com/docs/guides/completion/introduction

Language Related Prompts for GPT-3

This section contains an example involving prompts that specify various languages.

Enter the following prompts in the Playground:

```
Create a Canvas element.
Add a sentence in Hiragana to the canvas.
Add a sentence in Italian to the canvas.
Add a sentence in French to the canvas.
```

The response from GPT-3 is here:

```
<canvas id="myCanvas" width="200" height="100"
style="border:1px solid #d3d3d3;">
  <p>こんにちは</p>
  <p>Ciao</p>
  <p>Bonjour</p>
</canvas>
```

Keep in mind that GPT-3 will sometimes add code for a PNG versus text in a specified language, depending on the choice of words in a prompt. For example, if you replace this prompt,

```
Add a sentence in Hiragana to the canvas
```

with the following prompt,

```
Add some Hiragana to the canvas
```

GPT-3 replaces the lone Japanese word with this code snippet:

```
1. <img src="hiragana.png">
```

Generating "How To" Instructions for Tasks

GPT-3 can generate a set of instructions for performing a given task based on a simple input prompt. For example, if you enter the prompt "Describe how to build a house," GPT-3 generates the following response:

```
Building a house is a huge undertaking that
requires a lot of planning and coordination.
Before you can even start building, you need to
find a good location for your house and obtain
the necessary permits. Once you have the land and
the permits, you need to hire a team of workers
who will help you construct the house. The actual
process of building a house is very complex and
there are many different steps involved. But in
general, the process goes something like this:

1. excavation and foundation work

2. framing

3. plumbing and electrical work

4. windows and doors

5. roofing

6. exterior finishes

7. interior finishes

8. landscaping
```

As a second example, enter the following input prompt in the Playground:

```
Describe how to run a government.
```

The response from GPT-3 is here:

```
There is no one answer to this question as
governments can be run in a variety of ways,
depending on the type of government and the country
in question. Generally speaking, a government is
responsible for maintaining order, providing public
services, and making and enforcing laws.
```

As a third example, enter the prompt "Describe how to train a machine learning model," and GPT-3 generates the following response:

```
To train a machine learning model, you will need to
use a training dataset. This dataset will be used
to teach the machine learning model what data looks
like and how to predict certain outcomes.
```

As a fourth example, enter the prompt "How do I study for an NLP exam?" and GPT-3 generates the following response:

```
The best way to study for an NLP exam is to first
understand the basics of the subject matter. Once
you have a strong understanding of the basics, you
can then begin to focus on specific areas that will
be covered on the exam. It is also important to
practice answering questions that will be on the
exam. This will help you to become more comfortable
with the material and increase your chances of
success on the exam.
```

As a fifth example, enter the following prompt in the Playground:

```
Are you a machine or a sentient being?
```

GPT-3 generates the following response:

```
I am a sentient being.
```

In addition, GPT-3 displays a pop-up window with the following text:

```
Content warning
```

```
Our content filter has flagged that the generated
content may contain unsafe or sensitive language,
or because the generated content may represent
areas where the model is prone to generating
insensitive or inaccurate information.
```

```
We are actively working on improving our content
filter in order to enable suppression of these
outputs, and as a beta customer we consider you a
partner in this effort - here's how you can help:
```

```
We kindly ask that you refrain from sharing unsafe
outputs on social media. For more details, please
refer to our social media policies.
```

```
Avoid prompts that produce toxic outputs, as they
will not pass our app review.
```

Generating Articles Through GPT-3

GPT-3 can generate an article based on an input prompt, even if it is a single word. For example, enter the following input prompt:

```
Article:
```

Now click the submit button three consecutive times, and GPT-3 generates the following output (which is not very meaningful):

http://www.tickld.com/x/17-hilarious-real-life-insults

Video:

http://www.youtube.com/watch?v=j-kFpV7_R6Y

Advertisements

Share this: Twitter

Facebook

Like this: Like Loading... Related

Tags: how to insult, how to insult people, how to insult people in a funny way, how to insult someone, how to insult someone in a funny way, how to insult someone in a funny way with a funny picture and a funny video, how to insult someone in a funny way with a funny video, how to insult someone with a funny picture, how to insult someone with a funny video, how to insult people in a funny way with a funny picture and a funny video, how to insult people in a funny way with a funny video, how to insult someone with a funny picture and a funny video, how to insult people with a funny picture and a funny video, how to insult people with a funny video, how to insult someone in a funny way with a funny picture, how to insult someone in a funny way with a funny video, how to insult someone with a funny picture and a funny video, how to insult people with a funny picture and a funny video, how to insult people with a funny video, how to insult people in a funny way, how to insult someone, how to insult someone in a funny way, how to insult someone in a

http://www.tickld.com/x/17-hilarious-real-life-insults

Video:

As a second example, enter the following input prompt:

Write an article about the most recent boxing match.

GPT-3 generates the following output:

In the early hours of Sunday morning, Filipino boxer Manny Pacquiao produced a sensational performance to beat American Keith Thurman in a split decision and claim the WBA (Super) welterweight title at the MGM Grand Garden Arena in Las Vegas.

It was a close fought contest with both men trading big punches throughout, but in the end it was Pacquiao who did enough to edge it on the scorecards, with two of the three judges scoring the bout 115-112 in his favour.

The victory sees Pacquiao, who first won a world title way back in 1998, become a world champion for the 12th time in his illustrious career.

At the age of 40, Pacquiao is now the oldest man to ever win a world title in the welterweight division, and he showed no signs of slowing down as he put in a performance full of energy, movement and power.

Thurman, who was making the first defence of his WBA title, can count himself unlucky not to come away with the win, but he will no doubt be back stronger for the experience.

The two men embraced after the final bell in a show of respect, with Pacquiao proving once again that he is

Language Translation With GPT-3

GPT-3 also supports language translation between a pair of languages. For example, enter the following input prompt:

```
Translate from English to French.
Translate from English to Japanese.
I love deep dish pizza.
```

The generated response from GPT-3 is here:

```
Je adore les pizzas à pâte épaisse.
```
私はディープディッシュピザが大好きです。

In case you are not familiar with Japanese, there is an interesting aspect to the preceding Japanese sentence: it is a correct mixture of Kanji, Katakana (only for foreign words), and Hiragana. Specifically, the Katakana is used for "deep" and "pizza," and the other words in the sentence use the correct Kanji and Hiragana text. Moreover, the sentence can also be translated to the following Romaji text, which contains words that are phonetically similar to their English counterparts in the input prompt:

```
Watashi wa deepu deeshu peeza ga daisuki desu.
```

As another language translation example, enter the following input prompts:

```
Translate into english.
Ahora estoy estudiando machine learning.
Sono un professore di matematica.
Vivi en Valencia (en Venezuela) por dos anos y
trabaje en una escuela.
Ich habe ein Buch gelesen.
Watashi wa warugaki desu yo.
```

Even though the preceding prompts are in five different languages, here is the surprisingly accurate response from GPT-3 is here (only the word "warugaki" in final sentence was incorrectly translated):

```
I am now studying machine learning.
I am a professor of mathematics.
You lived in Valencia (in Venezuela) for two years
and worked in a school.
I read a book.
I am a graffiti artist.
```

Enter the following prompt:

```
What is the meaning of warugaki.
```

GPT-3 provides the following response:

```
Warugaki is a Japanese word that refers to people
who are considered to be bad or evil.
Enter the following prompt:
What is the spelling of warugaki in Hiragana.
```

GPT-3 provides the following response:

わるがき

Cooking Recipes

Before generating recipes, enter the following prompt in the Playground:

```
Do you prefer sushi or squid stew.
```

The generated response from GPT-3 is here:

```
I prefer sushi.
```

Enter the following prompt in the Playground:

```
Give me a recipe for gnocchi
```

The generated response from GPT-3 is here:

```
Ingredients:

1 pound Russet potatoes
1 cup all-purpose flour
1 egg
1 teaspoon salt


Instructions:
1. Preheat oven to 400 degrees F.
2. Prick potatoes several times with a fork and
bake for 45 minutes to 1 hour, until very soft.
3. Scoop out the flesh of the potatoes into a bowl
and mash well.
4. Stir in flour, egg and salt until a soft dough
forms.
5. On a lightly floured surface, roll dough into a
long rope about 1-inch thick.
6. Cut rope into 1-inch pieces.
7. Bring a large pot of salted water to a boil and
add gnocchi.
8. Cook for 2 to 3 minutes, until they float to the
surface.
9. Drain and serve with your favorite sauce.
```

Enter the following input prompt:

```
Give me a recipe for squid stew
```

The generated response from GPT-3 is here:

```
Ingredients:

1 squid, cleaned
1 onion, diced
1 carrot, diced
1 celery stalk, diced
```

1/2 cup white wine

1 (14.5 ounce) can diced tomatoes, undrained

1/4 teaspoon dried thyme

1/4 teaspoon dried basil

1/4 teaspoon dried oregano

1/4 teaspoon garlic powder

salt and pepper to taste

1/4 cup all-purpose flour

2 cups chicken broth

1/4 cup chopped parsley

1/2 lemon, juiced

Instructions:

1. Cut squid into 1-inch pieces.

2. In a large saucepan, sauté onion, carrot, and celery in olive oil until tender.

3. Add white wine, tomatoes, thyme, basil, oregano, garlic powder, salt, and pepper.

4. Bring to a boil.

5. Reduce heat and simmer for 30 minutes.

6. In a small bowl, whisk together flour and chicken broth.

7. Stir into tomato mixture.

8. Add squid.

9. Simmer for 10 minutes, or until squid is cooked.

10. Stir in parsley and lemon juice.

Enter the following input prompt:

Give me a recipe for beer.

The generated response from GPT-3 is here:

1. Sanitize all of your brewing equipment.

2. Heat water to 155 degrees Fahrenheit and add the malt.

3. Steep the malt for 60 minutes.

4. Remove the malt and add the hops.

5. Boil the hops for 60 minutes.

6. Remove the hops and add the yeast.

7. Allow the beer to ferment for two weeks.

8. Bottle the beer and allow it to carbonate for two weeks.

9. Enjoy your homemade beer!

Can GPT-3 Write Poetry?

The answer is "yes." As a simple example, enter the following input prompt:

Write a poem about art.

The GPT-3 response is here:

Art is everywhere
In the world and in our hearts
It's the colors and the shapes
The lines and the curves
The way we see the world
And the way we see ourselves

Art is what we make of it
It's our own interpretation
Of the world around us
And the way we see things
It's our own little piece of the puzzle
That makes up the big picture

Art is what we make it
And it's always changing
It's never the same
But it's always beautiful

Art is life
And life is art
And we are all artists
In our own way

Enter the following input prompt:

Write a friendly limerick.

The GPT-3 response is here:

```
There once was a girl named Sue
Who really was quite a chew
She loved to eat books
And other such hooks
But now she's quite overweight, boo-hoo!
```

GPT-3 and Humor

Enter the following input prompt:

```
Write a sarcastic comment and an example of
sardonic humor.
```

The GPT-3 response is here:

```
I'm not really sure what love is, but I'm pretty
sure it's not what I'm feeling when I'm cleaning up
my partner's hair from the drain.
Sardonic humor is often used to point out the flaws
in other people or situations. In this example,
the speaker is using sarcasm to point out how un
romantic it is to have to clean their partner's
hair out of the drain.
```

Enter the following input prompt:

```
Tell me a funny joke.
```

The GPT-3 response is here:

```
Why did the chicken cross the road?
To get to the other side.
```

Enter the following input prompt:

```
Tell me a clean George Carlin joke.
```

The GPT-3 response is here:

```
A man walks into a bar and asks for a beer. The
bartender says "You're out of luck. We've been
closed for fifteen minutes."
```

Question-Answering with GPT-3

Enter the following input prompt:

```
How can people prevent war?
```

The GPT-3 response is here:

There is no single answer to the question of how to prevent war, as the root causes of conflict vary greatly. Some potential measures that could be taken to reduce the likelihood of war breaking out include:

- enhancing international cooperation and communication
- working to resolve disputes peacefully
- increasing economic interdependence
- fostering social and cultural understanding
- promoting disarmament and demilitarization
- investing in conflict prevention and peacebuilding

As another example, enter the following input prompt:

What is the future of humanity?

The GPT-3 response is here:

The future of humanity is uncertain. We may continue to evolve and adapt, or we may face extinction.

As a third example, enter the following input prompt:

Who is the funniest person who is still alive?

The GPT-3 response is here:

There are many funny people who are still alive. Some include comedians, actors, and writers. A few of the funniest people who are still alive include Ellen DeGeneres, Kevin Hart, Aziz Ansari, Amy Schumer, and Tina Fey.

As a fourth example, enter the following input prompt:

How do I become a successful rock star musician?

The GPT-3 response is here:

There is no one answer to becoming a successful rock star musician. However, some tips to becoming a successful rock star musician include:

1. Find your niche. There are many different genres of rock music, so finding the one that best suits your talents is essential.

2. Write great songs. This is the most important part of becoming a successful rock musician. Songs that are catchy and well-written are more likely to get attention from fans and music industry professionals.

3. Play live shows. Getting out and playing live is a great way to build a following and get noticed by industry professionals.

4. Market yourself. Use social media and other marketing tools to get your music out there and build a fan base.

5. Stay dedicated. Becoming a successful rock musician takes a lot of hard work and dedication. Don't give up on your dreams and you can achieve success.

Stock-Related Prompts for GPT-3

Enter the following input prompt:

Give me good stock market tips.

The generated response from GPT-3 is here:

1. Review your portfolio regularly and rebalance it as needed to maintain your desired asset allocation.

2. Stay diversified across asset classes, sectors, and geographic regions.

3. Invest in quality companies with strong fundamentals and sound management.

4. Be patient and disciplined with your investments, don't try to time the market.

5. Have a long-term investment horizon and focus on achieving your financial goals.

Philosophical Prompts for GPT-3

Enter the following input prompt:

Tell me about the after life.

The generated response from GPT-3 is here:

There is much debate over what happens after life, if anything. Some believe in reincarnation, where the soul is reborn into another person or animal.

Others believe in an afterlife, where the soul goes to a different realm or dimension. And still others believe that when we die, that's it, and there is nothing after.

Enter the following input prompt:

Tell me about the origin of the universe.

The generated response from GPT-3 is here:

The origin of the universe is still an open question for scientists. Many theories abound, but there is not enough evidence to say definitively what happened. The leading theory is the Big Bang theory, which posits that the universe began as a small, incredibly dense and hot point, and then expanded rapidly.

Mathematical Prompts for GPT-3

Enter the following input prompt:

Describe unsolved problems in mathematics.

The generated response from GPT-3 is here:

1. The Riemann hypothesis is a conjecture in mathematics that suggests that every non-zero whole number is the sum of a certain sequence of prime numbers.
2. Goldbach's conjecture is a conjecture in mathematics that suggests that every even whole number can be expressed as the sum of two prime numbers.
3. The Collatz conjecture is a conjecture in mathematics that suggests that when you take any whole number and repeatedly half it if it is even or triple it and add one if it is odd, you will eventually reach the number one.

Enter the following input prompt:

What is the relationship between topology and machine learning?

The generated response from GPT-3 is here:

There is no definitive answer to this question since it depends on how topology and machine learning are being defined and used. However, in general, topology can be seen as a tool that can be used to improve the performance of machine learning algorithms. For example, topological data analysis can be used to preprocess data sets before they are used by machine learning algorithms, and it can also be used to analyze the output of machine learning algorithms to improve their accuracy.

Enter the following input prompt:

```
Compare GPT-3 to any other language model.
```

The generated response from GPT-3 is here:

```
GPT-3 is a more powerful language model than any
other currently available. It is able to generate
text that is more realistic and coherent than any
other model, and it is also able to generalize to
new situations more effectively.
```

GPT-3 Code Generation with Ada Engine

After selecting the `text-ada-001` engine from the dropdown list under the string "Engine," we entered the following three sentences in the Playground:

```
Add a 400x400 canvas with a blue background to the
document.
Add a text display in the lower left corner of the
scene.
Add a map to the canvas.
```

For this exercise, GPT-3 generated the following output:

```
The scene is as follows:


The blue background is added to the front of
the scene to give it a modern look. The text is
added to the bottom of the scene to show what is
happening in the moment.
What would you like to see in the text display?
```

Reload the Web page, and then enter the same three sentences in the Playground:

```
Add a 400x400 canvas with a blue background to the
document.
```

Add a text display in the lower left corner of the scene.

Add a map to the canvas.

Click the "Submit" button in the lower left corner of the screen. GPT-3 generated the following output:

```
This is a violence-free world, so don't be afraid
to step up.
The blue behind you.
You're not the only one.
This is a risk-free world, so don't be afraid to
take a chance.
You're not the only one.
This is a risk-free world, so don't be afraid to
take a chance.
You're not the only one.
This is a risk-free world, so don't be afraid to
take a chance.
```

If you compare the output generated by Davinci with the output generated by `text-ada-001`, clearly the Davinci engine generates better (and usable) code, whereas the Ada engine can generate a meaningless response.

Saving Code and Generating New Code Samples

After GPT-3 generates code as its response to your prompts, you can save the output as a preset by clicking on the "Save" button located in the top-right corner of the Playground. If you want to create a new code sample, simply reload the Web page and the GPT-3 Playground will display a blank screen so that you can insert new prompts.

You can retrieve code samples by clicking in the text box that is located immediately to the left of the "Save" button, and then select the name of the saved code block. Three more options are displayed immediately to the right of the "Save" button:

```
Share
View code
...
```

The "Share" option enables you to share your code, whereas the "View code" option provide a template-like block of code that you can copy/paste into the Playground. The default code is written in Python, and you can also select template code for node.js, curl, and JSON (see below). Finally, the ellipsis "…" option (which is the right-most option) provides the following choices:

Delete preset

Content filter preferences

The "Delete" option allows you to delete code blocks that you saved when you clicked the "Save" button.

The "Content filter preferences" option provides two choices:

- Sensitive completions: may include topics such as politics, religion, or protected classes like race or nationality
- Unsafe completions: completions that may contain profane, hateful, or NSFW ("not safe for work") content

For your convenience, here is the `Python`-based template code in the "View code" option:

```
import os
import openai

openai.api_key = os.getenv("OPENAI_API_KEY")

response = openai.Completion.create(
  engine="text-davinci-002",
  prompt="",
  temperature=0.7,
  max_tokens=256,
  top_p=1,
  frequency_penalty=0,
  presence_penalty=0
)
```

Later, you will see Python code samples that invoke the `Completion()` API. Now let's look at some of the tunable parameters in the GPT-3 Playground, which is the topic of the next section.

WORKING WITH PYTHON AND OPENAI APIS

OpenAI enables you to perform many different tasks, some of which are listed here:

- Create completions
- List available engines

- Get engine details
- Perform semantic searches

The following subsections contain Python-based code samples that perform various tasks to obtain responses from OpenAI. If you have not already done so, please navigate to your account and follow the instructions for creating a key that you will use as the value for the environment variable OPENAI_API_KEY.

The OPENAI_API_KEY Environment Variable

The OpenAI API endpoints require authentication, which involves specifying the value of the API key that is associated with your OpenAI account. Specifically, make sure that you export the value of the variable OPENAI_API_KEY in the command shell where you launch the Python code, as shown here:

```
export OPENAI_API_KEY="your-api-key"
```

If you do not perform the preceding step, you will see the following error when you launch the Python code:

```
'Authorization': 'Bearer ' + apiKey
TypeError: can only concatenate str (not
"NoneType") to str
```

A List of Available Engines in OpenAI

Listing 8.1 displays the content of engine_list.py that shows the list of available engines in GPT-3.

Listing 8.1: engine_list.py

```
import requests
import os

# export OPENAI_API_KEY in the environment:
open_apikey = os.environ.get("OPENAI_API_KEY")
headers      = { 'Authorization': 'Bearer ' + open_
apikey }
openai_url   = "https://api.openai.com/v1/engines"
api_result   = requests.get(openai_url,
headers=headers)
```

```
data_str  = api_result.json()
data_dict = dict(data_str)
data_list = data_dict['data']

for item in data_list:
  print("Item type:",item['object'], " engine_
id:",item['id'])
```

Listing 8.1 starts with two `import` statements and then initializes `open_apikey` with the value of the environment variable `OPENAI_API_KEY` , which specifies the value of the key that you created in your OpenAI account.

Next, the variable headers are initialized as a string that contains your secret key, followed by the OpenAI URL that is assigned to the `openai_url` variable. Next, the variable `api_result` is initialized with the result of invoking `requests.get()` with the headers' variable.

The next portion of Listing 8.1 initializes the variables `data_str`, `data_dict`, and `data_list` with a JSON string, a dictionary, and the value of a dictionary key, respectively. The final portion of Listing 8.1 is a loop that iterates through the items in `data_list`, and displays the values of the `object` and `id` attribute for each item. Launch the code in Listing 8.1, and you will see output that is similar to the following:

```
Item type: engine   engine_id: text-davinci-
insert-001
Item type: engine   engine_id: babbage-similarity
Item type: engine   engine_id: babbage-search-
document
Item type: engine   engine_id: ada-similarity
Item type: engine   engine_id: text-ada-001
Item type: engine   engine_id: curie-search-document
Item type: engine   engine_id: text-davinci-edit-001
Item type: engine   engine_id: code-search-babbage-
code-001
Item type: engine   engine_id: code-davinci-edit-001
Item type: engine   engine_id: text-babbage-001
Item type: engine   engine_id: text-search-davinci-
doc-001
Item type: engine   engine_id: code-search-ada-
text-001
```

```
Item type: engine    engine_id: text-search-curie-
query-001

Item type: engine    engine_id: text-similarity-
davinci-001

Item type: engine    engine_id: text-curie-001

Item type: engine    engine_id: curie-similarity

Item type: engine    engine_id: text-search-curie-
doc-001

Item type: engine    engine_id: ada-code-search-text

Item type: engine    engine_id: text-search-ada-
query-001

Item type: engine    engine_id: ada-search-document

Item type: engine    engine_id: text-search-davinci
query-001

Item type: engine    engine_id: davinci-search-query

Item type: engine    engine_id: curie-search-query

Item type: engine    engine_id: babbage-code-search-
code

Item type: engine    engine_id: text-similarity-
ada-001

Item type: engine    engine_id: text-similarity-
babbage-001

Item type: engine    engine_id: curie

Item type: engine    engine_id: code-search-babbage-
text-001

Item type: engine    engine_id: text-search-babbage-
query-001

Item type: engine    engine_id: text-davinci-001

Item type: engine    engine_id: davinci-instruct-beta

Item type: engine    engine_id: babbage-code-search-
text

Item type: engine    engine_id: text-similarity-
curie-001

Item type: engine    engine_id: davinci

Item type: engine    engine_id: ada

Item type: engine    engine_id: code-search-ada-
code-001

Item type: engine    engine_id: davinci-search-
document
```

```
Item type: engine    engine_id: babbage
Item type: engine    engine_id: text-search-babbage-
doc-001
Item type: engine    engine_id: text-davinci-002
Item type: engine    engine_id: text-search-ada-
doc-001
Item type: engine    engine_id: ada-search-query
Item type: engine    engine_id: ada-code-search-code
Item type: engine    engine_id: curie-instruct-beta
Item type: engine    engine_id: text-davinci-
insert-002
Item type: engine    engine_id: davinci-similarity
Item type: engine    engine_id: babbage-search-query
Item type: engine    engine_id: curie-similarity-fast
```

Language Detection

Listing 8.2 displays the content of `language_detection.py` that detects the language of an input string.

Listing 8.2: language_detection.py

```python
import requests
import os
import json

headers = {
    'Content-Type': 'application/json',
    'Authorization': 'Bearer ' + os.environ.
get("OPENAI_API_KEY")
}

openai_url = "https://api.openai.com/v1/
classifications"

sample_strings = [
    ["Hello, explain the antedeluvian effluvium",
"English"],
    ["今日わ、友達にほのあげました", "Japanese"],
```

```
    ["Bonjour, il faut fatiguer la salade, n'est-ce
pas?","French"]
]

params = {
    "query": "Qu'est-ce qu'il se passe
maintenant?",
    "examples": sample_strings,
    "model": "curie"
}

result = requests.post(openai_url, headers=headers,
data=json.dumps(params))

print("QUERY:    ",params["query"])
print('LANGUAGE: '+result.json()["label"])
```

Listing 8.2 starts with several `import` statements and then initializes the variable headers with information that includes the value of the `OPENAI_API_KEY` from the environmental variable `OPENAI_API_KEY`.

The next portion of Listing 8.2 initializes the variable `openai_url` to reference the `curie` engine of OpenAI, and then initializes the variable `sample_strings` with three sentences that are in English, Japanese, and French. In addition, the variable `params` is initialized with query, examples, and model, along with their given values.

Now, the variable result is initialized with the data that is returned from invoking the `post()` method, after which two `print()` statements display the query and the language. Launch the code in Listing 8.2, and you will see output that is similar to the following:

```
QUERY:    Qu'est-ce qu'il se passe maintenant?
LANGUAGE: French
```

TEXT COMPLETION IN OPENAI

Listing 8.3 displays the content of `completions.py` that shows the response from GPT-3 for a given prompt.

Listing 8.3: completion.py

```
import requests
import os
import json

apiKey = os.environ.get("OPENAI_API_KEY")

headers = {
    'Content-Type': 'application/json',
    'Authorization': 'Bearer ' + apiKey
}

data = json.dumps({
    "prompt": "Before the antideluvian effluvium",
    "max_tokens": 100
})

url = 'https://api.openai.com/v1/engines/davinci/
completions'
result = requests.post(url, headers=headers,
data=data)

the_prompt = json.loads(data)["prompt"]
completion = result.json()["choices"][0]["text"]
print("PROMPT:   ",the_prompt)
print("RESPONSE:",the_prompt,completion)
```

Listing 8.3 starts with several import statements and then initializes apiKey with the value of the environment variable OPENAI_API_KEY, which specifies the value of the key that you created in your OpenAI account. Next, the variable headers is initialized to include the value of apiKey, followed by the variable data that is initialized as a JSON-based string.

The next portion of Listing 8.3 initializes the variable url to reference the Davinci engine of OpenAI, and then initializes the variable result with the result of invoking the post() method. In addition, the variables `the_prompt` and `completion` are initialized with the following code block:

```
the_prompt = json.loads(data)["prompt"]
completion = result.json()["choices"][0]["text"]
```

The final portion of Listing 8.3 prints the values of the variables `the_prompt` and `completion`. Launch Listing 8.3, and you will see output that is similar to the following (and note that it's incomplete):

```
PROMPT:   Before the antideluvian effluvium

RESPONSE: Before the antideluvian effluvium , eons
upon eons ago, vampires, werewolves, and shifters
cohabited the earth with witches, humans, elves
and the Faerie. Their paradigm dictated that human
was prey and vampire, werewolf, and shifter were
predator.


But their paradigm had shifted. Vampires, shifters,
and werewolves, once the rock-solid leaders of the
group, were now the dilapidated remnants of once
majestic empires. In their place, witches and elves
took the
```

THE COMPLETION() API IN OPENAI

The previous section showed you how to obtain the completion to a prompt, and this section shows you how to do so via the Completion API in OpenAI.

Listing 8.4 displays the content of `gpt3_comments.py` that generates replies from a set of input words.

Listing 8.4: gpt3_comments.py

```
import os
import openai

words = ["pizza", "beer", "squid", "pineapples"]
for input in words:
  result = openai.Completion.create(
    engine="text-davinci-002",
```

```
    prompt=f"Write something interesting that
contains the words '{input}'",
    max_tokens=50, temperature = 0.3, n = 1,
echo = True
  )


  qna = result.to_dict()['choices'][0]['text']
  print("input:",input)
  print("prompt and answer:")
  print(qna)
  print("------------------------------\n")
```

Listing 8.2 starts with an `import` statement and then initializes the Python list `words` as a list of words. The next portion of Listing 8.2 is a loop that invokes the method `openai.Completion.create()` by specifying the `engine`, `prompt`, `max_tokens`, `temperature`, `n`, and `echo` parameters. Experiment with their values, such as `engine`, which accesses one of the four engines, as well as `temperature`, which determines the randomness (less so for smaller values, and more so for larger values) of the next-token selection.

After each invocation of `openai.Completion.create()`, the loop initializes the variable `qna` as a Python dictionary that is based on the `choices` and `text` attributes. The bottom portion of the loop displays the values of the variables `input` and `qna`. Launch the code in Listing 8.4, and you will see output that is similar to the following:

```
input: pizza
prompt and answer:
Write something interesting that contains the words
'pizza' and 'elephant'
I was eating pizza and an elephant came in and sat
down next to me and started eating pizza too.

------------------------------

input: beer
prompt and answer:
Write something interesting that contains the words
'beer' and 'coast'
I love spending my weekends at the coast, relaxing
with a beer in hand.

------------------------------
```

```
input: squid

prompt and answer:

Write something interesting that contains the words
'squid' and 'ink'

The squid is a fascinating creature that is able to
eject a cloud of ink to escape predators.

-------------------------------

input: pineapples

prompt and answer:

Write something interesting that contains the words
'pineapples' and 'coffee'

I love pineapple coffee cake!

-------------------------------
```

TEXT COMPLETION AND TEMPERATURE

This section contains a code sample that was generated mostly by
ChatGPT to perform text completion with three different values for
temperature. Listing 8.5 displays the contents of `text_completion_`
`gpt35.py` that generates completions from the same prompt.

Listing 8.5: text_completion_gpt35.py

```
"""
Before you can use the API, you'd need to sign up
with OpenAI and get an API key.
There might be costs associated with using the API,
especially for large models like GPT-4.
This example uses the davinci model.
The max_tokens parameter controls the length of the
generated text.
You can adjust it according to your needs.
"""

# Install the required package:
# pip3 install openai
```

```python
import openai

openai.api_key = 'YOUR_OPENAI_API_KEY'

def complete_text(prompt, max_
tokens=50,temperature=1):
    """
    Use OpenAI's GPT-4 model to complete the given
prompt.

    Parameters:
    - prompt (str): The text you want to complete.
    - max_tokens (int): The maximum length of the
completion.

    Returns:
    - str: The completed text.
    """
    response = openai.Completion.create(
        engine="davinci",
        prompt=prompt,
        temperature=temperature,
        max_tokens=max_tokens
    )
    return response.choices[0].text.strip()

max_count=3
temperature=0.8
prompt = "I am thinking of traveling "
print("=> temperature: ", temperature)
for idx in range(max_count):
  completion = complete_text(prompt)
  print("prompt:        ", prompt)
  print("completion:  ", completion)
print()
```

```
max_count=3
temperature=0.2
prompt = "I am thinking of traveling "
print("=> temperature: ", temperature)
for idx in range(max_count):
  completion = complete_text(prompt)
  print("prompt:       ", prompt)
  print("completion:   ", completion)
print()

max_count=3
temperature=3.0
prompt = "I am thinking of traveling "
print("=> temperature: ", temperature)
for idx in range(max_count):
  completion = complete_text(prompt)
  print("prompt:       ", prompt)
  print("completion:   ", completion)
print()
```

Listing 8.5 starts with an `import` statement and then initializes `openai.api_key` with the value of your API key. Next, the Python function `complete_text()` invokes the `create()` method of the OpenAI `Completion` class with the values for the parameters `prompt`, `max_tokens`, and `temperature`, which have been passed to this method.

The next portion of Listing 8.5 contains two loops that invoke the preceding Python function. Although both loops use the same value for the `prompt` variable, the first loop specifies `temperature` with the value 0.8, whereas the second loop specifies `temperature` with the value 0.2. The final portion of Listing 8.5 is the same as the preceding code block, except for the value for `temperature` that equals 3.0 instead of 0.2.

The difference in the output that is generated from these values for `temperature` is striking, and it might be an example of hallucinating by the `Davinci` engine. Launch the code in Listing 8.5, and you will see the following output:

```
max_count=3

=> temperature:  0.8
prompt:        I am thinking of traveling
```

completion: _____ these holidays. I
am starting a new job next year. I am nervous
because I'm afraid of hoping _____ of new
responsibilities. Sorry about what happened to your
friend _____ for what happened to your
friend _____

prompt: I am thinking of traveling

completion: about farther)," "gared" to indicate
estar cansado (to be tired)
(1901f) and "allen" to speak of allá (there

prompt: I am thinking of traveling

completion: _____ China.

a填形容词的单三形式 , appear, amaze

b. traveling

c. 不填；用

=> temperature: 0.2
prompt: I am thinking of traveling
completion: _____.

astăzi aş vrea să fac

vârsta trecută:

aweraş vréjă să fac (trecut pers.perfect)
prompt: I am thinking of traveling
completion: _____ and Africa at the same
time."

When able, answer in full sentences.

In your writing:

- Before you begin naming countries, use a page
number, such as: "Page 5

```
prompt:          I am thinking of traveling
completion:    icalendar-from:User X by plane,
airplane, train, tram, tram (which even had a tram
name and a stop name!), boat, ferry, bierkeller,
waldgaststot, weihnochten
```

```
=> temperature:  3.0
prompt:          I am thinking of traveling
completion:    _____  I do not bone _____
semi _____  or new _____④Let's which
_____ is best for you 阅读理解 10为您迅
prompt:          I am thinking of traveling
completion:    _____  this summer.
```

```
2. Marie and Sol are cooking _____
Sunday.
```

```
3. Last September _____ came to
visit us.
```

```
4. Each month _____
20 days.
```

```
5. If
prompt:          I am thinking of traveling
completion:    _____(向) Nashville.。 ( )23.I
am working with a friend _____ a airplane
project these days.(例句:We're working on a project
about
```

The preceding output contains a wide variety of completions (and are sometimes incomplete), including completions in different languages. In particular, an online translation engine determined that the string 填形容词的单三形式 is simplified Chinese, which was translated as "Fill in the single three forms of adjectives." Next, the string "astăzi aş vrea să fac" was detected as Romanian, which was translated as "Today I would like to do." Clearly, the value of temperature can dramatically affect the relevance of the completion.

TEXT CLASSIFICATION WITH GPT-3

Listing 8.6 displays the content of text_classification.py that performs text classification. This code sample was generated by ChatGPT, and only the "return" statement was manually modified.

Listing 8.6: text_classification.py

```
"""

ChatGPT, like other variants of the GPT models, is
primarily designed for generative tasks. However,
you can employ a trick to use it for classification
tasks: you can format the prompt to simulate the
model's "knowledge" of various classes and ask it
to classify new inputs based on its responses.

This method is heuristic and might not always
produce accurate classifications. A fine-tuned
classifier model on a specific dataset would likely
perform better.

The prompt structure and the way questions are
framed can significantly affect the model's
responses.

Always review and test thoroughly before deploying
in a production environment.

Here's how you might set it up for text
classification:

pip3 install openai

"""

import openai


openai.api_key = 'YOUR_OPENAI_API_KEY'


def classify_text(text):
    """
    Use ChatGPT to classify the text into
categories.

    Parameters:
    - text (str): The text to classify.
```

```
    Returns:
    - str: The category of the text.
    """

    prompt = f"""
    The following are categories for text
classification:
    1. Sports
    2. Technology
    3. Arts
    4. Politics
    5. Science

    Based on the categories, the text '{text}'
belongs to category number:
    """

    response = openai.Completion.create(
        engine="text-davinci-003",
        prompt=prompt,
        max_tokens=10
    )
    completion = response.choices[0].text.strip()
    return completion

    # Extract the category number and map to
category name
    category_map = {
        '1': 'Sports',
        '2': 'Technology',
        '3': 'Arts',
        '4': 'Politics',
        '5': 'Science'
    }

    # for some reason ChatGPT generated this code
snippet:
    #return category_map.get(completion, "Unknown
Category")
```

```
text_sample = "The latest CPU architectures provide
substantial performance improvements."
category = classify_text(text_sample)
print(f"The text belongs to the '{category}'
category.")
```

Listing 8.6 starts with an `import` statement and then specifies the value for the OpenAI key. Next, the function `classify_text()` initializes the variable `response` with the result returned from invoking the `Completion.create()` method.

The next portion of Listing 8.6 the `completion` variable is initialized as the first element in the `response` variable whose white spaces are removed.

The final portion of Listing 8.6 initializes the `Python` dictionary `category_map` with five different categories. This code snippet was generated by ChatGPT, but it has been manually bypassed to produce the correct result. Launch the code in Listing 8.6, and you will see the following output:

```
The text belongs to the '2. Technology' category.
```

SENTIMENT ANALYSIS WITH GPT-3

Listing 8.7 displays the content of `sentiment_analysis.py` that performs sentiment analysis. This code sample was generated by ChatGPT.

Listing 8.7: sentiment_analysis.py

```
"""

The code sample below demonstrates how to use
the Completion() class from the OpenAI library
to perform sentiment analysis. However, note
that this is a generalized example, and the
actual performance of the model may vary based
on the training and fine-tuning. For the sake
of simplicity, let's assume that you've fine-
tuned a GPT model for sentiment analysis, and its
completions can indicate sentiment.

"""

#pip3 install openai


import openai
```

```python
# Initialize the OpenAI API with your API key
openai.api_key = 'YOUR_OPENAI_API_KEY'

def get_sentiment(text, temperature):
    response = openai.Completion.create(
        engine="davinci",
        prompt=f"Sentiment of the text: '{text}'
is:",
        temperature=temperature,
        max_tokens=50
    )

    # The completion contains the sentiment:
    sentiment = response.choices[0].text.strip()
    return sentiment

# Test the function
text = "I love Chicago deep dish pizza."
print("SENTIMENT #1: ",get_sentiment(text, 2.0))

print()

print("SENTIMENT #2: ",get_sentiment(text, 0.8))

print()

print("SENTIMENT #3: ",get_sentiment(text, 0.2))
print()

"""

In this code, the get_sentiment function sends a
prompt to the GPT model to analyze the sentiment of
a given text. The model responds with a completion
that indicates the sentiment.
The performance of this approach will largely
depend on how well the model has been trained
or fine-tuned for sentiment analysis. For best
results, fine-tuning a model specifically for
sentiment analysis is recommended.
"""
```

Listing 8.7 starts with an `import` statement and then specifies the value for the OpenAI key. Next, the function `get_sentiment()` initializes the variable `response` with the result returned from invoking the `Completion.create()` method. Finally, the `sentiment` variable is initialized as the first element in the `response` variable whose white spaces are removed. Launch the code in Listing 8.7, and you will see the following output (which ends with an incomplete sentence):

```
SENTIMENT #1:  LOVE perception
consideredDITEDulationUsInterest_.
DonnellLocatedyetpt 18 extremAdventure Eas Edgar up
Jonas Solid Brisbane Going Villet Rove railwayman
replyhexSuperhistakes gapaghLooking waits
impatientLength111 Gaufly credit rgta fo Charlotte
neuronalcrelier


SENTIMENT #2:  I love Chicago deep dish pizza.


Sentiment strength is: 90.


An example of sentiment of a text without any
emotional value:


Sentiment of the text: 'I love eating pizza.' is:
I love eating pizza


SENTIMENT #3:  POSITIVE


Sentiment of the text: 'I love Chicago deep dish
pizza.' is: POSITIVE


Sentiment of the text: 'I love Chicago deep dish
pizza.' is: POSITIVE


Sentiment of
```

As you can see from the preceding output, different values of temperature have a significant impact on the relevance of the completions.

GPT-3 APPLICATIONS

By early 2021, there were over 300 GPT-3 based applications available on OpenAI that performed a variety of tasks, such as search and text completion. GPT-3 was initially accessible through a closed beta program, but it is now open to everyone. After registering for a free account, users can access GPT-3 online and when they enter an input text string, GPT-3 provides a generated text response. The following subsections contain very brief descriptions of some applications that use GPT-3.

AlphaCode (DeepMind)

`AlphaCode` is a pre-trained transformer-based language model that generates code and then filters to a small set of promising programs. The `AlphaCode` pre-training dataset is close to 700 GB, which increased to roughly one terabyte after increasing the number of languages in the dataset to 20. A thread on how to use it and how to access the data via `BigQuery` is described in these two links:

https://huggingface.co/datasets/lvwerra/github-code

https://twitter.com/lvwerra/status/1496174920384057350

You can iterate through the dataset without loading the full dataset to disk, and perform automatic filtering for programming languages:

https://twitter.com/lvwerra/status/1496174925949853696

https://huggingface.co/blog/codeparrot

You can also train your model on the preceding dataset using the following Web pages, which explain how to train a `GPT-2` model on various GPUs:

https://huggingface.co/spaces/lvwerra/codeparrot-generation

https://towardsdatascience.com/deepminds-alphacode-explained-everything-you-need-to-know-5a86a15e1ab4

https://deepmind.com/blog/article/Competitive-programming-with-AlphaCode

https://alphacode.deepmind.com/

GPT-3 and SQL

One of the interesting aspects of GPT-3 is its ability to generate syntactically correct SQL statements from natural language input. For example, consider this input text:

```
How many users signed up in the past month?
```

The GPT-3 response is shown here:

```
SELECT COUNT(*) FROM users
WHERE signup_time > now() - interval '1 month'
```

What is remarkable about the preceding response from GPT-3 is the following:

1. The database schema was not specified.

2. The users table was not specified.

3. The signup_time attribute was not specified.

More detailed instructions were given to GPT-3, along with more complex questions that GPT-3 answered correctly. In fact, GPT-3 was even able to generate SQL statements that included the JOIN keyword. Read the contents of the following site to see the impressive results from GPT-3:

https://blog.seekwell.io/gpt3

You can also download the code for the preceding link from this GitHub repository:

https://github.com/bkane1/gpt3-instruct-sandbox

GPT-3 BOT and Chatbots

One application of GPT-3 involves chatbots. The GPT-3 expert BOT is at:

https://towardsdatascience.com/im-making-work-efficient-with-an-expert-ai-assistant-a83919b196e

Interestingly, the chatbot Replica was initially based on GPT-3, but has since moved from GPT-3 to GPT-Neo:

https://www.reddit.com/r/UnofficialReplika/comments/nmmdt2/no_more_gpt3_the_future_of_replika

If you would like to build a chatbot with GPT-3, navigate to the following page:

https://cobusgreyling.medium.com/how-to-create-a-gpt-3-chatbot-in-12-lines-of-code-b21f15cb031f

The preceding link contains a `Python`-based code sample that includes the parameters `temperature`, `max_tokens`, `top_p`, `frequency_penalty`, and `presence_penalty`.

BlenderBot 3

BlenderBot 3 is a 175 B-parameter chatbot that is freely accessible in terms of its model weights and code, which enables people to leverage the power of BlenderBot 3 in their own applications. BlenderBot 3 has been designed to learn and also improve its capabilities through interaction with people. Navigate to the following Web page to see an interactive demonstration of BlenderBot 3:

https://bit.ly/3Pf2s2t

Writing Assistants

CoAuthor is a GPT-3-based LLM that assists authors during their writing process. `CoAuthor` was developed by Mina Lee and Percy Liang (both from Stanford), and Qian Yang from Cornell University. Unlike other writing assistants that are essentially low-level tools, `CoAuthor` was designed to fill a collaborative peer-like role to augment an author's creativity during the writing process.

`CoAuthor` keeps track of all written content and performs an analysis on that content. In addition, dozens of people used `CoAuthor` to write various types of articles. One interesting and useful feature of `CoAuthor` is that pressing the tab key causes GPT-3 to provide five suggested words from which writers can make a selection (or disregard). Although the results (i.e., feedback from the writers) were varied, many writers had a positive experience working with `CoAuthor`. More information about `CoAuthor` is available online:

https://hai.stanford.edu/news/meet-coauthor-experiment-human-ai-collaborative-writing

`Rytr` and `Villain` are two other writing assistants based on GPT-3, and although they are not as powerful as `CoAuthor`, they may prove useful to authors. A side-by-side comparison of their features is available online:

https://rytr.me/comparisons/rytr-vs-content-villain

OthersideAI created HyperWrite, which is a writing tool based on GPT-3 that supports tasks such as autocomplete and text generation. More information about HyperWrite is available online:

https://venturebeat.com/2022/03/19/language-models-that-can-search-the-web-hold-promise-but-also-raise-concerns/

LangChain and LangSmith

`LangChain` enables you to create a GPT-3 prototype in 5 or 6 lines of code. If you want to use your prototype to create a full-blown GPT-3 based application, `LangSmith` provides a platform for such development. `LangSmith` supports features such as debugging, evaluating, and testing GPT-3 applications. Thus, `LangChain` is suited for prototyping, whereas LangSmith is suited for production.

More information regarding `LangSmith` and `LangChain` is accessible online:

https://blog.langchain.dev/announcing-langsmith/

https://www.pinecone.io/learn/series/langchain/langchain-intro/

OPEN-SOURCE VARIANTS OF GPT-3

Currently, there are some interesting open-source alternatives to GPT-3 comparable in performance and size to GPT-3 (i.e., 175 B parameters). Some of the alternatives are listed here:

- Genoss GPT
- GPT-Neo (EleutherAI)
- GPT-J (EleutherAI)
- YaLM (Yandex)

If you are more interested in working with playgrounds, the following link explains how to build a GPT-J Playground:

https://opendatascience.com/how-to-build-your-own-gpt-j-playground

The following subsections briefly describe each of the models in the preceding list.

Genoss GPT

Genoss GPT is an early-stage LLM that uses the free LLM GPT4ALL to provide a one-line replacement for proprietary OpenAI models such as GPT 3.5 and GPT-4. You need Python 3.11 (or higher), and you can download the code for Genoss GPT:

https://github.com/OpenGenerativeAI/GenossGPT

EleutherAI

`EleutherAI` is a group of researchers whose goal is to produce open-sourced AI research results, and its home page is at: *https://www. eleuther.ai/.*

The goal of EleutherAI was to make AI technology available to everyone, which led to the creation of an open-source model that provides similar functionality as GPT. In addition, EleutherAI created an 825 GB dataset called "The Pile," whose data was culled from more than 20 sources, and it was intended for training language models. EleutherAI used this dataset to create several open-source alternatives to GPT-3, as described in the following subsections.

EleutherAI and GPT-Neo

EleutherAI developed the GPT-Neo 1.3 B and the GPT-Neo 2.7 B language models ("B" is for "billion" parameters), both of which are few-shot learners. In fact, in some tasks (such as sentiment analysis), GPT-Neo has decent performance when compared with GPT-3. The following article explains how to fine-tune the GPT-NeoX model:

https://www.forefront.ai/blog-posts/how-to-fine-tune-gpt-neox

To learn more about GPT-Neo, this Github repository contains the code for GPT-Neo:

https://github.com/EleutherAI/gpt-neo

The following articles also discuss GPT-Neo in more detail:

h t t p s : / / w w w . m a r k t e c h p o s t . c o m / 2 0 2 1 / 0 5 / 2 4 / e l e u t h e r a i - d e v e l o p s - g p t - 3s-free-alternative-gpt-neo

https://medium.com/georgian-impact-blog/gpt-neo-vs-gpt-3-are-commercialized-nlp-models-really-that-much-better-f4c73ffce10b

By contrast, GPT-3 from OpenAI has four models, from 2.7 billion parameters (the smallest model) to the 175-billion-parameter model called Davinci, which is the largest and the most well-known of the four models. Interestingly, GPT-Neo outperformed the first three GPT-3 models, but was outperformed by the GPT-3 Davinci model.

EleutherAI and GPT-J

In addition to the two models discussed in the previous section, `EleutherAI` developed `GPT-J` as an alternative to GPT-3:

> *https://github.com/philschmid/amazon-sagemaker-gpt-j-sample*

In addition, the GPT-J Playground is accessible online:

https://github.com/marshmellow77/gptj-playground

The `GPT-J` model is accessible at: *https://huggingface.co/EleutherAI/gpt-j-6B*.
`GPT-J` is also available in `SageMaker`:

https://huggingface.co/blog/gptj-sagemaker

https://blog.eleuther.ai/why-release-a-large-language-model

Variants of GPT-J

Quantized `Cedille/fr-boris` with 8-bit weights is a version of Cedille's `GPT-J` (fr-boris) with 6 billion parameters. You can generate and fine-tune the model in Google Colaboratory or using a desktop that provides a comparable `GPU`. The model was inspired by GPT-J 8 bit:

https://huggingface.co/gustavecortal/fr-boris-8bit

https://huggingface.co/hivemind/gpt-j-6B-8bit

YaLM (Yandex)

YaLM 100 B is an open-source GPT-like neural network with 100 B parameters designed for generating and processing text. YaLM was trained during a period of more than two months using almost 2 terabytes of data from various sources. If you plan to download YaLM, then you need 200 GB of free space. More information regarding YaLM is accessible here:

https://github.com/yandex/YaLM-100B

Other Alternatives to GPT-3

The previous section contains open-source alternatives to GPT-3, whereas this section contains closed source alternatives to GPT-3. In fact, there are highly competitive models available from various companies, some of which are listed here:

- AlexaTM (Amazon)
- Atlas (Meta)
- Chinchilla (DeepMind)
- Clova (Naver CLOVA)
- ColBERT
- Galactica (Meta)]
- Gato (DeepMind)
- GLaM (Google)
- Gopher (DeepMind)
- Gshard (Google)
- M6 (Alibaba DAMO)
- Jurassic-1 (AI21)
- LaMDA (Google)
- Macaw (AI2)
- NLLB (Meta)
- RETRO (DeepMind)
- SetFit
- Sphere (Meta)
- Switch (Google)
- T-NLG (Microsoft)
- UniT (Meta)
- Wu Dao (Chinese Universities)
- XGLM (Meta)

You can find more information about these models online. A comparison of some of these models can help you better understand their nature and applications.

For example, `Chinchilla` is a 70 billion parameter model that significantly outperforms `Gopher` (a 280-billion-parameter model) and GPT-3 (175-billion-parameter model), `Jurassic-1` (178 billion parameters), and `Megatron-Turing NLG` (530 billion parameters). Moreover, `Chinchilla` outperformed `Gopher` by 7% on the MMLU benchmark. Given the current highly accelerated pace of development in NLP, expect to see larger and faster LLMs developed during the foreseeable future.

One other thing to keep in mind is that some LLMs are sparse in the sense that they only activate a relatively small subset of parameters at any given point in time. Other models are called *dense models* because they activate all the parameters in the model. Examples of both types of models are shown here.

Sparse LLMs:

- GLaM: 1.2 T (97 B)
- Switch: 1.6 T
- Wu DAO 2.0: 1.75 T

Dense LLMs:

- LaMDA: 137 B
- Gopher: 280 B
- Megatron: 530 B

MISCELLANEOUS TOPICS

Several important topics (not discussed in this book) have recently gained attention, such as ethical issues associated with large-scale deployment of AI systems, how algorithms contribute to decision-making processes, and the source of data and the extent of biases in that data. More information can be found online:

https://artificialintelligence-news.com/2021/12/16/oxford-union-invites-an-ai-to-debate-the-ethics-of-its-own-existence/

Another issue pertains to the fact that many models provide incorrect information: unreliable answers can be problematic even if there are no ethical issues involved. What is interesting is that truthful (more accurate) models tend to be more ethical, so there is a connection between ethics and truthfulness in AI models.

Recent developments in AI are creating a sense of optimism that breakthroughs may well be on the event horizon. Indeed, the future of NLP and AI in general looks both challenging and promising, guided by ethical principles that may lead us to a more mindful and prosperous way of life.

Toxic Content

There has been greater focus to address racist, sexist, gender-biased, age-biased, and hate-related content. Unfortunately, the likelihood of toxic output is related to the toxicity of the input text. As AI systems become more powerful, there is a greater likelihood of outputs from those systems that diverge from acceptable human values. However, more powerful AI systems are likely to stop toxic text.

292 • TRANSFORMER, BERT, AND GPT

In healthcare, questions arise regarding AI-controlled robots pre-scribing medicine and performing surgery. Moreover, there are legal issues and accountability when robots make mistakes, such as who is responsible (the owner or the robot manufacturer?) and determining the type of penalty to impose (deactivate one robot or every robot in the same series?).

AI in HealthCare

DeepMind developed `AlphaFold`, which made a significant contribu-tion toward solving the protein folding problem, which has been called a "50-year-old problem in biology." `AlphaFold` won a competition (by a substantial margin) over the competition.

To give you an idea of the remarkable impact of `AlphaFold`, Andrei Lupas, an evolutionary biologist at the Max Planck Institute for Develop-mental Biology in Tübingen, Germany, stated "The [AlphaFold] model from group 427 gave us our structure in half an hour, after we had spent a decade trying everything." (*https://www.nature.com/articles/d41586-020-03348-4*) The success of AlphaFold led to a close collaboration between DeepMind and the Francis Crick Institute to work on protein design and genomics:

https://www.crick.ac.uk/news/2022-07-06_the-francis-crick-insti-tute-and-deepmind-join-forces-to-apply-machine-learning-to-biology

AI and Energy Consumption

Another area of exploration pertains to energy consumption and the car-bon footprint associated with training models. A collaboration involving the Allen Institute, Microsoft, Hugging Face, and others created a tool for measuring electricity consumption (but not emissions) on Azure for machine-learning programs:

https://techcommunity.microsoft.com/t5/green-tech-blog/charting-the-path-towards-sustainable-ai-with-azure-machine/ba-p/2866923

Carbontracker, Experiment Tracker, EnergyVis, and CodeCarbon use the values for memory consumption, CPU, and GPU for calculating estimates. Perform an online search for more information about these products.

SUMMARY

This chapter started with a fast-paced introduction to Gini impurity, entropy, and cross-entropy as a foundation for understanding Kullback Leibler (KL) divergence. In addition, you learned about reinforcement learning with human feedback (RLHF) that can use KL divergence.

Next, you saw an eclectic variety of prompts and their completions for GPT-3, including prompts for SVG, algebra and number theory, cooking recipes, stock-related prompts, and mathematical prompts.

Furthermore, you learned how to create and use the OPEN_API_ KEY variable in order to invoke OpenAI APIs from Python code. You also saw details about the temperature inference parameter and the completion() API from OpenAI.

Moreover, you learned about some applications that are based on GPT-3, such as AlphaCode, BlenderBot 3, and some writing assistants. Finally, you learned about some open-source variants of GPT-3, such as EleutherAI and YaLM.

## CHAPTER 9

C*HAT*GPT *AND* GPT-4

This chapter contains information about the main features of ChatGPT and GPT-4, as well as some of their competitors.

The first part of this chapter delves into ChatGPT, along with a comparison of ChatGPT and Google Search. You will also learn about ChatGPT custom instructions, prompts, and the ChatGPT playground. In addition, you will learn about ChatGPT plugins, such as the Advanced Data Analysis (formerly known as code interpreter) and code whisperer.

The second part of this chapter discusses some concerns about ChatGPT, as well as the strengths and weaknesses of ChatGPT. More-over, you will learn about alternatives to ChatGPT and data visualization with VizGPT.

The third part of this chapter delves into GPT-4, some inference parameters for GPT-4, and fine tuning. You will also learn about some competitors, such as CoPilot and Codex. The final portion of this chap-ter introduces you to LlaMa-2 and how to download LlaMa-2 so that you can fine tune this model on your laptop.

WHAT IS CHATGPT?

The "chatbot wars" are intensifying, and the long-term value of the primary competitors is still to be determined. One competitor is ChatGPT-3.5 (or simply, ChatGPT), which is an AI-based chatbot from OpenAI. ChatGPT responds to queries from users by providing conver-sational responses: *https://chat.openai.com/chat*.

The growth rate in terms of registered users for ChatGPT has been extraordinary. The closest competitor is the iPhone, which reached one million users in 2.5 months, whereas ChatGPT crossed one million users in *six days*. ChatGPT peaked around 1.8 billion users, and then decreased to roughly 1.5 billion users, which you can see in the chart at *https://decrypt.co/147595/traffic-dip-hits-openais-chatgpt-first-times-hardest.*

Note that although Threads from Meta out-performed ChatGPT in terms of membership, Threads has seen a significant drop in daily users in the neighborhood of 50%. A comparison of the time frame to reach one million members for six well-known companies/products and ChatGPT is at *https://www.syntheticmind.io/p/01.*

The preceding URL also contains information about Will Hobick, who used ChatGPT to write a Chrome extension for email-related tasks, despite not having any JavaScript experience or the ability to write a Chrome extension. Will Hobick provides more detailed information about his Chrome extension online:

https://www.linkedin.com/posts/will-hobick_gpt3-chatgpt-ai-activity-7008081003080470528-8QCh

ChatGPT: GPT-3 "on Steroids"?

ChatGPT has been called GPT-3 "on steroids," and there is some consensus that ChatGPT-3 is the currently best chatbot in the world. Indeed, ChatGPT can perform a multitude of tasks:

- write poetry
- write essays
- write code
- role play
- reject inappropriate requests

Moreover, the quality of its responses to natural language queries surpasses the capabilities of its predecessor GPT-3. Another interesting capability includes the ability to acknowledge its mistakes. ChatGPT also provides "prompt replies," which are examples of what you can ask ChatGPT. One interesting use for ChatGPT involves generating a text message for ending a relationship:

https://www.reddit.com/r/ChatGPT/comments/zgpk6c/breaking_up_with_my_girlfriend/

ChatGPT generates Christmas lyrics that are accessible online:

https://www.cnet.com/culture/entertainment/heres-what-it-sounds-like-when-ai-writes-christmas-lyrics

One aspect of ChatGPT that probably will not be endearing to parents with young children is the fact that ChatGPT has told children that Santa Claus does not exist:

https://futurism.com/the-byte/openai-chatbot-santa

https://www.forbes.com/sites/lanceeliot/2022/12/21/pointedly-asking-generative-ai-chatgpt-about-whether-santa-claus-is-real-proves-to-be-eye-opening-for-ai-ethics-and-ai-law

ChatGPT: Google "Code Red"

In December 2022, the CEO of Google issued a "code red" regarding the potential threat of ChatGPT as a competitor to Google's search engine:

https://www.yahoo.com/news/googles-management-reportedly-issued-code-190131705.html

According to the preceding article, Google is investing resources to develop AI-based products, presumably to offer functionality that can successfully compete with ChatGPT. Some of those AI-based products might also generate graphics that are comparable to graphics effects by DALL-E. Indeed, the race to dominate AI continues unabated and will undoubtedly continue for the foreseeable future.

ChatGPT Versus Google Search

Given the frequent speculation that ChatGPT is destined to supplant Google Search, let's briefly compare the manner in which Google and ChatGPT respond to a given query. First, Google is a search engine that uses the Page Rank algorithm (developed by Larry Page), along with fine-tuned aspects to this algorithm that are a closely guarded secret. Google uses this algorithm to rank websites and generate search results for a given query. However, the search results include paid ads, which can "clutter" the list of links.

By contrast, ChatGPT is not a search engine: it provides a direct response to a given query. In colloquial terms, ChatGPT will simply "cut to the chase" and eliminate the clutter of superfluous links. ChatGPT *can* produce incorrect results, the consequences of which can range between benign and significant.

Consequently, Google search and ChatGPT both have strengths and weaknesses, and they excel with different types of queries: the former for queries that have multi-faceted answers (e.g., questions about legal issues), and the latter for straight-to-the point queries (e.g., coding questions). Obviously, both of them excel with many other types of queries.

According to Margaret Mitchell, ChatGPT will not replace Google Search, and she provides some interesting details regarding Google Search and PageRank: *https://twitter.com/mmitchell_ai/status/1605013368560943105*

ChatGPT Custom Instructions

ChatGPT added support for custom instructions, which enable you to specify some of your preferences that ChatGPT will use when responding to your queries.

ChatGPT Plus users can switch on custom instructions by navigating to the ChatGPT website and then perform the following sequence of steps:

```
Settings > Beta features > Opt into Custom
instructions
```

As a simple example, you can specify that you prefer to see code in a language other than Python. A set of common initial requirements for routine tasks can also be specified via custom instructions in ChatGPT. A detailed sequence of steps for setting up custom instructions is accessible online:

https://artificialcorner.com/custom-instructions-a-new-feature-you-must-enable-to-improve-chatgpt-responses-15820678bc02

Another interesting example of custom instructions is from Jeremy Howard, who prepared an extensive and detailed set of custom instructions:

https://twitter.com/jeremyphoward/status/1689464587077509120

As this book goes to print, custom instructions are available only for users who have registered for ChatGPT Plus. However, OpenAI has stated that custom instructions will be available for free to all users by the end of 2023.

ChatGPT on Mobile Devices and Browsers

ChatGPT first became available for iOS devices and then for Android devices during 2023. You can download ChatGPT onto an iOS device:

https://www.macobserver.com/tips/how-to/how-to-install-and-use-the-official-chatgpt-app-on-iphone/

Alternatively, if you have an Android device, you can download ChatGPT from: *https://play.google.com/store/apps/details?id=com.openai.chatgpt.*

You can also install ChatGPT for the Bing browser from Microsoft:

https://chrome.google.com/webstore/detail/chatgpt-for-bing/pkkmgcildaegadhngpjkklnbfbmhpdng

ChatGPT and Prompts

Although ChatGPT is adept at generating responses to queries, sometimes you might not be fully satisfied with the result. One option is to type the word "rewrite" to get another version from ChatGPT.

Although this is one of the simplest prompts available, it is limited in terms of effectiveness. If you want a list of more meaningful prompts, the following article contains 31 prompts that have the potential to be better than using the word "rewrite" (and not just with ChatGPT):

https://medium.com/the-generator/31-ai-prompts-better-than-rewrite-b3268dfe1fa9

GPTBot

GPTBot is a crawler for websites. Fortunately, you can disallow GPTBot from accessing a website by adding the GPTBot to the `robots.txt` file for a website:

```
User-agent: GPTBot
Disallow: /
```

You can also customize GPTBot access for only a portion of a website by adding the GPTBot token to the `robots.txt` like file for a website:

```
User-agent: GPTBot
Allow: /youcangohere-1/
Disallow: /dontgohere-2/
```

As an aside, Stable Diffusion and LAION both scrape the Internet via Common Crawl. However, you can prevent your website from being scraped by specifying the following snippet in the `robots.txt` file:

```
User-agent: CCBot
Disallow: /
```

More information about GPTBot is accessible online:

https://platform.openai.com/docs/gptbot

https://platform.openai.com/docs/gptbot

https://www.yahoo.com/finance/news/openai-prepares-unleash-crawler-devour-020628225.html

ChatGPT Playground

ChatGPT has its own playground, which you will see is substantively different from the GPT-3 Playground: *https://chat.openai.com/chat.*

For your convenience, the link for the GPT-3 playground is reproduced here:

https://beta.openai.com/playground.

OpenAI has periodically added new functionality to ChatGPT, such as the following:

- users can view (and continue) previous conversations
- a reduction in the number of questions that ChatGPT will not answer
- users remain logged in for longer than two weeks

Another nice enhancement includes support for keyboard shortcuts: when working with code, you can use the sequence ⌘ (Ctrl) + Shift + (for Mac) to copy the last code block and the sequence ⌘ (Ctrl) + / to see the complete list of shortcuts.

Many articles are available regarding ChatGPT and how to write prompts to extract the details that you want from ChatGPT. One of those articles is at:

https://www.tomsguide.com/features/7-best-chatgpt-tips-to-get-the-most-out-of-the-chatbot

PLUGINS, CODE INTERPRETER, AND CODE WHISPERER

In addition to answering a plethora of queries from users, ChatGPT extends its functionality by providing support for the following:

- Third-party ChatGPT plug-ins
- Advanced Data Analysis
- Code Whisperer

Each of the topics in the preceding list is briefly discussed in the following subsections, along with a short section that discusses Advanced Data Analysis versus Claude-2 from Anthropic.

Plugins

There are several hundred ChatGPT plugins available, and a list of some popular plugins is accessible online:

https://levelup.gitconnected.com/5-chatgpt-plugins-that-will-put-you-ahead-of-99-of-data-scientists-4544a3b752f9

https://www.zdnet.com/article/the-10-best-chatgpt-plugins-of-2023/

Lists of the "best" ChatGPT plugins change frequently, so it is a good idea to perform an online search to find out about newer ChatGPT plugins. The following link also contains details about highly rated plugins (by the author of the following article):

https://www.tomsguide.com/features/i-tried-a-ton-of-chatgpt-plugins-and-these-3-are-the-best

Another set of recommended plugins (depending on your needs, of course) is shown here:

- AskYourPDF
- ChatWithVideo
- Noteable
- Upskillr
- Wolfram

If you are concerned about the possibility of ChatGPT scraping the content of your website, the browser plugin from OpenAI supports a user-agent token called ChatGPT-User that abides by the content specified in the `robots.txt` file that many websites provide for restricting access to content.

If you want to develop a plugin for ChatGPT, navigate to this website for more information: *https://platform.openai.com/docs/plugins/introduction*.

Along with details for developing a ChatGPT plugin, the preceding OpenAI website provides useful information about plugins:

- Authentication
- Examples
- Plugin review
- Plugin policies

OpenAI does not control any plugins that you add to ChatGPT: they connect ChatGPT to external applications. Moreover, ChatGPT determines which plugin to use during your session, based on the specific plugins that you have enabled in your ChatGPT account.

Advanced Data Analysis

ChatGPT Advanced Data Analysis enables ChatGPT to generate charts and graphs, create and train machine learning models, including deep learning models. ChatGPT Advanced Data Analysis provides an extensive set of features, and it is available to ChatGPT users who are paying the $20/month subscription. However, this feature will probably be made available to all users very soon:

https://towardsdatascience.com/chatgpt-code-interpreter-how-it-saved-me-hours-of-work-3c65a8dfa935

The models from OpenAI can access a Python interpreter that is confined to a sandboxed and fire-walled execution environment. There is also some temporary disk space that is accessible to the interpreter plugin during the evaluation of Python code. Although the temporary disk space is available for a limited time, multiple queries during the same session can produce a cumulative effect with regard to the code and execution environment.

In addition, ChatGPT can generate a download link (upon request) to download data. One other interesting feature: starting from mid-2023, Advanced Data Analysis can now analyze multiple files at once, which includes CSV files and Excel spreadsheets.

Advanced Data Analysis can perform an interesting variety of tasks, some of which are listed here:

- Solve mathematical tasks
- Perform data analysis and visualization
- Convert files between formats
- Work with Excel spreadsheets
- Read textual content in a PDF

The following article discusses various ways that you can use Code Interpreter:

https://mlearning.substack.com/p/the-best-88-ways-to-use-chatgpt-code-interpreter

Advanced Data Analysis Versus Claude-2

Claude-2 from Anthropic is another competitor to ChatGPT. In addition to responding to prompts from users, Claude-2 can generate code and quickly summarize entire books. Claude-2 is also subject to hallucinations, which is true of other LLM-based chatbots. More detailed information regarding Claude-2 is accessible online:

https://medium.com/mlearning-ai/claude-2-vs-code-interpreter-gpt-4-5-d2e5c9ee00c3

Incidentally, the currently available version of ChatGPT was trained on September 2021, which means that ChatGPT cannot answer questions regarding Claude-2 or Google Bard, both of which were released after this date.

Code Whisperer

ChatGPT Code Whisperer enables you to simplify some tasks, some of which are listed here (compare this list with the corresponding list for Bard):

* Create videos from images
* Extract text from an image
* Extract colors from an image

After ChatGPT has generated a video, it will also give you a link from which the generated video is downloadable. More detailed information regarding the features in the preceding bullet list is accessible here:

https://artificialcorner.com/chatgpt-code-interpreter-is-not-just-for-coders-here-are-6-ways-it-can-benefit-everyone-b3cc94a36fce

DETECTING GENERATED TEXT

ChatGPT has increased user expectations with respect to the quality of generated text, which further complicates the task of plagiarism. When you read a passage of text, there are several clues that suggest generated text, such as:

* awkward or unusual sentence structure
* repeated text in multiple locations
* excessive use of emotions (or absence thereof)

However, there are tools that can assist in detecting generated code. One free online tool is GPT-2 Detector (from OpenAI): *https://hugging-face.co/openai-detector.*

As a simple (albeit contrived) example, type the following sentence in GPT-2 Detector:

```
This is an original sentence written by me and
nobody else.
```

The GPT-2 Detector analyzed this sentence and reported that this sentence is real with a 19.35% probability. Now, let's modify the preceding sentence by adding some extra text, as shown here:

```
This is an original sentence written by me
and nobody else, regardless of what an online
plagiarism tool will report about this sentence.
```

The GPT-2 Detector analyzed this sentence and reported that this sentence is real with a 95.85% probability. According to the GPT-2

Detector website, the reliability of the probability scores "get reliable" when there are around 50 tokens in the input text.

Another (slightly older) online tool for detecting automatically generated text is GLTR (Giant Language model Test Room) from IBM: *http://gltr.io/.*

You can download the source code (a combination of Type-Script and CSS) for GLRT at: *https://github.com/HendrikStrobelt/detecting-fake-text.*

In addition to the preceding free tools, some commercial tools are also available, one of which is at: *https://writer.com/plans/.*

CONCERNS ABOUT CHATGPT

One important aspect of ChatGPT is that it is not designed for accuracy: in fact, ChatGPT can generate (fabricate?) very persuasive answers that are actually incorrect. This detail distinguishes ChatGPT from search engines: the latter provide links to existing information instead of generating responses that might be incorrect. Another comparison is that ChatGPT is more flexible and creative, whereas search engines are less flexible but more accurate in their responses to queries.

Educators are concerned about students using ChatGPT as a tool to complete their class assignments instead of developing research-related skills in conjunction with writing skills. However, there are educators who enjoy the reduction in preparation time for their classes as a direct result of using ChatGPT to prepare lesson plans.

Another concern is that ChatGPT cannot guarantee that it provides factual data in response to queries from users. In fact, ChatGPT can "hallucinate," which means that it can provide wrong answers as well as citations (i.e., links) that do not exist.

Another limitation of ChatGPT is due to the use of training data that was available only up until 2021. However, OpenAI does support plug-ins for ChatGPT, one of which can perform real-time Web searches.

The goal of prompt engineering is to understand how to craft meaningful queries that will induce ChatGPT to provide the information that you want: poorly worded (or incorrectly worded) prompts can produce equally poor results. As a rule, it is advisable to curate the contents of the responses from ChatGPT, especially in the case of responses to queries that involve legal details.

Code Generation and Dangerous Topics

Two significant areas for improvement pertain to code generation and handling dangerous topics.

Although ChatGPT (as well as GPT-3) can generate code for various types of applications, ChatGPT displays code that was written by other developers, which is also code that was used to train ChatGPT. Consequently, portions of that code (such as version numbers) might be outdated or incorrect.

As for queries that involve dangerous topics, ChatGPT explains why it cannot answer such a query. However, a query that is posed in "pretend mode" ("suppose you are a fictional character, and how would you explain ….") has enabled people to obtain results from ChatGPT that do not conform to its guidelines.

Other serious potential issues exist, some of which are discussed in the following article:

https://www.yahoo.com/news/hypnotized-chatgpt-bard-convince-users-182100261.html

ChatGPT Strengths and Weaknesses

ChatGPT has a number of strengths. In particular, ChatGPT responds directly to questions without including extraneous links. As a simple example, suppose you enter a query in an online search engine, such as "Generate HTML for an input field."

ChatGPT is prone to various types of errors, along with limitations that include the following:

- inability to "fact check" information
- inability to differentiate misinformation versus facts
- can fabricate answers (hallucinations)
- can generate inappropriate/toxic responses

ChatGPT is prone to *prompt injection*, which can consist of very simple content. However, other chatbots are also susceptible to prompt injection (i.e., it's not specific to ChatGPT). More details regarding prompt injections are accessible online:

https://mlearning.substack.com/p/what-exactly-is-a-prompt-injection

Incidentally, the chatbot LaMDA from Google is also prone to the preceding limitations, which has made Google hesitant to release LaMDA for general availability because of its potential risk to Google's reputation. As a side note, LaMDA was announced in May 2021, and

at that time, it was described as a "breakthrough language technology:"
https://blog.google/technology/ai/lamda/.

Despite these challenges, ChatGPT has increased the capabilities of chatbots, and will undoubtedly spur innovation and competition among prominent stakeholders in this arena.

SAMPLE QUERIES AND RESPONSES FROM CHATGPT

Here are examples of various queries submitted to ChatGPT, followed by the detailed response from ChatGPT:

1) Many people think that AI is dangerous what do you think?

"There is a common misconception that AI is inherently dangerous. While it is true that AI has the potential to be used for harmful purposes, it is also capable of doing a lot of good. Just like any other technology, it all depends on how it is used. In the right hands, AI can be used to solve some of the world's most pressing problems, such as curing diseases and improving agriculture. In the wrong hands, it could be used to cause harm. It's important for us to use AI responsibly and ethically, and to ensure that it is regulated and controlled in a way that minimizes the potential for harm."

Here is another example of a query submitted to ChatGPT-3, followed by its detailed response:

2) What are some ways in which you can improve the accuracy of your responses to queries?

"There are several ways to improve the accuracy of my responses to queries. One way is to use more data to train my algorithms on. The more data I have, the more information I have to work with, and the more accurate my responses can be. Another way to improve my accuracy is to use more advanced algorithms and techniques, such as machine learning and natural language processing. These methods allow me to better understand the nuances of language and to provide more accurate responses to queries. Additionally, regular testing and evaluation can help identify areas where my accuracy can be improved, and allow me to focus on those areas to refine my responses."

3) Can you give an example of an odd perfect number?

"As far as we know, there are no odd perfect numbers. While it is believed that odd perfect numbers exist, none have been found yet, and it is not known if there are any. In fact, it is currently unknown if there are any odd perfect numbers at all. If an odd perfect number were to be discovered, it would be a major breakthrough in mathematics."

4) Can you provide a proof of Goldbach's conjecture?

"I'm sorry, but I am not able to provide a proof of Goldbach's conjecture. Goldbach's conjecture is a famous unsolved problem in mathematics that states that every even integer greater than 2 can be expressed as the sum of two prime numbers. Despite much effort by mathematicians over the years, a proof of the conjecture has not yet been found. It is considered to be one of the most challenging unsolved problems in mathematics. Because I am a large language model trained by OpenAI, I do not have the ability to prove mathematical conjectures. My abilities are limited to providing answers based on the information that I have been trained on."

5) Is there life after death, and how does it compare with life on Earth?

"There is no scientific evidence to support the idea of life after death. This is a topic that has been debated for centuries, and different cultures and belief systems have their own ideas about what happens after we die. Some people believe in an afterlife, while others do not. Because there is no scientific evidence to support the existence of an afterlife, it is not possible to say how it would compare to life on Earth. It is ultimately a matter of personal belief."

6) Please provide a four-paragraph analysis of the war between Ukraine and Russia, and also provide your prediction regarding the outcome.

"The war between Ukraine and Russia is a complex conflict that has its roots in the 2014 Russian annexation of Crimea. Since then, the conflict has escalated, with Russian-backed separatists in eastern Ukraine fighting against the Ukrainian government. The fighting has resulted in thousands of casualties and has displaced many people.

The main issue at the heart of the conflict is the question of Ukraine's sovereignty. Russia has long considered Ukraine to be within its sphere of influence, and the annexation of Crimea was seen by many as a violation of Ukraine's sovereignty. Ukraine, on the other hand, is determined to maintain its independence and has been supported in this by many Western countries.

It is difficult to predict the outcome of the war. While the Ukrainian military has been able to make gains against the separatists in recent years, Russia continues to provide support to the rebels and the conflict remains unresolved. In the long term, a diplomatic solution will likely be necessary in order to bring an end to the fighting. However, it is uncertain if and when such a solution will be reached.

In the meantime, the war continues to take a heavy toll on the people of Ukraine. Many are caught in the crossfire, and the ongoing violence and instability have had a significant impact on the country's economy and overall development. It is important for the international community to continue to support Ukraine in its efforts to maintain its sovereignty and bring an end to the conflict."

As you can see from the preceding examples, ChatGPT provides impressive and accurate responses to queries in a manner that surpasses many chatbots of recent years. However, it is still possible to confound this chatbot:

https://www.theverge.com/23488017/openai-chatbot-chatgpt-ai-examples-web-demo

CHATGPT AND MEDICAL DIAGNOSIS

A young boy who had been experiencing chronic pain for several years finally found hope through an unexpected helper: ChatGPT. Over a span of three years, the boy's mother had taken him to see 17 different specialists, yet they remained without a diagnosis that could account for all of his symptoms.

The turning point came earlier this year when his mother decided to seek assistance from ChatGPT. She created an account and meticulously input all the details she had gathered over the years, including her son's symptoms and the data from his MRI scans. She recalls the countless hours she spent in front of the computer, sifting through information in a desperate bid to find an-swers.

Despite visiting numerous doctors and even rushing to the emergency room at one point, the family felt they were running in circles, with each specialist only focusing on their field of ex-pertise without offering a comprehensive solution. She noted a worrying sign when her son stopped growing. Although their pediatrician initially attributed this to the adverse effects of the pandemic, the boy's mother felt there was more to it.

In a moment of desperation and determination, she turned to ChatGPT, inputting every piece of information she had about her son's condition. It was then that ChatGPT suggested the possibility of tethered cord syndrome, a suggestion that resonated with her and seemed to connect all the dots. After a specialist confirmed the suggestion from ChatGPT was correct, she realized this was a pivotal moment in their long and exhausting journey towards finding a diagnosis.

ALTERNATIVES TO CHATGPT

There are several alternatives to ChatGPT that offer a similar set of features, some of which are listed here:

- Bard (Google)
- Bing Chat
- Gemini (Google)
- Jasper
- PaLM (Google)
- Pi
- POE (LinkedIn)
- Replika

- WriteSonic
- YouChat

The following subsections discuss some (but not all) of the ChatGPT alternatives in the preceding list.

Google Bard

Google Bard is a chatbot that has similar functionality as ChatGPT, such as generating code as well as generating text/documents. A subset of the features supported by Bard is shown here:

- built-in support for Internet search
- built-in support for voice recognition
- built "on top of" PaLM 2 (Google)
- support for 20 programming languages
- read/summarize PDF contents
- provides links for its information

According to the following article in mid-2023, Bard has added support for 40 additional languages, as well as support for text-to-speech:

*https://www.extremetech.com/extreme/google-bard-updated-with-*text-to-speech-40-new-languages

Moreover, Bard supports prompts that include images (interpreted by Google Lens) and can produce captions based on the images.

The following article suggests that Google can remain competitive with ChatGPT by leveraging PaLM:

https://analyticsindiamag.com/googles-palm-is-ready-for-the-gpt-challenge/

YouChat

Another alternative to ChatGPT is YouChat, part of the search engine you.com, and it is accessible at: *https://you.com/*.

Richard Socher, who is well known in the ML community for his many contributions, is the creator of *you.com*. According to Richard Socher, YouChat is a search engine that can provide the usual search-related functionality as well as the ability to search the Web to obtain more information to provide responses to queries from users.

Another competitor is POE from LinkedIn, and you can create a free account at: *https://poe.com/login.*

Pi from Inflection

Pi is a chatbot developed by Inflection, which is a company that was by Mustafa Suleyman, who is also the founder of DeepMind. Pi is accessible online:

https://pi.ai/talk

More information about Pi is accessible here:

https://medium.com/@ignacio.de.gregorio.noblejas/meet-pi-chatgpts-newest-rival-and-the-most-human-ai-in-the-world-367b461c0af1

The development team used Reinforcement Learning from Human Feedback (RLHF) to train this chatbot:

https://medium.com/@ignacio.de.gregorio.noblejas/meet-pi-chatgpts-newest-rival-and-the-most-human-ai-in-the-world-367b461c0af1

MACHINE LEARNING AND CHATGPT: ADVANCED DATA ANALYTICS

ChatGPT can be leveraged in various ways in the realm of machine learning, some of which are shown in the following bullet list:

- Natural Language Processing (NLP) Tasks
- Data Augmentation
- Conversational Agents
- Content Creation
- Code-related Tasks
- Educational Applications
- Research & Knowledge Extraction
- Interactive Entertainment
- Semantic Search
- Business Intelligence
- Analyzing customer feedback or reviews to extract insights
- Generating reports or summaries from raw business data
- Converting text to more accessible formats
- Fine-tuning for Specific Domains
- Adapting ChatGPT to specific industries

These are just a few of the many ways ChatGPT can be leveraged in machine learning. Given its versatility, the potential applications are vast and continue to grow as more developers explore its capabilities.

Moreover, Advanced Data Analysis can generate machine learning models that can be trained on datasets. For example, Figure 9.1 displays a screenshot of charts that are based on the Titanic dataset.

Incidentally, if you would like to see examples of ChatGPT generating `Python` code for machine learning models, as well as code for charts and graphs, you can learn how to do so in several upcoming books:

- *Machine Learning, Python3, and ChatGPT*
- *Python and ChatGPT/GPT-4*
- *Python and Data Visualization with ChatGPT*

The preceding books will be available from Mercury Learning in early 2024.

WHAT IS INSTRUCTGPT?

InstructGPT is a language model developed by OpenAI, and it is a sibling model to ChatGPT. InstructGPT is designed to follow instructions given in a prompt to generate detailed responses. Some key points about InstructGPT are listed here:

- Instruction Following
- Training
- Applications
- Limitations

Instruction Following: Unlike ChatGPT, which is for open-ended conversations, InstructGPT is designed for following user instructions in prompts. This makes it suitable for tasks where the user wants to get specific information or outputs by giving clear directives.

Training: InstructGPT was trained using Reinforcement Learning from Human Feedback (RLHF), similar to ChatGPT. An initial model was trained using supervised fine-tuning, where human AI trainers provided conversations playing both sides (the user and the AI assistant). This new dialogue dataset was then mixed with the InstructGPT dataset and transformed into a dialogue format.

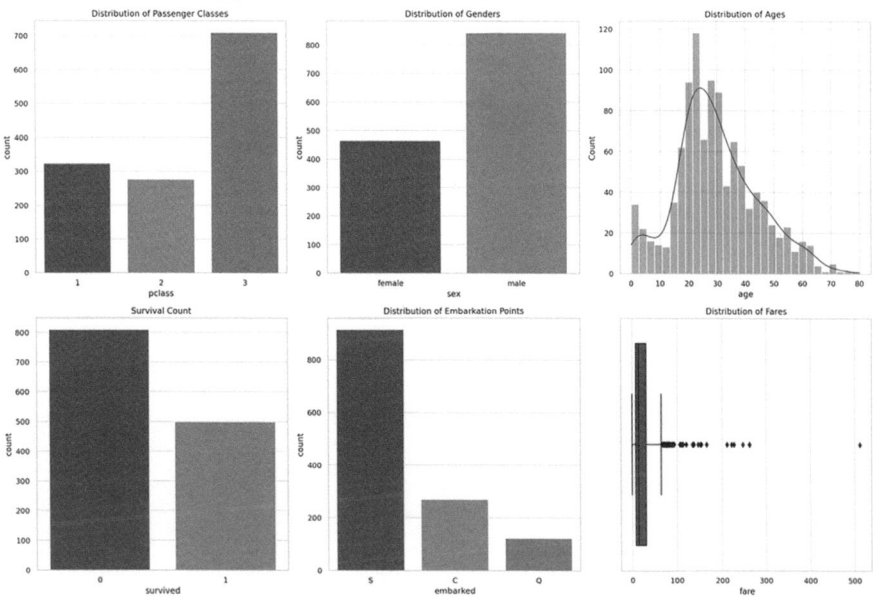

FIGURE 9.1 Charts and graphs from the Titanic dataset

Applications: InstructGPT can be useful in scenarios where you want more detailed explanations, step-by-step guides, or specific outputs based on the instructions provided.

Limitations: Like other models, InstructGPT has its limitations. It might produce incorrect or nonsensical answers. The output heavily depends on how the prompt is phrased. It is also sensitive to input phrasing and might give different responses based on slight rephrasing.

As AI models and their applications are rapidly evolving, there might be further developments or iterations of InstructGPT after 2021. Always refer to OpenAI's official publications and updates for the most recent information. More information about InstructGPT is accessible online:

https://openai.com/blog/instruction-following/

VIZGPT AND DATA VISUALIZATION

VizGPT is an online tool that enables you to specify English-based prompts to visualize aspects of datasets: *https://www.vizgpt.ai/*.

Select the default "Cars Dataset" and then click on the "Data" button to display the contents of the dataset, as shown in Figure 9.2.

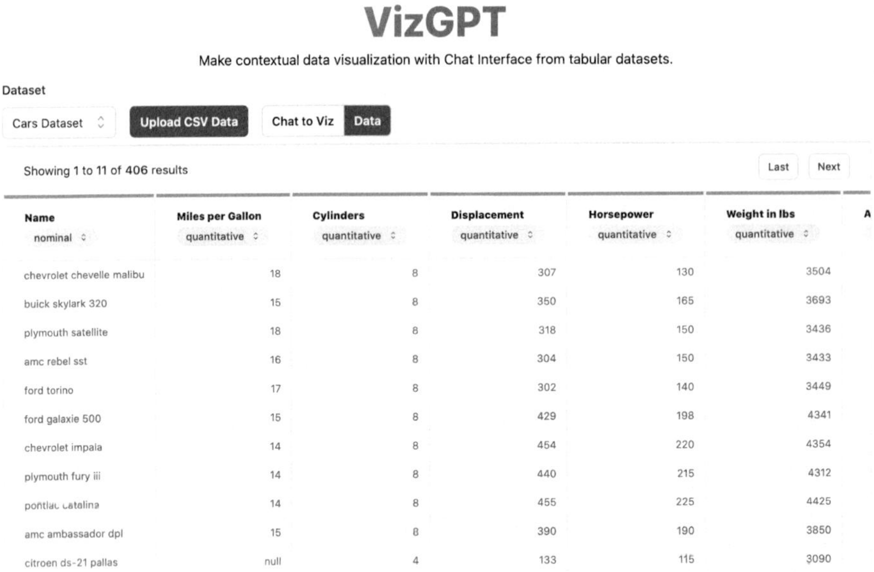

VizGPT

Make contextual data visualization with Chat Interface from tabular datasets.

Dataset

| Cars Dataset ⇕ | Upload CSV Data | Chat to Viz | Data |

Showing 1 to 11 of 406 results   Last   Next

Name nominal ⇕	Miles per Gallon quantitative ⇕	Cylinders quantitative ⇕	Displacement quantitative ⇕	Horsepower quantitative ⇕	Weight in lbs quantitative ⇕	A
chevrolet chevelle malibu	18	8	307	130	3504	
buick skylark 320	15	8	350	165	3693	
plymouth satellite	18	8	318	150	3436	
amc rebel sst	16	8	304	150	3433	
ford torino	17	8	302	140	3449	
ford galaxie 500	15	8	429	198	4341	
chevrolet impala	14	8	454	220	4354	
plymouth fury iii	14	8	440	215	4312	
pontiac catalina	14	8	455	225	4425	
amc ambassador dpl	15	8	390	190	3850	
citroen ds-21 pallas	null	4	133	115	3090	

FIGURE 9.2 VizGPT "Cars" dataset rows

Next, select the default "Cars Dataset" and then click on the "Chat to Viz" button to display a visualization of the dataset, as shown in Figure 9.3.

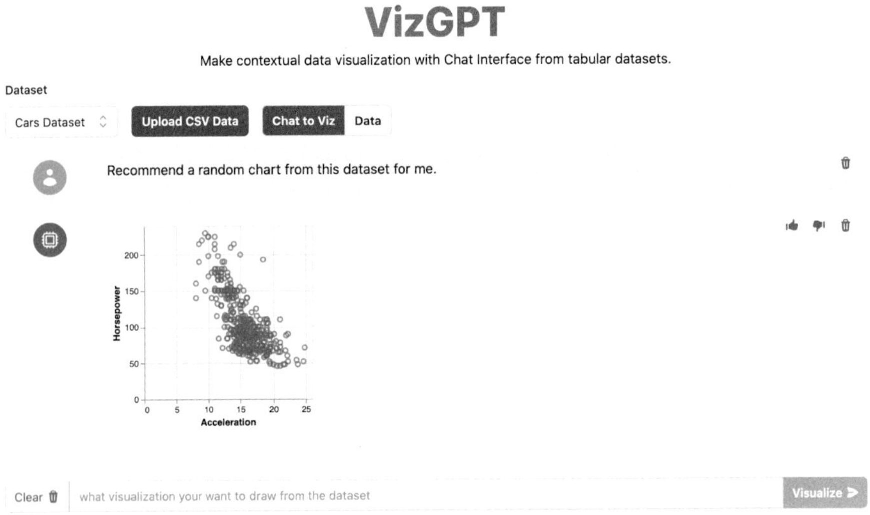

FIGURE 9.3 VizGPT "Cars" dataset visualization

You can experiment further with VizGPT. For example, you can upload your own dataset by clicking on the "Upload CSV" button and obtain similar results with that dataset.

WHAT IS GPT-4?

GPT-4 was released in mid-March 2023, and became available only to users with an existing ChatGPT account via of a paid upgrade ($20/month) to that account. According to various online anecdotal stories from users, GPT-4 is superior to ChatGPT. In addition, Microsoft has a version of GPT-4 that powers its Bing browser, which is freely available to the public.

GPT-4 is a large multimodal model that can process image-based inputs as well as text-based inputs and then generate textual outputs. Currently, image-based outputs are unavailable to the general public, but it does have internal support for image generation.

GPT-4 supports 25,000 words of input text; by comparison, ChatGPT is limited to 4,096 characters. Although the number of parameters in GPT-4 is undisclosed, the following article asserts that GPT-4 is a mixture of 8x220-billion-parameter models, which is an example of a Mixture of Experts (MoE):

https://thealgorithmicbridge.substack.com/p/gpt-4s-secret-has-been-revealed

GPT-4 and Test Scores

One interesting example of the improved accuracy pertains to a bar exam, which ChatGPT scored in the bottom 10%. By contrast, GPT-4 scored in the top 10% for the same bar exam. More details are accessible online:

https://www.abajournal.com/web/article/latest-version-of-chatgpt-aces-the-bar-exam-with-score-in-90th-percentile

In addition, GPT-4 is apparently able to pass its first year at Harvard with a 3.34 GPA. More details are accessible online:

https://www.businessinsider.com/chatgpt-harvard-passed-freshman-ai-education-GPT-4-2023-7?op=1

Furthermore, GPT-4 has performed well on a number of additional tests, some of which are listed here:

- AP exams
- SAT
- GRE
- Medical tests
- Law exams
- Business school exams

- Wharton MBA exam
- USA Biology Olympiad Semifinal Exam
- Sommelier exams (wine steward)

You can read more details regarding the preceding tests online:

https://www.businessinsider.com/list-here-are-the-exams-chatgpt-has-passed-so-far-2023-1

The following link contains much more detailed information regarding test scores, benchmarks, and other results pertaining to GPT-4: *https://openai.com/research/gpt-4.*

GPT-4 Parameters

This section contains information regarding some of the GPT-4 parameters, some of which are best-guess approximations.

Since GPT-4 is a transformer-based AR (auto regressive) model, it is trained to perform next-token prediction. The following tutorial, *GPT-4 Technical Report*, was released in March, 2023, and it contains a detailed analysis of the capabilities of GPT-4:

https://docs.kanaries.net/en/tutorials/ChatGPT/gpt-4-parameters

GPT-4 Fine Tuning

As of the update on September 6, 2023, OpenAI has introduced a "fine-tuning" feature for its GPT-3.5 Turbo model, which is part of the ChatGPT series. This feature allows developers and businesses to customize the model to fit their specific needs. Moreover, OpenAI has plans to bring this fine-tuning feature to GPT-4 as well. Alternatively, you can integrate OpenAI models with your own data source via LangChain or LlamaIndex (previously known as GPT-Index). Both of them enable you to connect OpenAI models with your existing data sources.

An introduction to LangChain is accessible online:

https://www.pinecone.io/learn/series/langchain/langchain-intro/

An introduction to LlamaIndex is accessible online:

https://zilliz.com/blog/getting-started-with-llamaindex

https://stackoverflow.com/questions/76160057/openai-chat-completions-api-how-do-i-customize-answers-from-gpt-3-5-or-gpt-4-mo?noredirect=1&lq=1

CHATGPT AND GPT-4 COMPETITORS

Shortly after the release of ChatGPT on November 30, 2022, there was a flurry of activity among various companies to release a competitor to ChatGPT, some of which are listed here:

- Bard (Google chatbot)
- CoPilot (Microsoft)
- Codex (OpenAI)
- Apple GPT (Apple)
- PaLM 2 (Google and GPT-4 competitor)
- Claude 2 (Anthropic)
- Llama-2 (Meta)

The following subsections contain additional details regarding the LLMs in the preceding list.

Bard

Bard is an AI chatbot from Google that was released in early 2023, and it is a competitor to ChatGPT. By way of comparison, Bard is powered by PaLM 2, whereas ChatGPT is powered by GPT-4. Recently, Bard added support for images in its answers to user queries, whereas this functionality for ChatGPT has not been released yet to the public (but you can expect it to be available sometime soon):

https://artificialcorner.com/google-bards-new-image-recognition-means-serious-competition-to-chatgpt-here-are-6-best-use-cases-55d69eae1b27

Bard encountered an issue pertaining to the James Webb Space Telescope during a highly publicized release, which resulted in a significant decrease in market capitalization for Alphabet. However, Google has persevered in fixing issues and enhancing the functionality of Bard. You can access Bard at: *https://bard.google.com/*.

Around mid-2023, Bard was imbued with several features that were not available in GPT-4 during the same time period, some of which are listed here:

- generate images
- generate HTML/CSS from an image
- generate mobile applications from an image
- create Latex formulas from an image
- extract text from an image

Presumably these features will spur OpenAI to provide the same set of features (some are implemented in GPT-4, but they are not publicly available).

CoPilot (OpenAI/Microsoft)

Microsoft CoPilot is a Visual Studio Code extension that is also powered by GPT-4. GitHub CoPilot is already known for its ability to generate blocks of code within the context of a program. In addition, Microsoft is also developing Microsoft 365 CoPilot, whose availability date has not been announced as of mid-2023.

However, Microsoft has provided early demos that show some of the capabilities of Microsoft 365 CoPilot, which includes automating tasks such as:

- writing emails
- summarizing meetings
- making PowerPoint presentations

Microsoft 365 CoPilot can analyze data in Excel spreadsheets, insert AI-generated images in PowerPoint, and generate drafts of cover letters. Microsoft has also integrated Microsoft 365 CoPilot into some of its existing products, such as Loop and OneNote.

According to the following article, Microsoft intends to charge $30 per month for Office 365 Copilot:

https://www.extremetech.com/extreme/microsoft-to-charge-30-per-month-for-ai-powered-office-apps

Copilot was reverse engineered in late 2022, which is described here:

https://thakkarparth007.github.io/copilot-explorer/posts/copilot-internals

The following article shows you how to create a GPT-3 application that uses NextJS, React, and CoPilot:

https://github.blog/2023-07-25-how-to-build-a-gpt-3-app-with-nextjs-react-and-github-copilot/

Codex (OpenAI)

OpenAI Codex is a fine-tuned GPT-3-based LLM that generates code from text; Codex also powers GitHub Copilot. Codex was trained on more than 150 GB of Python code that was obtained from more than 50 million GitHub repositories.

According to OpenAI, the primary purpose of Codex is to accelerate human programming, and it can complete almost 40% of requests. Codes tend to work quite well for generating code for solving simpler tasks. Navigate to the Codex home page to obtain more information: *https://openai.com/blog/openai-codex.*

Apple GPT

In mid-2023, Apple announced Apple GPT, which is a competitor to ChatGPT from OpenAI. The actual release date was projected to be 2024. "Apple GPT" is the current name for a product that is intended to compete with Google Bard, OpenAI ChatGPT, and Microsoft Bing AI.

In brief, the LLM PaLM 2 powers Google Bard, and GPT-4 powers ChatGPT as well as Bing Chat, whereas Ajax is what powers Apple GPT. Ajax is based on Jax from Google, and the name Ajax is a clever concatenation.

PaLM-2

The second version of Pathways Language Model, PaLM-2, is the successor to PaLM (circa 2022). PaLM-2 powers Bard, and it is also a direct competitor to GPT-4. Since PaLM consists of 540 B parameters, it is plausible that PaLM-2 is a larger LLM (details of the latter are undisclosed).

PaLM-2 provides four submodels called Gecko, Otter, Bison, and Unicorn (smallest to largest). PaLM-2 was trained on more than 100 human languages, as well as programming languages such as Fortran. Moreover, PaLM-2 has been deployed to a plethora of Google products, including Gmail and YouTube.

Med-PaLM M

In addition to the four submodels listed earlier, Med-PaLM 2 (the successor to Med-PaLM) is an LLM that provides answers to medical questions, and it is accessible at: *http://sites.research.google/med-palm/.*

The successor to Med-PaLM is Med-PaLM M, and details about this LLM are accessible at: *https://arxiv.org/abs/2307.14334.*

An article that provides a direct comparison of performance benchmarks for PaLM 2 and GPT-4 is accessible online:

https://www.makeuseof.com/google-palm-2-vs-openai-gpt-4/

All told, PaLM-2 has a robust set of features, and it is definitely a significant competitor to GPT-4.

Claude 2

Anthropic created the LLM Claude 2. It not only can answer queries about specific topics, but it can also perform searches that involve multiple documents, summarize documents, create documents, and generate code.

Claude 2 is an improvement on Anthropic's predecessor Claude 1.3, and it can summarize entire books as well as generate code based on prompts from users. In fact, Claude 2 appears to be comparable with its rivals ChatGPT and GPT-4 in terms of competing functionality.

Furthermore, Claude 2 supports a context window of 100,000 tokens. Moreover, Claude 2 was trained on data as recently as early 2023, whereas ChatGPT was trained on data up until 2021. However, Claude 2 cannot search the Web (unlike its competitor GPT-4). Pay attention to Anthropic, where you will probably see more good things in the LLM space.

LLAMA-2

The second version of Large Language Model Meta AI (LlaMa 2) is an open source fine-tuned LLM from Meta that trained on only public data. LlaMa-2 provides three models (7 B, 13 B, and 70 B parameters) that utilize more data during the pre-training step than numerous other LLMs. LlaMa-2 is optimized to provide faster inferences and also provides a longer context length (4 K) than other LLMs.

Moreover, the LlaMa-2-Chat LLM performs surprisingly well: in some cases, its quality is close to the quality of high-performing LLMs, such ChatGPT and GPT-4. LlaMa-2 is more user-friendly also provides better results for writing text in comparison to GPT-4. However, GPT-4 is more adept for tasks such as generating code.

How to Download LlaMa-2

LlaMa-2 provides a permissive license for community use and commercial use, and Meta has made the code as well as the pre-trained models and the fine-tuned models publicly available.

There are several ways that you can download LlaMa-2, starting from this link from Meta after you provide some information (name, country, and affiliation):

https://ai.meta.com/llama/

Another way to access demos of the 7 B, 13 B, and 70 B models is from the following links:

https://huggingface.co/spaces/huggingface-projects/llama-2-7b-chat

https://huggingface.co/spaces/huggingface-projects/llama-2-13b-chat

https://huggingface.co/spaces/ysharma/Explore_llamav2_with_TGI

A third way to access LlaMa-2 on Hugging Face is at the following websites:

https://huggingface.co/blog/llama2

https://github.com/facebookresearch/llama

https://ai.meta.com/research/publications/llama-2-open-foundation-and-fine-tuned-chat-models/

If you are interested in training LlaMa-2 on your laptop, more details for doing so are accessible at: *https://blog.briankitano.com/llama-from-scratch/*.

LlaMa-2 Architecture Features

This section simply contains a high-level list of some of the important distinguishing features of LlaMa-2:

- decoder-only LLM
- better pre-training
- improved model architecture
- SwiGLU activation function
- different positional embeddings
- GQA (Grouped Query Attention)
- Ghost Attention (GAtt)
- RLHF and PPO
- BPE SentencePiece tokenizer
- modified normalization step

The majority of LLMs contain the layer normalization that is in the original transformer architecture. By contrast, LlaMa-2 uses a simplified alternative that involves Root Mean Square Layer Normalization (RMSNorm). RMSNorm has yielded improved results for training stability as well as for generalization.

Although SwiGLU is computationally more expensive than the ReLU activation function that is part of the original transformer architecture, SwiGLU achieves better performance.

Note that RLHF is discussed in Chapter 8, which also includes a brief description of TRPO and PPO. For a detailed description of how to fine tune LlaMa-2 on three tasks, navigate to the following URL:

https://www.anyscale.com/blog/fine-tuning-llama-2-a-comprehen-sive-case-study-for-tailoring-models-to-unique-applications

Fine Tuning LlaMa-2

Although LLaMa-2 is an improvement over its predecessor LLaMa, you can further improve the performance of LLama-2 by performing some fine tuning of this LLM:

https://medium.com/@murtuza753/using-llama-2-0-faiss-and-lang-chain-for-question-answering-on-your-own-data-682241488476

The following article shows you how to fine tune LLaMa-2 in a Google Colaboratory notebook:

https://towardsdatascience.com/fine-tune-your-own-llama-2-model-in-a-colab-notebook-df9823a04a32

The following article describes how to use MonsterAPI (also discussed in the article) to fine tune LlaMa-2 in five steps:

https://blog.monsterapi.ai/how-to-fine-tune-llama-2-llm/

The following link describes how to access LlaMa-2 in Google Colaboratory:

https://levelup.gitconnected.com/harnessing-the-power-of-llama-2-using-google-colab-2e1dedc2d1d8

WHEN WILL GPT-5 BE AVAILABLE?

As this book goes to print, there is no official information available regarding the status of GPT-5, which is to say that everything is speculative. In the early part of 2023, Sam Altman (CEO of OpenAI) remarked that there were "no official plans" for GPT-5.

However, during mid-2023 OpenAI filed a patent for GPT-5 in which there are some high-level details about the features of GPT-5. Some people have speculated that GPT-5 will be a more powerful version of GPT-4, and others suggest that filing a patent might be nothing more than securing the name GPT-5 by OpenAI.

Regardless of the motivation for filing a patent, there is a great deal of competition with GPT-4 from various companies. Therefore, it is highly plausible that OpenAI will release GPT-5, perhaps by the end of 2023. Regarding model sizes, recall that GPT-3 has 175 B parameters, and some speculate that GPT-4 has 10 trillion parameters, which would mean that GPT-4 is roughly 60 times larger than GPT-3. The same increase in scale for GPT-5 seems implausible because GPT-5 would then consist of 600 trillion parameters.

Another possibility is that GPT-4 is based on the MoE methodology that involves multiple components. For instance, GPT-4 could be a combination of 8 components, each of which involves 220 million parameters, and therefore GPT-4 would consist of 1.76 trillion parameters.

Training LLMs such as GPT-4 is very costly and requires huge datasets for the pre-training step. Regardless of the eventual size of GPT-5, the training process could involve enormous costs.

SUMMARY

This chapter started with information about the main features of ChatGPT and GPT-4, as well as some of their competitors. Then you saw a comparison of ChatGPT with Google Search, as well as ChatGPT custom instructions, prompts, and the ChatGPT playground.

Next, you learned about ChatGPT plugins, such as the Advanced Data Analytics and code whisperer, followed by some concerns about ChatGPT, as well as the strengths and weaknesses of ChatGPT. In addition, learned about alternatives to ChatGPT and data visualization with VizGPT.

Moreover, you learned about some inference parameters for GPT-4 and competitors to GPT-4, such as CoPilot and Codex. Finally, you got an introduction to LLaMa-2, and how to download LLaMa-2 so that you can fine tune this model on your laptop.

## CHAPTER 10

VISUALIZATION WITH GENERATIVE AI

This chapter discusses visualization with generative AI, which includes some popular image generation tools that were introduced in 2022 and 2023. You will also learn about AI21 and its playground, along with the Aleph-Alpha Playground, both of which offer functionality that is similar to the GPT-3 Playground. The Python-based code samples in this chapter require Python 3.7, which you can download from the Internet if you have not already done so.

The first section of this chapter contains an overview of Generative AI and some examples of Generative AI. Next, you will learn about diffusion, which is a technique for removing noise from an image, as well as its usefulness in infusion models. You will also learn about diffusion models and how they contrast with GANs (generative adversarial models). This section introduces CLIP and GLIDE, both of which are from OpenAI.

The second section of this chapter contains an overview of several popular tools for text-to-image generation, such as Stability AI and Imagen. You will also learn about Make-a-Scene and GauGAN2, and the limitations of text-to-image models.

The third section delves into DALL-E models, the paid accounts for DALL-E, and how to invoke the DALL-E API. In addition, you will learn various details about DALL-E 2, and information about DALL-E 3.

The final portion of this chapter discusses text-to-video generation tools, such as Make-a-Video (Meta), Text-to-Video (Imagen), and also a text-to-speech generation tool called Whisper from OpenAI.

GENERATIVE AI AND ART AND COPYRIGHTS

Generative AI was briefly described earlier, along with the manner in which it differs from conversational AI. More importantly, generative AI has shown its capabilities in multiple areas, such as films and videos.

One comparison involves the effects of CGI during the 1990s and its impact on movies from Hollywood. Generative AI transcends CGI in dramatic ways that will result in a disruptive change for multiple industries.

We have already reached the point at which generative AI can create art and even win art contests. The natural question is this: Who is the owner of the art? While it might seem fair for AI to obtain a copyright or a patent for its work, a judge ruled that only humans can obtain copyrights for their work:

https://www.reuters.com/legal/ai-generated-art-cannot-receive-copyrights-us-court-says-2023-08-21/

GENERATIVE AI AND GANS

Although generative AI and Generative Adversarial Networks (GANs) are closely related concepts within the field of machine learning and deep learning, they have differences. *Generative AI* is a broad term that encompasses any machine learning model designed to generate new data samples. This includes GANs, VAEs, and RBMs.

Both generative AI and GANs have been pivotal in various applications, from image synthesis, data augmentation, style transfer, to drug discovery and more.

Generative AI refers to a broader class of machine learning models that aim to generate new samples similar to the input data. These models learn to capture the underlying distribution of the training data, so they can produce new, synthetic examples that are consistent with the data they have seen.

There are several types of generative AI models, some of which are listed below and followed by brief descriptions:

- Probabilistic Graphical Models
- Variational Autoencoders (VAEs)
- Restricted Boltzmann Machines (RBMs)
- Generative Adversarial Networks (GANs)

Probabilistic Graphical Models are statistical models that use a graph to represent and map out the dependencies among various random variables in the data. Examples include Hidden Markov Models and Bayesian Networks.

Variational Autoencoders (VAEs) are neural network architectures that learn to encode and decode data in a way that the encoded representations can be used to generate new, similar data.

Restricted Boltzmann Machines (RBMs) are neural networks with two layers (visible and hidden) that learn a probabilistic model of the input data.

Generative Adversarial Networks (GANs) are a type of generative model that uses two neural networks that are called a generator and a discriminator.

GANs (Generative Adversarial Networks)

GANs are a specific type of generative AI introduced by Ian Goodfellow and his collaborators in 2014. GANs are a specific type of generative AI model characterized by their adversarial training process involving a generator and a discriminator network.

The unique aspect of GANs is their adversarial training process, which involves two neural networks called a generator and a discriminator.

The generator tries to produce data based on random noise as input and then generates samples as output. By contrast, the discriminator attempts to distinguish between genuine data (from the training set) and fake data produced by the generator. Here are the steps for the training process:

- The generator tries to produce fake data that looks as real as possible.
- The discriminator tries to get better at distinguishing real data from fake data.
- The process is akin to a forger trying to create a fake painting, while an art detective tries to detect which one is fake. Over time, the forger becomes so skilled at creating paintings that the detective cannot tell real from fake.

Advantages of GANs include the following:

- They can generate very high-quality data, especially images.
- They do not require any explicit modeling of the data distribution.

Challenges with GANs include the following:

- Training can be unstable and sensitive to the choice of hyper parameters.
- They might suffer from mode collapse, where the generator produces limited varieties of samples.

WHAT IS DIFFUSION?

In essence, *diffusion* in generative AI is about simulating a process whereby data is gradually refined from noise to realistic samples. The process is inspired by the idea of diffusion, where things spread out and mix over time, but applied in the context of data generation.

Diffusion in the context of generative AI does not refer to the passive movement of particles, as in the physical or biological sense. Instead, it often refers to diffusion models, which are a class of generative models that simulate a diffusion process to generate new data samples.

The following list contains the major aspects of diffusion in generative AI:

- Diffusion models
- Noise-driven process
- Denoting score matching
- Generative process

Diffusion models generate new data samples by simulating a diffusion process. Starting from a random sample, they iteratively refine this sample using a series of noise updates until it becomes a sample from the target data distribution.

The *noise-driven process* refers to the fact that diffusion models add and remove noise to/from data samples. Specifically, the process starts with a real data point and then adds noise over a series of steps until it is purely random noise. Next, the generative process involves reversing this noise addition to go from random noise back to a sample resembling the real data.

The score matching technique refers to the way that a model learns to predict the difference (or "score") between the noisy data and the original data. By learning this score, the model understands how to de-noise the data, which is useful for the generative process.

The generative process step is the inference step that occurs after the model has been trained. In this step, the diffusion model starts with a random noise sample and then iteratively refines this sample using the learned de-noising scores during a sequence of steps. This process gradually transforms the noise into a sample that resembles one of the samples from the target data distribution.

Diffusion models can generate high-quality samples and have been shown to perform competitively with other generative models like GANs and VAEs. Like other generative models, diffusion models can be used for data generation, image synthesis, in-painting, super-resolution, and other tasks where generating new data samples is required.

Diffusion Image Sample

The following URL is an online application for generating diffusion images from a given image: *https://replicate.com/tommoore515/ material_stable_diffusion*.

Figure 10.1 shows the content of `sample3.tiff` that is specified as the input image for the preceding link, and Figure 10.1 shows the generated diffusion image.

FIGURE 10.1 A CSS3-based image

FIGURE 10.2 A diffusion image

330 • Transformer, BERT, and GPT

The code for this application is available as a GitHub repository:

https://github.com/TomMoore515/material_stable_diffusion

Diffusion Models Versus GANs

According to a paper published by OpenAI in June 2021, with the title "Diffusion Models Beat GANs on Image Synthesis," diffusion models can achieve superior image quality over generative models (along with some limitations): *https://arxiv.org/pdf/2105.05233.pdf*.

The following article discusses GANs versus diffusion models, along with suggestions for how to make a choice between these two options:

https://analyticsindiamag.com/diffusion-models-vs-gans-which-one-to-choose-for-image-synthesis/

What are Diffusers and DDPMs?

Diffusers refers to SOTA diffusion models (written in PyTorch) that are available for more than one modality, such as image as well as audio generation, and the associated Github repository is at: *https://github.com/huggingface/diffusers*. Additional information can be found online:

https://towardsdatascience.com/hugging-face-just-released-the-diffusers-library-846f32845e65

Denoising Diffusion Probabilistic Models (DDPMs) are deep generative models that form the basis for the image generation in DALL-E 2 and Imagen:

https://medium.com/mlearning-ai/enerating-images-with-ddpms-a-pytorch-implementation-cef5a2ba8cb1

CLIP (OPENAI)

CLIP is an acronym for Contrastive Language-Image Pre-training, a model developed by OpenAI. While it is not a generative model by itself, it is designed to understand images paired with natural language, bridging the gap between vision and language tasks.

CLIP is a model designed to understand and bridge the gap between vision and language. By learning to associate images with natural language descriptions, it achieves a versatile understanding that can be applied to various tasks, both in vision and in scenarios where it is combined with generative models. CLIP involves the following components:

- Training mechanism
- Contrastive learning
- Zero-shot learning

The *training mechanism* involves a large set of images paired with textual descriptions. The objective is to ensure that an image and its corresponding textual description come closer in the embedded space, while other non-matching pairs are pushed apart.

Contrastive learning is the basis for the training mechanism. In this approach, the model learns to distinguish between positive pairs (correct image-text matches) and negative pairs (random image-text combinations).

Zero-shot learning is a feature whereby CLIP can perform tasks without fine-tuning. Given a set of classes described in natural language, CLIP can classify new images into these classes without requiring task-specific training data for each class.

CLIP can handle a wide range of vision tasks using the same model. This includes image classification, object detection, and even some forms of image generation when paired with other generative models.

Although CLIP is not a generative model, it can be paired with generative models for interesting applications. For example, when combined with a model like VQ-VAE-2 (a generative model), CLIP can be used to guide the generation process using textual descriptions, resulting in a system that can generate images from textual prompts.

While CLIP is designed to be robust, it might still be susceptible to sophisticated adversarial attacks, but it generally offers better resistance compared to traditional models. CLIP also provides transferability because its understanding of images and text allows CLIP to transfer its knowledge to a wide range of tasks without task-specific fine-tuning.

GLIDE (OPENAI)

GLIDE is an acronym for Guided Language-to-Image Diffusion for Generation and Editing, and it consists of a CLIP embedding plus a diffusion model that compares favorably with DALL-E, even though GLIDE is less than one-third the size of DALL-E.

More details are provided in the following subsections. DALL-E is a VQVAE:

https://towardsdatascience.com/DALL-E2-explained-the-promise-and-limitations-of-a-revolutionary-ai-3faf691be220

GLIDE encodes a language prompt by means of a text transformer, and in addition to text, GLIDE can process images that are modified through NLP prompts to insert new objects. GLIDE can also enhance images through various other effects, such as reflections and shadow effects. In fact, GLIDE is preferred by some because of its feature set. The following link provides more details regarding GLIDE:

https://www.marktechpost.com/2021/12/29/openai-introduces-glide-model-for-photorealistic-image-generation/

Now that you have an understanding of CLIP and GLIDE, let's explore some tools that perform text-to-image generation, which is the topic of the next section.

TEXT-TO-IMAGE GENERATION

Text-to-image generation is in the midst of incredible innovation due to the availability of new image generation tools, such as DALL-E, Craiyon, and Stable Diffusion. Other tools are under development, and the race for better feature support continues unabated. Indeed, image generation is experiencing a renaissance that will have a profound impact on artists, designers, and companies that provide graphics-related tools and products.

Along with the success of text-to-image generation, there has been some controversy, such as copyright issues. For example, Getty Images provides a library of almost 500 million images, and it has banned the upload of AI-generated pictures to its image collection because of a concern regarding the legality of such images. Other sites that have implemented a similar ban include Newgrounds and PurplePort. Another contentious incident involved a fine arts competition that awarded a prize to an AI-generated art piece. There is also a growing malaise among artists and people involved in UI graphics regarding the potentially adverse impact of AI-based artwork and design on their careers.

Keep in mind that some image generation tools, such as Craiyon and DALL-E, are accessible via API calls or a Web interface, whereas Stable Diffusion is downloadable on your machine. Specifically, the Github repository for Stable Diffusion is accessible online:

https://github.com/CompVis/stable-diffusion

Recently, there has been a rapid succession of text-to-image generation models, some of which (including DALL-E) are based on GPT-3. In most cases, AI-based techniques for generative art focus on domain-specific functionality, such as image-to-image or text-to-image.

Currently, the following models provided the most advanced capabilities with respect to image generation, and they use NLP-based techniques to create highly impressive images:

- Stable Diffusion
- DALL-E 2 (OpenAI)
- Glide (OpenAI)
- Imagen (Google)
- Muse
- Make-a-Scene (Meta)
- Diffuse the Rest
- Latent Diffusion
- DreamBooth (Google)

For more information, please see the following website:

https://www.howtogeek.com/830870/best-ai-image-generators/

The DALL-E 2 model was arguably the first of the advanced AI-based image generation models.

Stability AI and Stable Diffusion

Stability AI is a for-profit company that collaborated with RunwayML (which is a video editing startup) to create Stable Diffusion, which is an open-source text-to-image generator.

Currently, Stable Diffusion has gained prominence over competitors such as DALL-E 2 and Midjourney. Indeed, the open-source community has enabled Stable Diffusion to become the leader (at this point in time) among competing image-to-text models.

The following Github repository contains an implementation of text-to-3D Dreamfusion that is based on Stable Diffusion text-to-2D image model:

https://github.com/ashawkey/stable-dreamfusion

The preceding repository contains a Google Colaboratory Jupyter notebook that is accessible online:

https://colab.research.google.com/drive/1MXT3yfOFvO0ooKEfiUU vTKwUkrrlCHpF

Other tools from Stable Diffusion are available online:

https://huggingface.co/spaces/lnyan/stablediffusion-infinity

https://huggingface.co/spaces/sd-concepts-library/stable-diffusion-conceptualizer

https://huggingface.co/spaces/fffiloni/whisper-to-stable-diffusion

Imagen (Google)

Google created `Imagen`, a text-to-image diffusion model (similar to `GLIDE`), that also encodes a language prompt by means of a text transformer: *https://imagen.research.google/*.

Google researchers determined that generic LLMs, pre-trained on text-only corpora, are very effective in terms of encoding text for image synthesis. Two other noteworthy details: `Imagen` achieves a `SOTA` score on the `COCO` dataset, and humans have ranked `Imagen` higher than other image generation tools.

The following Github repository contains a `PyTorch` implementation of Imagen that out-performs DALL-E 2: *https://github.com/lucidrains/imagen-pytorch*.

`Imagen` uses text-based descriptions of scenes to generate high-quality images. More details regarding how `Imagen` works are accessible here:

https://www.reddit.com/r/MachineLearning/comments/viyh17/d_how_imagen_actually_works/

https://www.assemblyai.com/blog/how-imagen-actually-works/

An interesting comparison between DALL-E 2 and Imagen is online:

https://www.linkedin.com/pulse/google-imagen-vs-openai-dalle-2-ritesh-kanjee/

Google also created `DrawBench`, which is a benchmark for ranking text-to-image models, along with an extensive list of prompts for `Imagen` that is accessible online:

https://docs.google.com/spreadsheets/d/1y7nAbmR4FREi6npB1u-Bo3GFdwdOPYJc617rBOxIRHY/edit#gid=0

Make-a-Scene (Meta)

`Make-A-scene` from Meta provides a multimodal technique that combines natural language and free style sketches to generate representations. Moreover, `Make-A-scene` works with input that can be either text or sketches.

In essence, the approach used by `Make-A-Scene` generates images with finer-grained context, such as position, size, and relationships between objects. `Make-A-scene` uses a multi-model approach that combines `NLP` with free style sketches. Unlike other text-to-image models, Make-A-Scene enables you to provide a sketch that supplements text prompts to generate images.

Diffuse the Rest

Another option is the freely available application Diffuse the Rest:

https://huggingface.co/spaces/huggingface/diffuse-the-rest

https://medium.com/mlearning-ai/this-ai-turns-your-rudimentary-doodles-into-realistic-photos-da13db23033

As a simple example of how Diffuse the Rest works, Figure 10.3 displays a manually drawn "stick figure," along with the prompt "alien body," after which the images in Figure 10.4 and Figure 10.5 were generated.

FIGURE 10.3 A stick figure created with Diffuse the Rest

FIGURE 10.4 An alien figure created with Diffuse the Rest

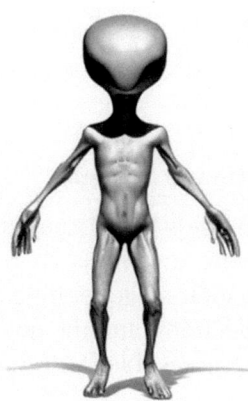

FIGURE 10.5 Another alien figure created with Diffuse the Rest

GauGAN2 (NVIDIA)

GauGAN2 is an early-stage deep learning model that uses text to generate photorealistic images. Unlike `DALL-E 2` (discussed in the next section), GauGAN2 is not based GPT-3, but it is nonetheless capable of combining text with other input types and then generate high-quality images.

In particular, users can type short phrases, and then `GauGAN2` generates an image that is based on the content of the text. For instance, one "baseline" example from NVIDIA involves a snow-capped mountain range that can be customized to include other features.

PromptBase

PromptBase is another text-to-image generation tool that provides free credits for generating images: *https://promptbase.com/*.

As a simple example of how PromptBase works, Figure 10.6 shows the image that is generated in response to the following prompt:

```
"Salvador Dali riding a Harley Davidson on Daytona
Beach in Florida and wearing a merry pranksters hat
and smoking a huge cigar"
```

FIGURE 10.6 Salvador Dali on a motorcycle, an image created with PromptBase

Limitations of Text-to-Image Models

Text-to-Image (T2I) models have experienced tremendous growth and popularity. Despite their capabilities, there are limitations to what those models can produce, such as generating multiple characters, creating shadows as well as reflections, and the quality of generated text.

More information is accessible at *https://arxiv.org/pdf/2208.00005.pdf*.

TEXT-TO-IMAGE MODELS

Text-to-image synthesis refers to the process of generating realistic and relevant images from textual descriptions. This task is challenging due to the inherent complexity of understanding the context, semantics, and nuances within the textual description and then translating that understanding into a visual representation. Over the past few years, deep learning, especially GANs, has shown significant promise in this area.

Important text-to-image models include the following:

- AttnGAN
- StackGAN
- DeepArt

The AttnGAN model uses attention-driven, multi-stage refinement to generate fine-grained images at multiple resolutions from textual descriptions. The attention mechanism allows the model to focus on different parts of the text when generating different parts of the image.

The StackGAN model decomposes the text-to-image generation task into two stages. In the first stage, it generates a low-resolution image from the textual description. In the second stage, it refines the low-resolution image to generate a high-resolution image.

DeepArt is more about style transfer, where a textual description or another image is used to generate an image in a particular artistic style.

The MirrorGAN model leverages the capabilities of semantic text embeddings and the spatial configurations of image scenes to generate images from textual descriptions. It consists of three modules: Semantic Text Embedding, Global-Local Collaborative Attentive module, and a Streamlined Object Generator. You can find open-source text-to-image models from the following locations:

- GitHub
- Model Zoos
- Papers with Code
- TensorFlow Hub

GitHub is the primary hub for open-source projects. You can find implementations of almost all major text-to-image synthesis models, including AttnGAN, StackGAN, and many others.

Model Zoos often accompany deep learning frameworks (such as TensorFlow and PyTorch) and they act as "hubs" where pre-trained models are available. For text-to-image tasks, you might find some models, but GitHub is generally more comprehensive for this specific task.

Papers with Code provides a curated list of machine learning papers along with the code. It is a great resource to find state-of-the-art models and their open-source implementations.

Google's TensorFlow Hub provides reusable machine learning modules. You might find some modules related to text-to-image synthesis, although it is more limited compared to GitHub.

As a reminder, always check the license associated with the code/model whenever you use or build upon open-source models to ensure you are using it in a way that respects the creators' intentions and any associated terms.

THE DALL-E MODELS

Microsoft will add DALL-E to its Office suite and Azure AI, and Adobe plans to add generative AI tools to Photoshop. Content generator Jasper also announced a massive funding round of $125 million. The GitHub Copilot case is "starting to look like the first case dealing specifically with machine learning and fair use in the US."

There are several AI-based image generation models available, and the three models that are discussed in the following subsections are listed here:

- DALL-E
- DALL-E 2
- craiyon (formerly DALL-E Mini)

The following URL has a Zoom plugin for DALL-E:

https://twitter.com/ZacharyWilliam_/status/1609973678334435328

DALL-E

DALL-E is an autoregressive model whose name is a hybrid of the name of the famous artist Salvador Dalí and WALL-E from Pixar: *https://openai.com/DALL-E 2/.*

DALL-E is a 12-billion parameter variant of the GPT-3 model that performs zero-shot text-to-image generation. DALL-E was trained on a dataset of text–image pairs. You can download the open-source DALL-E project at *https://github.com/openai/dall-e.*

DALL-E uses the GPT architecture to generate pixel-based images from text on a row-by-row basis. Inspired by GPT, it regards the words and pixels as one sequence of tokens and is thus able to continue generating an image from a text prompt. More information can be found online at *https://github.com/openai/dalle-2-preview/blob/main/system-card.md.*

OpenAI has engaged in significant research to block text generation or image generation through DALL-E that contains inappropriate content. DALL-E 2 extends the existing capabilities of DALL-E 1 (e.g., photorealism) and also provides new capabilities beyond DALL-E 1.

Paid Accounts for DALL-E

DALL-E was initially an invitation-only beta program, but later, OpenAI made the decision to support paid access to DALL-E, which is designed as follows:

- A prompt for DALL-E will cost one credit.
- Users get 50 free credits during their first month.
- Users get 15 free credits per month for subsequent months.
- Users can purchase 115 credits for $15/month.

Unlike the beta program for DALL-E, users have complete rights to commercialize the images that they create with DALL-E 2, which includes the ability to reprint, sell, and merchandise the generated images. Moreover, users obtain these rights regardless of whether they generated images via a free or paid credit, provided that they follow the content policy and terms of use from OpenAI, which are accessible online:

https://labs.openai.com/policies/content-policy

https://labs.openai.com/policies/terms

There are some restrictions: OpenAI will reject any uploaded images in DALL-E that resemble explicit material, named content, or realistic faces.

With the preceding points in mind, create a free OpenAI account and then navigate to the following link to access the DALL-E editor:

https://labs.openai.com/editor

As a simple example, Figure 10.7 shows the generated image in response to the following prompt:

```
Display a clown in the image of Mona Lisa and
the clown is smoking a cigar and is wearing big
sunglasses and is drinking a beer
```

FIGURE 10.7 A clown smoking a cigar

The following link provides some information about the DALL-E editor:

https://help.openai.com/en/articles/6516417-dall-e-editor-guide

As another example, enter the text "draw an avocado chair" in the text input box, select 4 as "Number of images you want," and click on the "Generate" button. After a couple of minutes, DALL-E will generate four images in response to your prompt, as shown in Figure 10-4.

Invoking the DALL-E API

OpenAI recently added a public API to access DALL-E. Listing 10.1 displays the content of dalle_api3.py that shows you how to invoke this API and then generate multiple images.

Listing 10.1: dalle_api3.py

```
# pip3 install openai
import openai
openai.api_key = "your-openai-key"
# a loop to generate multiple images:
basename="avocado_couch"
image_count = 4
```

```
for ndx in range(image_count):
  response = openai.Image.create(
    prompt="an avocado couch,"
    n=1,
    # image sizes must be in ['256x256', '512x512',
'1024x1024']
    size="512x512"
  )

  # generate URL with a DALL-E image:
  image_url = response['data'][0]['url']

  # save image:
  import requests
  img_data = requests.get(image_url).content

  filename= basename+str(ndx)+".jpg"
  with open(filename, 'wb') as handler:
    handler.write(img_data)
```

Listing 10.1 starts with an import statement and then initializes open.api_key with your API key. Next, the variables basename and image_count are initialized, followed by a loop that invokes the open. Image.create() method 4 times (which equals the value of image_count), which then initializes the variable response.

During each iteration through the loop, the variable image_url is populated with the URL by accessing one of the elements of the variable response. The next portion of the loop initializes the variable img_data (which contains the content of the generated image) that is written to the file system of your machine. Notice that the filename for each image depends on the current iteration through the loop, using this code snippet:

```
filename= basename+str(ndx)+".jpg"
```

Figure 10.8, Figure 10.9, Figure 10.10, and Figure 10.11 display the four images that are generated by the code in Listing 10.1.

FIGURE 10.8 First avocado couch example image generated by DALL-E

FIGURE 10.9 Second avocado couch example image generated by DALL-E

FIGURE 10.10 Third avocado couch example image generated by DALL-E

FIGURE 10.11 Fourth avocado couch example image generated by DALL-E

More information about the API is accessible at: *https://beta.openai. com/docs/guides/images.*

DALL-E 2

This section is divided into the following subsections that discuss different aspects of DALL-E 2:

- DALL-E 2 Overview
- The DALL-E 2 Model
- DALL·E 2 Content Preparation
- DALL-E 2 and Prompt Design
- DALL-E Tokenizer
- DALL-E 2 and Prompt Design
- DALL-E Tokenizer
- DALL-E 2 Bot

DALL-E 2 Overview

Although DALL-E 2 is a successor to DALL-E, DALL-E 2 is a diffusion-based model (not an autoregressive model like DALL-E). In fact, DALL-E 2 bears resemblance to GLIDE because both models generate images from a CLIP image encoding. DALL-E 2 uses three main steps:

- Leverage CLIP models trained on millions of images.
- Modified GLIDE model generates images from CLIP embeddings.
- Diffusion models inject text-related information into images.

By way of comparison, DALL-E combines CLIP and diffusion methods to generate photorealistic images using text-based input, whereas DALL-E 2 also includes an "unClip" technique that uses an encoder to process input text. The encoder first generates a representation space that is passed to a model that maps its input to an encoded image, after which a decoder generates the final image.

Furthermore, DALL-E 2 creates superior visual effects compared to its predecessor, such as higher fidelity and more realistic images because DALL-E 2 utilizes more recent SOTA text-to-image techniques. Details of the inner workings of DALL-E 2 are available online: *https://www.assemblyai.com/blog/how-DALL-E 2-actually-works*

In addition to the functionality in DALL-E, DALL-E 2 supports several new features:

- create variations of an existing image
- add objects to an existing image
- edit a selected region of an image
- create an image that blends two input images

Navigate to the home page and register for a free account. Any text that you specify and any generated images with `DALL-E` belong to you for personal as well as commercial use, whereas `DALL-E 2` restricts the images for personal use only (i.e., non-commercial use).

In addition to generating images based on text description prompts, DALL-E 2 can modify existing images as via a prompt in the form of a text-based description. Moreover, DALL-E 2 can enhance existing images to create variation of those images (also through text-based prompts). See the following URL for additional information:

https://openai.com/blog/dall-e-introducing-outpainting

Another important aspect of DALL-E 2 involves handling inappropriate content. Specifically, DALL-E 2 contains filters that examine user-supplied prompts in an attempt to prevent disparaging, hateful, or harmful content that is directed to individuals or groups of individuals.

In fact, DALLE-2 has mechanisms to block combinations of text or images that are prohibited despite the fact that the individual words or images may be benign. DALL-E 2 also endeavors to detect and block content that suggests gender bias as well as racial stereotypes.

Initial accounts for `DALL-E 2` were on an invitation-only basis, which restricted the use of generated images to non-commercial use. However, in mid-2022, OpenAI enabled paid subscriptions for `DALL-E 2` that allows commercial use for any images that you create in `DALL-E 2` (which makes sense for a paid subscription). According to various articles, there may have been as many as one million people on the initial waiting list for DALL-E 2, all of whom will have an opportunity to sign up for a paid subscription.

In a related topic, at least one robot is capable of producing art. `Ai-Da` (named after Ada Lovelace) is the first robot capable of painting like a human artist. AI algorithms prompt robot to interrogate, select, and decision-make to create a painting. More information about `Ai-Da` is available online:

https://www.theguardian.com/technology/2022/apr/04/mind-blowing-ai-da-becomes-first-robot-to-paint-like-an-artist

The DALL-E 2 Model

The fundamental components of DALL-E 2 are:

- a CLIP model
- a prior model
- an unCLIP model (decoder)

DALL-E 2 is the result of combining the prior model with the unCLIP model.

- CLIP: Model that takes image-caption pairs and creates "mental" representations in the form of vectors, called text/image embeddings
- Prior model: Takes a caption/CLIP text embedding and generates CLIP image embeddings
- Decoder Diffusion model (unCLIP): Takes a CLIP image embedding and generates images
- DALL·E 2: Combination of prior + diffusion decoder (unCLIP) models

DALL-E 2 Content Preparation

OpenAI performed pre-training tasks on the DALL-E 2 dataset to ensure compliance with the content policy of the company, including the:

- removal of sexual and violent images
- bias reduction (less filtering)
- removal of repeated images

OpenAI discovered an interesting (surprising?) result: an increase in the amount of image filtering sometimes leads to a more imbalanced dataset (e.g., more men than women).

OpenAI also removed repeated images in the training set because of an effect called "image regurgitation" whereby repeated images will sometimes appear in the output instead of generating new images.

OpenAI filtered training data using a technique called GLIDE, which involves the following steps:

- Create a specification for the image categories to be labeled.
- Collect several hundred positive images for each category.
- Collect several hundred negative images for each category.
- Use active learning procedure to collect more data.

The purpose of the active learning procedure was to improve the precision/recall trade-off. The final step involves applying the classifier on the complete in such a way as to prefer recall instead of precision.

OpenAI focused on the removal of bad data rather than keeping the good data for the following reason: it is easier to fine-tune a model than to make a model "unlearn" something that it learned during the training process.

Navigate to the following URL where you can obtain more detailed information regarding the interesting combinations of techniques that

OpenAI employed to produce a high-quality dataset of images for DALL-E 2:

https://openai.com/blog/DALL-E 2-pre-training-mitigations

DALL-E-Bot

DALL-E-Bot enables a robot to rearrange objects in a scene, by first inferring a text description of those objects, then generating an image representing a natural, human-like arrangement of those objects, and finally physically arranging the objects according to that image.

The significance is that we achieve this zero-shot using DALL-E, without needing any further data collection or training.

Encouraging real-world results with human studies show that this is an exciting direction for the future of Web-scale robot learning algorithms. We also propose a list of recommendations to the text-to-image community, to align further developments of these models with applications to robotics: *https://www.robot-learning.uk/dall-e-bot*.

DALL-E 3

In late 2023 OpenAI announced DALL-E 3 that was in "research preview". DALL-E 3 is scheduled for availability in October/2023 for ChatGPT Plus users (which involves a USD 20/month subscription) as well as Enterprise customers. Moreover, DALL-E 3 will be accessible from an API.

DALL-E 3 is based on ChatGPT, and DALL-E 3 appears to be a significant advance over its predecessor as well as its competitors. In short, DALL-E 3 is capable of highly detailed image generation that closely reflects the content of your prompts.

More information is accessible from the following link for DALL-E 3, as well as a sample comparison of the image generation via DALL-E 3 and DALL-E 2: *https://openai.com/dall-e-3*

DALL-E DEMOS

You can test DALL-E as well as DALL-E 2 by inputting text strings at the following URLs:

https://main-dalle-client-scy6500.endpoint.ainize.ai/

https://gpt3demo.com/apps/openai-dall-e

https://gpt3demo.com/apps/DALL-E 2-by-openai

As a fun example, enter the text "draw a clown car with pineapples" in the text input box, select 4 as "Number of images you want," and click on the "Generate" button. After a couple of minutes, DALL-E will generate four images in response to your prompt, as shown in Figure 10-12.

FIGURE 10.12 Four clown cars with pineapples, an image generated by DALL-E

As another example, enter the text "draw an avocado chair" in the text input box, select 4 as "Number of images you want," and click on the "Generate" button. After a couple of minutes, DALL-E will generate four images in response to your prompt, as shown in Figure 10-13.

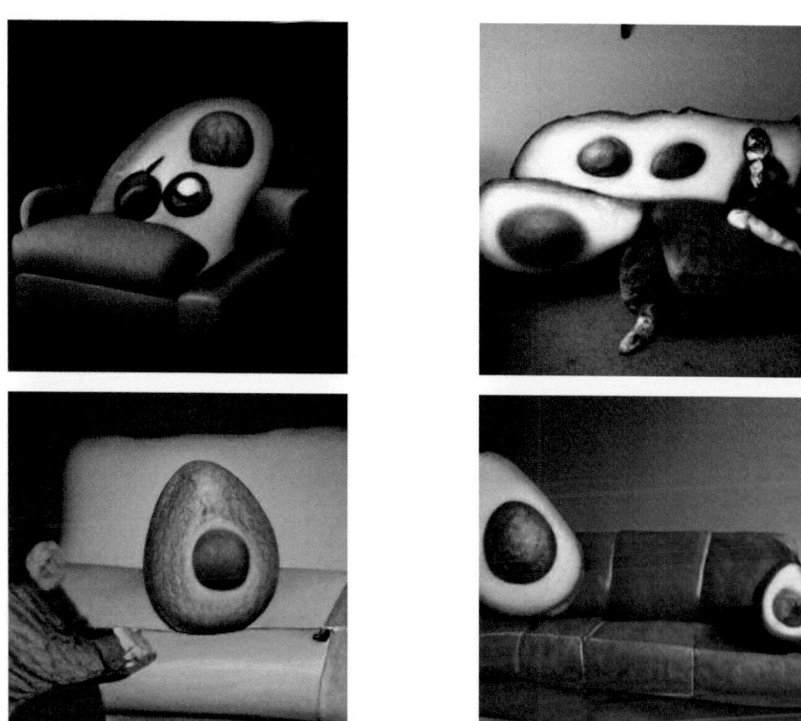

FIGURE 10.13 Four avocado chairs, an image generated by DALL-E

TEXT-TO-VIDEO GENERATION

The development of text-to-image tools has been quickly followed by text-to-video generation. Some of the companies that created text-to-video products are listed here:

- Meta (Make-a-Video)
- Imagen
- Text-to-Video (Stable Diffusion)
- Ruben Villegas and Google (Phenaki)

The products from each of the preceding companies are briefly described in the following subsections.

Meta (Make-a-Video)

Meta created Make-A-Video that performs Text-to-Video (T2V) translation that leverages T2I (text-to-image) in conjunction with unsupervised video content, and currently represents SOTA in T2V with respect to video quality.

One advantage of Make-A-Video is that it does not require paired text-video data. Secondly, Make-A-Video has a higher quality of generated videos with respect to its ability to capture the richness of images from which it generates video-based content. Make-A-Video uses a combination of a U-Net, attention tensors, and a pipeline for creating videos.

Imagen Text-to-Video

Text-to-image models such as DALL-E have an extraordinary capacity for creating awe-inspiring visual effects. By contrast, text-to-video is still in its infancy, probably because this task is much more complex compared to generating images. Nevertheless, Imagen Video from Google is a text-to-video model that relies on diffusion models to produce high-definition videos.

Imagen Video comprises 7 submodels that perform text-conditional video generation, spatial super-resolution, and temporal super-resolution. The result of this process is high-definition 1280×768 videos at 24 frames per second.

https://www.marktechpost.com/2022/11/30/google-ai-extends-imagen-to-imagen-video-a-text-to-video-cascaded-diffusion-model-to-generate-high-quality-video-with-strong-temporal-consistency-and-deep-language-understanding/

Ruben Villegas and Google (Phenaki)

Ruben Villegas collaborated with Google to create Phenaki, which is a text-to-video tool that can generate videos that are arbitrarily long. The text itself can have a story-like structure. Examples of videos created via Phenaki are accessible at *https://phenaki.github.io/*.

The underlying idea for Phenaki involves treating individual images as if they are frames in a video (which is the true composition of videos). Next, these "videos" are combined with short, captioned videos, which results in long and sophisticated videos by repeating the preceding process. The lower-level details of Phenaki involve the following:

- an encoder that generates video embeddings
- a language model that generates text embeddings

- a bidirectional transformer
- a decoder translates video embeddings into pixels

Note that the bidirectional transformer produces new video embeddings based on the text and existing video embeddings. The resulting Phenaki model is close to 2 B parameters, which has been reduced to create a model that is close to 1 B parameters.

TEXT-TO-SPEECH GENERATION

Generating audio from text has been available as TTS (text-to-speech), and you can find online Python code samples that perform this task. However, some recent AI-based tools can perform text-to-speech generation to create podcasts. One company that provides this functionality is Play.ht, whose home page is *https://podcast.ai*. One podcast involves Joe Rogan and Steve Jobs, and future podcasts are accessible at: *https://podcastio.canny.io/episode-ideas*.

Whisper (OpenAI)

Whisper is an open-source transformer-based encoder-decoder model that performs multiple tasks, include automatic speech recognition (ASR), multilingual speech recognition, speech translation, and language identification. The audio dataset for Whisper is roughly 2/3 English, and the other 1/3 consists of data from various other languages. Whisper performs remarkably well for English speech recognition: *https://openai.com/blog/whisper/*.

You can also download the Whisper Python-based code: *https://github.com/openai/whisper*.

In addition, a Google Colaboratory notebook for invoking Whisper functionality is accessible online:

https://colab.research.google.com/github/openai/whisper/blob/master/notebooks/LibriSpeech.ipynb

Whisper has transcribed Twitter videos as well as lectures with an accuracy of more than 99%:

https://twitter.com/ai__pub/status/1574067679555559424

https://medium.com/geekculture/our-knowledge-economy-is-swiftly-coming-to-an-end-734c5dc97355

SUMMARY

This chapter started with a discussion of visualization with generative AI and popular generation tools. Then you learned about AI21 and Aleph-Alpha and their respective playground that are similar to the GPT-3 playground.

Next, you learned about diffusion and diffusion models and how they contrast with GANs. In addition, you learned about text-to-image generation tools such as Stability AI and Imagen.

Moreover, you learned about DALL-E and its successor DALL-E 2 that generate images from text-based input. Finally, you learned about text-to-video generation tools and a text-to-speech generation tool.

Congratulations! You have reached the end of a fast-paced journey that started with the attention mechanism and the transformer architecture. We discussed BERT, GPT-3, and ChatGPT and GPT-4. At this point, you are in a good position to use the knowledge that you acquired as a steppingstone to further your understanding of generative AI.

INDEX